# Face Value

# Face Value
## The Politics of Beauty

Robin Tolmach Lakoff
and Raquel L. Scherr

**Routledge & Kegan Paul**
Boston, London, Melbourne and Henley

*For Samuel and Beatrice B. Tolmach*

*and in memory of*
*Juana Estela Salgado de Scherr*
*Max Scherr*

*with love and gratitude*

*First published in 1984*
*by Routledge & Kegan Paul plc*

*9 Park Street, Boston, Mass. 02108, USA*

*14 Leicester Square, London WC2H 7PH, England*

*464 St Kilda Road, Melbourne,*
*Victoria 3004, Australia and*

*Broadway House, Newtown Road,*
*Henley-on-Thames, Oxon RG9 1EN, England*

*Set in Linotron Century*
*by Input Typesetting Ltd, London SW19 8DR*
*and printed in the United States of America*

*Library of Congress Cataloging in Publication Data*

*Lakoff, Robin Tolmach.*
*Face value, the politics of beauty.*

*Bibliography: p.*
*Includes index.*
*1. Beauty, Personal. I. Scherr, Raquel L.*
*II. Title.*
*RA778. L24 1984 302.5 84-9784*
*British Library CIP Data also available.*

*ISBN 0–7100–9742–5*

# Contents

# Illustrations

# Preface

Writing a book necessarily has its painful as well as its joyous and exhilarating moments. Here we would like to thank some of the many people who made the painful parts less so, and the exhilaration greater.

First, there were many – students, friends, and others – who shared their stories and their feelings with us in interviews that shaped our ideas and the form of this book. We cannot name all, as some have requested anonymity, but we do want to thank: Carl R., Sergio K. S., Elaine I., Cecile E., Terry M., Richard O., Marlo M., Marty, Margaret, Leonore, Rosana, Judy, Juana, Barbara, and George.

Also, Patricia W., Ellyn Z., Margie G., Amy S., Gina D., Oggie K., Lynn Marie M., Laurie M., Patricia P., Susan H., Esther S., and Azita B.

Those who anonymously answered our written questionnaire are also gratefully acknowledged.

We would especially like to thank Barbara Christian and Margaret Wilkerson for sharing their ideas with us, as well as Dr Greta Clarke, Yolanda J. Moses, Clara Sue Kidwell and Ron Bygum.

Our friends have played a multiple and invaluable role: they have encouraged us in difficult moments, provided a sympathetic ear and an inspiring voice, as well as providing amusement and distraction when those were called for. But more than this, they have reminded us, by their own anecdotes and recollections, that what we were doing mattered, that we should persevere. It would be impossible to mention all. Below are a few: Mandy Aftel; Mildred Ash, M.D.; Gloria Bowles; Naomi Cutner; Nora Krasnapolsky; Deirdre Lashgari; Maurice Marcus, M.D.; Marlo Martin; Françoise Meltzer; Peggy McCurdy; June McKay; Margaret Newman; Grace Robinson; Catherine Rodriguez-Nieto; Peter D. Scott; Sandra Silberstein; Emily Stoper; Jayne Walker; and Tobey Wiebe.

Our families, too, were solace and help. This book could certainly not have been written without Carl Uggla (Chalte), who calmly endured our exhilaration and despair, believing always in the importance of the project. David, Sergio, Nancy Herman, and Irvin Scherr were also sources of support. Andy Lakoff was, as usual, a loving and wise critic, and a hope for the future. And finally, this book would not have been possible without the encouragement, advice and support of our agent, Frances Goldin, and Philippa Brewster and Helen Armitage of Routledge & Kegan Paul.

## Acknowledgments

The authors and publisher are grateful to Michael Yeats and Macmillan London Limited, and Macmillan Publishing Company (USA) (copyright 1924 by Macmillan Publishing Co., Inc., renewed 1952 by Bertha Georgie Yeats) for permission to reproduce material from 'A Prayer for My Daughter' by W. B. Yeats; and to Michael Yeats and Macmillan London Limited, and Macmillan Publishing Company (USA) (copyright 1933 by Macmillan Publishing Co., Inc., renewed 1961 by Bertha Georgie Yeats) for material from 'For Anne Gregory' by W. B. Yeats. We are also grateful to the following for permission to reproduce the plates: BBC Hulton Picture Library (plates 3.1, 3.7, 3.16, 4.1a, 4.1b, 4.2, 4.3a, 4.3b, 4.4a, 4.4b, 4.4c, 4.5a, 4.5b, 4.6, 4.7, 4.8, 4.9, 4.10, 4.11a, 4.11b, 4.11c, 4.12); the National Gallery, London (plates 3.2, 3.3, 3.11, 3.13); The Vatican Museum (plate 3.4); Documentation photographique de la Réunion des musées nationaux (Musée du Louvre), (plates 3.5, 3.18); Staatliche Kunstsammlungen, Dresden, Gemäldegalerie Alte Meister (plate 3.6); Gemäldegalerie, Kassel (Staatliche Kunstsammlungen), (plate 3.8); Städelsches Kunstinstitut, Frankfurt a.M., photo by Ursula Edelmann (plate 3.9); Budapest Museum of Fine Arts (plate 3.10); Musée Condé, Chantilly, photo by Lauros-Giraudon (plate 3.12); the Prado, Madrid (plate 3.14); the Kunsthistorisches Museum, Vienna (plate 3.15); the Rijksmuseum, Amsterdam (plate 3.17). We are extremely grateful to Condé Nast for their kind permission to use quotations from *Vogue* magazine and other related material.

Part 1
# The History of Beauty

# Chapter 1

# Why This Book?

## Raquel

Beauty. I had not, it seemed, thought about it in years. Perhaps I was retreating from the old high-school days of pom-poms and football games, when self-worth could be measured by how many football players you could catch or, maybe, I somehow had become convinced that it was simply unintelligent for a woman to think about things like that. After all, there were so many other important things to think about.

But on that hot July day as I was trudging up the hill to Robin's house for dinner and conversation, my mind would not stop thinking about beauty. As I thought about my face, about my full lips, my cinnamon-colored skin, and traces of my mother's Indian in my eyes, I began to feel ugly. Of course, it did not help much that I had just leaped over thirty and that the man with whom I had been involved for twelve years had suddenly cast aside his utter devotion and taken off with a blond six years younger than me.

'Blonds. . . more fun,' I thought, and began to feel that to be condemned to my dark self for the rest of my life was to be condemned to a life of misery. Indeed, as thoughts of beauty wore on I became more and more miserable. But why? I had the notion that I had always been comfortable with my looks – at times, even rather pleased with people's reactions towards my appearance. 'You look exotic. Where are you from?' I was often asked. I suppose that my face wore the mixture of my Jewish-Mexican parentage rather well, for when I told them they were not surprised. 'An interesting combination,' they'd say.

The thought did not comfort me. Being interesting meant being different. While I imagined that I had always delighted in the different, at the moment it wasn't me but a blond, however insignificant she looked, who with her bleached mane was having all the fun. Jealousy? No, not exactly. It was not just a blond, it was, I realized, *all* blonds who made me feel different and that difference, at that moment, translated itself into inadequacy. I tried to seek refuge from my thoughts, to escape such stupid emotions, to think of happier times. How could I succumb to such pettiness. . . beauty and blonds?

It was not always this way. During my late teenage years I would invent faces for the mirror in practice for a brief courtship with the camera. I quit modeling almost as soon as I had started. 'Do not get involved in anything which centers only on your looks,' my mother once told me. 'Why?' I asked. 'Because you'll suffer. There will always be someone better looking and beauty which depends on youth doesn't last.' It was less my mother's warning than my awkward movements in front of the camera, my inability to look seductively in its eye, that sent me off in search of books instead of bookings.

Earlier, too, grown-ups had always thought of me as a pretty little girl. Kids liked me. Little boys would chase me around the school yard trying to catch me, but I was fast and would run and hide, laughing all the while as I learned the cues of coquetry. In my Spanish-speaking home my mother would call me '*princesa*' and, not knowing that it was only a term of endearment, I almost believed her, believed that I was waiting for someone to discover the princess I really was. After all, I had read of such things in fairy tales. Why not me?

Well, the most immediate problem was that princesses are always blond – at least the good ones – and they certainly don't have the features that I had. They are beautiful in their fluffy pink and white dresses. Even then I must have looked at myself in the mirror and known that I was barred from the kingdom of beauty.

No matter what other people might have thought of me, picture books told me differently and, no doubt, they spoke the truth when they spoke of fine features, yellow hair, rosy cheeks, blue eyes, and cotton-candy dresses. Here I was with my dark unruly hair, dark eyes, cinnamon-colored skin, and a mouth that was big enough to hold the whole secret of my emerging agony. I must have been confused, I thought, as I walked bent in meditation. It must have hurt to know that it was for others, not me, to live happily ever after.

After grade school I held tight to my secret; I almost convinced myself that my features weren't really that 'off.' Sometimes it was as if, after staring at the mirror a long enough time, my face would undergo a magical transformation: the eyes began to look lighter, the nose finer, the hair straighter, and the mouth. . . well, the mouth in repose looked fleshy but if I smiled it stretched and the lips appeared thinner. By concentrating hard enough I could wish my 'bad' looks away.

Still, despite all my secret maneuverings, my appearance did not seem to offend people's aesthetic sensibilities, or affect my ability to attract people to me. Somehow there seemed to be a contradiction between the way other people saw me and the way I saw myself. But this, too, I subjected to scrutiny. Growing up in Berkeley in the 1960s was an unusual experience. People seemed to appreciate or, at least, tolerate differences in others. In school I was singled out by teachers in a nice way. Because I spoke Spanish they often asked me to go before the class to tell my classmates a little about Mexican culture. It made me feel kind of special – a 'specialness' which spilled over to other activities.

Yet underneath it all, underneath the pretenses that differences were tolerated, I was not allowed to forget that I was different and I was made to feel, I realized, somewhat freakish. As I labored to unravel my obsession with beauty I remembered one incident which deeply hurt me, which made me know that my differences could never be covered up or wished away, that at any moment they could be used against me.

I was thirteen and had just won election to the student body of my junior high school. I remember that I was sitting on a bench eagerly waiting for a bus to take me home. I could hardly wait to tell my mother the exciting news. It was a warm spring day and I was wearing a full skirt that I had matched with a yellow blouse which showed to advantage the contours of my growing body. I felt a sense of pride and satisfaction.

But the feeling seemed to round itself out only for an instant before it was rudely ruptured by the sound of two girlfriends of mine who positioned themselves on the other side of the street hurling taunts that at first I could not understand. The words 'Aunt Jemima' interrupted the steady hiss of the cars that were swooshing past me, making it difficult at first to get a glimpse of my ex-friends whose mouths were poised on these abusive words, 'Aunt Jemima.' It was the first time that my differences had been so clearly cast in racial terms. Unable to figure out how else to torment me, they settled on my looks, which gave them ammunition enough. I looked different from them, and 'Aunt Jemima' forcefully captured that difference. No more had to be said.

Instead of entering my home bragging about my victory, I walked in bent with defeat. My mother at first didn't understand, nor do I know if she ever did understand why I cried and hurled abuse at my curly hair. But now I realized that somehow I had been silently blaming my mother for my different looks.

My mother had died just a few months earlier, and the memory of her life was still painful to me. As I reviewed my obsession with beauty I was filled with remorse at my inability to tell her that I remembered so much more than those sometimes troubled silences when I found myself staring at her and assessing the curve of her cheekbones, the impenetrable black color of her Indian eyes and long hair, the fullness of her body. I remembered that when I was small she looked so beautiful to me as she would bend her head to brush her long black hair; she had bearing, poise that I had rarely encountered. But as I grew older and began to see that the curve of her brow, the outline of her cheeks were like mine, her looks pleased me less well. As I thought about the confusion that had beset my childhood, I began to feel a rage and resentment that I remember feeling only once before, when I came home that day suddenly transformed into Aunt Jemima. Then, I swore that I wouldn't let it bother me. I gathered those friends who hadn't split from me and proposed that for our year book our motto should be 'To free the slaves.' Even then I wanted to free those who had bound themselves to the slavish mentality of judging acceptability on the basis of looks, on the basis of racial prejudice. Yet here I was unknowingly enslaved to the same mentality that I proposed to protest.

Now, I began to see that despite years of popularity and success with both men and women, I *had* let it bother me. I felt a deep resentment towards those who bore the privilege of their whiteness. I felt that the battle of beauty and ugliness was really a battle between the haves and have nots, between those who could aspire to the toothpaste smiles that Madison Avenue and Hollywood sold and those who had long practiced keeping their mouths shut.

My reflections now led me back to Boston and a conversation I had with an Argentinian friend of mine. 'Raquel,' she said, 'I really like the Indian in your looks. There is something rather special about them.' I acted complimented as I was supposed to but privately I felt anxious and uneasy. 'She was insulting me,' I thought, 'telling me I am ugly and disguising it as a compliment.' 'Thank you,' I said aloud, feeling a strange mixture of shame and pride in my Indian looks. But the problem, I realized, was less hers than mine, and it was something that I knew I would have to work out in due time. Besides, I was more troubled by her next observation: 'I think that discrimination based on beauty is more prevalent than discrimination based on race.' I was outraged by the remark. 'How can you possibly say that?' I countered, insisting that our notion of beauty was determined to a large extent by racial prejudice. We had come to no conclusions about the nature of either beauty or racism, and I had pretty much wiped the conversation from my memory. But now I felt sharply the intensity of my anger. 'Discrimination based on beauty,' I thought, 'is rooted in racism.' Blonds have more fun, I felt, because they are free to have more fun, because billboards and magazine covers and TV ads have made it legitimate to be blond, so that everywhere they look they are reminded of their legitimacy. No identity crises for them.

This narrow argument didn't satisfy me. There was more to it, much more. My friend was onto something, ill-expressed perhaps. After all, the whole matter of beauty was troubling her as it had troubled other friends of mine who wore their privileges easily. But these women didn't talk about it; they were just vaguely troubled by it. I felt different. I had to talk about it. It was as if my mental meanderings, my anger had to be transformed into action, given some form. My pace quickened. I turned the corner to Robin's house.

I knocked on the door. When she opened it was as if a

terrible spell had finally been broken. 'Robin,' I said with a sense of urgency. 'Do you want to write a book with me?' I waited for a response. 'What about?' she asked. 'About beauty.'

## Robin

There is a photograph of myself as a child of three, sitting on a tricycle. The child is dimpled, plumpish, brown-haired and dark-eyed, gazing confidently out at the camera. It seems a rather unremarkable portrait, except that family legend has it that it was a photograph that was submitted in a children's beauty contest, and subsequently won third prize (a pair of roller skates). It was a small local contest, hardly a spectacular victory, but none the less the fact that I was entered in and won (even third prize) in a beauty contest seems to me today not merely astonishing, but irreconcilable with my feelings about my looks from childhood to the present. For a child to be entered in a beauty contest means that her parents think highly enough of her looks, and consider looks important enough, for them to make the not-inconsiderable effort. For the child to win means that, at the tender age of three, she has already absorbed many of the assumptions of American womanhood, knows how to flirt with the camera (and the photographer besides), wants to be beautiful badly enough to make the not-inconsiderable effort to win. Again, I don't think any of this is particularly unusual or remarkable: surely many readers share similar early experiences. But it is remarkable from the point of view of what happened thereafter.

What happened is that, from very shortly after that triumphant moment, there exist virtually no pictures of me by myself, and only one or two with the other members of my family (in which, presumably, my presence was unavoidable). On the evidence of these few remaining photos, my whole response to the camera, to the event of picture-taking, has changed altogether. The little girl no longer confronts the camera, or if she does, she glares at it with suspicion and hostility. Mostly, though, she gives the impression that she is not present at all, or at least is not a participant in the event: she is looking elsewhere, her gaze downcast, her demeanor suggesting she wants nothing more than invisibility, that she does not belong in the picture and is hardly an adornment to it. Nothing could be further from her mind or hopes than that the picture being taken could establish her as a beauty – she seems to suspect, or fear, the reverse, and by withdrawing emotionally, if not physically, from the event, she hopes to minimize the blow of the inevitable verdict. To this day I cringe in the presence of a camera.

Then, at the age of three, did I give up forever on every young girl's dream? If I did not entirely give up on beauty, how did I come to terms with the split between the dream and the observed physical reality? Or, on the other hand, how *did* my conscious abandonment of the dream alter the physical reality?

These are questions not easily answered, not even from the vantage point of thirty-six years and much reflection later. What changes in a child when she knows she is not able to live up to the world's expectations of her?

There was the hoping against hope: my decision at age seven or so to be a movie actress when I grew up (although certainly I knew already in my heart the unlikelihood of that); my fascinated reading, a few years after that, of teenage novels about aspiring models; and a note in a diary I kept when I was eleven or twelve, about a wedding, or a big dressy party I attended in a flowered pink chiffon dress, with lacy puff sleeves and an apple-green silk sash: 'Everyone said I looked like a princess.' Do these represent the last stirrings of hopefulness, or the denial of a child who has already turned her back on the aspirations of womanhood?

The 'princess' dress aside, I took certain steps to shield myself from the bitterest disappointment. I felt that if I claimed homeliness as my own choice, under my control, it would hurt less. (I certainly never articulated this consciously, but looking back, it seems clear enough that I worked pretty hard toward that goal.) When I was ten or so I let my hair grow long, but stopped brushing or combing it, so that it finally matted into a tangle that no comb could penetrate. I wore clothes in any state of disrepair, and my reluctance to take care of them was my mother's futile despair. At the same time, curiously, after it was found that I needed to wear glasses, I fought ferociously for a year against wearing them, with a passion that suggested a life-and-death issue, because I was afraid they would make me look 'different.' Of course, I already looked different enough, but at least some of that was by my own choice (of sorts), while the glasses were imposed on me by someone else.

From seventh through twelfth grade I went to an all-girls' school, and so avoided directly confronting the problem of popularity most of the time. In the summer, however, my family lived in a community of about seventy-five families which was both homogeneous (Jewish, middle-class, professional) and static in its membership (most of us had been together summers from the time we were toddlers). There were some thirty boys and girls of my age, who from early childhood had attended the community day camp together and consequently had known each other for years, probably too well. So we acknowledged no real possibility of personality change. Your role in the group, your popularity, your talents, remained constant. You were perceived as being what you were when you were five, forever.

In school, during the winter, I gradually came to feel respected for my scholarly and creative talents, and (amazingly enough) well-liked by a respectable number of people, elected by my senior year to offices of importance. In that school, appearance really was secondary: while we voted, among other superlatives, for the 'most attractive' senior, I recall feeling somewhat at a loss to decide. It had never been a matter for attentive discussion, and wasn't considered any sort of crowning achievement. We voted on it because that was what you did, one of the things you mentioned in a year book, but not because most of us took it terribly seriously. So for those years I flourished, feeling I was somehow able – however impermanently – to escape the losing confrontation with beauty.

In the summer, though, the business resurfaced in all its lurid melancholy. As we entered adolescence, the fifteen or so young women of my age came to be aware of a pecking order, based increasingly on popularity with boys. That in turn was presumably based on 'personality,' but in fact we knew better. Any of us could have given a list of ourselves in order of looks, and the pecking order following directly from that. I knew perfectly well – I could read the signs clearly, above it all as I theoretically was – that I was last on the list, and there was nothing I could do to change it. I nurtured my various eccentricities of character (which remained quiescent during the school year), figuring if they wouldn't like me, they would at least have their hands full putting up with me: I would choose to make myself unlovable as well as unlovely, and I must say I did an impressively complete job of it. (Here too I didn't really choose to choose, but took the only choice I felt I had.)

Because appearance, and fashion, were downplayed in school, I felt I could experiment with them along with everyone else. I wore the same circle skirts, saddle shoes, angora sweaters, as my classmates; we waffled our bottoms with the same number of layers of crinolines that were *de rigueur* for teenagers during the 1950s. I probably wore less make-up, did less with my hair than many of my contemporaries, but I recall wearing lipstick regularly and sleeping on the large rollers that were essential equipment during those years before the home blow-dryer.

If I stopped to think about it, though, I assumed during those years that the world of flirtation, love and marriage was unlikely to be mine. But it didn't trouble me terribly, since I had other, more glamorous ambitions and these were encouraged by my successes in school.

When I got to college, however, things changed rather dramatically. College was a women's school within a large men's university of unquestionable academic repute, the women according to legend brighter than the men (and also, by legend, avoided by them in favour of women from other schools in the area who were less intellectually daunting and more interested in the feminine graces appropriate to the doctors', lawyers' and stockbrokers' wives that were those men's destiny). Despite our reputation for high intellectuality and little concern for appearances, dating and marriage were of paramount importance, especially as we drew closer to graduation, and looks were a matter of concern. To my astonishment, I actually found myself married before I graduated. But I couldn't understand why he wanted me, and as I reflect on it now, the main reason I wanted him was that I felt marriage to him was my only chance to achieve respectability. But I spent eleven years smoldering in that marriage before it ended, despising first myself and then him for my predicament but unwilling to make a move towards ending it.

And as I fell into this largely-unconscious despair and self-disgust, other things predictably went with it: I cut my hair for my wedding; then not again for eleven years. (I cut it again about a month before my husband announced he was leaving me.) I bought virtually no clothing for the duration, except for a few absolutely necessary maternity clothes. Of course I stopped wearing make-up. My ostensible reasons were simple: I was married. Why did I need to play the game any longer? My husband encouraged this point of view. But of course I saw many examples to the contrary, which I was not at all tempted to follow.

If I were to see the person I have described as a stranger, if I were to draw conclusions from external impressions and nothing else, I might well be tempted to declare that person the exception to a main argument of this book: that the desire for beauty, or at least for attractiveness, possesses every woman, that every woman considers her looks a vital part of herself, that to fail to realize one's full potential for beauty is to feel oneself a failure as a woman and a human being. I don't, I think, perceive myself as a failure; but I consider myself strikingly homely, and do as little as is humanly possible to overcome that.

How am I to account for the contradiction? I think it is no contradiction, and I have already explained why it is not. Denial of a pressing concern does nothing to dispel it; in fact, it exacerbates it, recreating the fear anew time and again. I don't think I have ever – in my childhood, or now – transcended the anguish of appearances, I have merely learned to work around it, by means of believing that I was in control of those appearances. Of course, I have never really been.

Therefore it might have seemed surprising to an outsider that I reacted as I did to Raquel's suggestion, as she entered my house for dinner that evening.

## Our story

In the spring of 1979 we were team-teaching a course. Twice a week, before the class met, we would get together to plan what to do during that meeting. Of course, before we got down to serious business, we'd engage in a little 'small talk' – and after a while, noticed the same topics recurring. How terrible I look today; I have to get a haircut, but can't figure out what kind of a haircut would make me look good/tolerable/less disgusting; I can't find clothes that I like that make me look halfway decent; my breasts are too small; I have to lose weight; so-and-so, who is blond, seems to be having more fun. . . and so on, and so on. Then, after a couple of minutes of this, we'd stop and smile at each other, sheepishly. What drivel, we'd say. Here are two professional women with PhD's, meeting to talk about serious and professional matters, and the best we can do is to get bogged down in trivia about our looks and our feelings about them! We call ourselves feminists, we'd say ruefully. If anybody else we knew – any of our feminist friends – could just hear this conversation! We felt embarrassed, ashamed of ourselves as women and as scholars.

But finally – unable to kick the habit – we thought again. Why was this topic, alone among the others we commiserated with each other about, during a time of great personal stess for both of us, the only one we couldn't respect ourselves for talking about? Why did we feel the way we felt after such talks – a pang of fear at the self-revelation, shame at the subject matter, but over all, relief at having mentioned it? And why had both of us – who each had a circle of trusted friends with whom we could discuss 'anything' – never, in fact, discussed these topics except for a fleeting moment or two, with anyone else?

It was self-indulgent, we told ourselves. It was reinforcing the bad old stereotypes – women as vain and self-absorbed. It was the evil stepmother looking in the mirror, bemoaning the signs of wear and tear. It brought back the lessons learned at mothers' knees, from the media: women are in competition with one another and can never be true friends, and looks are the arena in which the battle is fought. Hence, women cannot openly discuss their looks with each other. It would be giving too much away to the competition. And even the women's movement, our rediscovery of sisterhood in so many other powerful ways, had not erased this unease in this one area. Truly, and shockingly, we had exposed the last taboo – what neither feminists nor any other women could admit to openly: our feelings about how we and other women looked, our fantasies, our pleasures, our fears, our endless obsession.

It was time to look into the mirror again, but to ask it a different sort of question.

We had talked about it often enough before, of course, but informally and personally. We hadn't thought of beauty as a problem, or a Problem – not a feminist issue, not at all something you brought up as a serious thought in public. It was what you agonized about privately, with yourself, hardly even in words, when you woke at 3 a.m.; it was what flitted through your mind as you tried to shut it out, looking in the mirror the next morning. It was what nagged at you as you turned the page of the glossy magazine, nudged you in the ribs as you watched the diet soft-drink commercial on TV. But it wasn't something you had or were expected to have a fleshed-out, publicly-visible opinion about. Anyhow there was only one opinion, though apparently a different one in different circles. And it was not a topic for political discussion anywhere. For anyone.

Maybe with close friends, as we had become over two years of team-teaching, the thoughts too private for words could be given a voice, but always, up till that moment, as defining your individual neurosis, your secret shame. We had spent time, of course, in consciousness-raising groups in earlier years, and in them we had thought we had dealt with *every* woman's secret, every hidden shame, desire, fear, hope. . . and yet the subject had never to our recollection been mentioned, not in those groups of thoughtful, feminist, politically-savvy and angry women. That in itself was curious, we were eventually to realize, but not yet. At first it was just with a personal sense of relief that we realized that there were words for it, that someone else had thought the same thoughts, felt the same anguish, hope, fear, fury – and never spoken of it to another soul.

Why could you discuss the other taboos – masturbation,

menstruation, things too unspeakable to contemplate until recently – with your women friends and consider it politically valid and intellectually enriching to do so – and not this? If it was a feminist triumph of sorts that these topics had become defused and shorn of their mystery, why did this last taboo remain? Why, that evening, did we have to give each other reasons, to believe that the topic of beauty was serious and not insulting to a woman? We weren't quite convinced ourselves – not yet.

We had talked enough to each other to realize that our working pretense, that beauty was not important or interesting to intelligent women, was only a defense. We were beginning to understand more fully that however you dealt with it, it kept coming back, it was never solved. We had been told, often enough, that the way to deal with a problem that wouldn't go away was to turn and confront it head-on: to transform it from an emotional bogeyman to an intellectual conundrum. In that way too the book made sense to us: bring the questions we tormented ourselves with into the light of day, and they would recede – for ourselves and, if we could do a good job of it, for other people too.

But we still felt some unease. We acknowledged our fears and yearnings about beauty, and acknowledged our relief in their recognition. But we really hadn't approached other people in any depth. Perhaps we were unique in the world, or members of a small cult of diehard neurotics? Maybe what we had tentatively identified as the last great taboo, the anguish that separates women from themselves, men, and each other, was no more than a twitch, a minor annoyance. Why make a heart attack out of a little indigestion? We reproached ourselves. To agonize over your looks is narcissistic, self-indulgent – those adjectives that have been hurled at women, by men and woman alike, since the beginning of language. Was it not even more so to worry about worrying about appearance? Meta-narcissism, perversity indeed! To justify to ourselves the worth of expending time on the effort, we had to believe that other people – most other people – found the business of looks a painful one, and that the pain was a real interference with productive living. So we started talking to people, questioning them as closely as we were questioning ourselves. We got results that might have surprised us – in fact they did, come to think of it. Our surprise just goes to show the extent of the implicit assumptions and propaganda we had encountered all our lives, that we had never thought to examine. For example, that self-adornment was a pleasure for women, simple and fun. Women's vanity is legend. But we found it to be more and less. Some of us openly and consciously agonize about our looks; some of us merely look in the mirror in states of mind varying from mild anxiety to all-out panic, squeezing a pimple here, pulling out a gray hair there; some of us blanket a vanity table with expensive cosmetics, making ourselves over from head to foot; others do more, a week at the fat farm, ten days in the hospital recovering from a face-lift or a fanny-tuck. Some of us seem to rise above it all: we wear no make-up, none at all, let our hair go gray and our crow's feet triumph, buy clothing only to protect ourselves from the elements and the vice squad. Surely this diversity of responses shows we were mistaken, we thought. There is no universal feminine terror, no widespread neurosis. We've come to terms with it, lots of us, in lots of ways. It's not a problem. Thank goodness! *Something's* not a problem!

But then we started listening more carefully, to ourselves and everyone else. We noticed a few funny things. One: we had believed that serious women, intellectuals, feminists (ourselves) weren't interested in the topic. But we'd mention to our friends (who matched this description) that we were thinking about beauty, and we couldn't stop them. They begged to be interviewed. They begged to read the manuscript. They told us anecdotes – unbidden, uncensored. And as they talked, memories came back to them, incidents they had buried. They laughed. They cried. It became clearer every time how much looks, and people's own responses to their looks, were intertwined in their personalities, affected everything they had accomplished and hoped for themselves in the future. It wasn't the dichotomy: looks *or* brains, frivolous *or* serious. No, the most serious and the brainiest of us had confronted the matter of looks, and hadn't quite come to terms with it.

We found other interesting responses. Some people got angry. Why were we interested in beauty? They never thought of it. Never – you hear? Never! Looks didn't matter. It was what was inside that counted. Inside – you hear? We were perfectly willing to take these statements at face value and indeed, they represented some of the most frequently-reiterated beliefs of humankind, so we felt a responsibility to put credence in them. Only one thing deterred us, and that was the intensity with which such opinions were offered – odd to offer platitudes with such a passion, we thought.

It was clear enough that some of us consciously and actively worried about our looks. Were we undesirable? Did we do enough? Would we eventually end up undesirable, or could we stave off that day, maybe forever? It was worth a good deal to do so, but what if we couldn't? These questions tormented some of us, mildly bothered others, but clearly they were present for many.

But how about the others, the ones who wore no make-up, cut their hair when it got in their eyes, put on any old thing, and explicitly couldn't care less? Weren't those of us who didn't play into the stereotype free from it? We prided ourselves on that, until we looked a little further. More often than not, the apparent conquest of vanity revealed at its source a fear: that all the vanity in the world could not make its possessor presentable, so that it was better not even to try. But this decision hardly brought relief, only a sense of missed opportunity and general dissatisfaction. In short, no one was immune, and the more immune you think you are, the more severely afflicted you will turn out to be. That is not to say, of course, that the pursuit of beauty knows no delight, for there can be and often is pleasure in catching the admiring glance, or even pleasure in being pampered, cosseting yourself with things that look good and feel good and smell good. But we should not pretend that there is no conflict because on the surface none can be discerned.

We decided then to write this book, for ourselves as much as our readers. And as we began, more and more that we had never really understood or even been fully aware of began to make sense to us. As we began to understand, some of the pain we had felt started to ebb. And we hope that, as you read, the same things will happen to you.

The first title to occur to us was *The Politics of Beauty*. The reason it struck us as apt was perhaps the same as the reason we eventually demoted it to subtitle: the ubiquity of *Politics*, at that time, in titles. But embarrassing as the imputation of faddishness might be, we were loath to abandon that title altogether, as it seemed in many ways to encapsulate our position. We were writing a political document, looking at beauty as a political issue.

Still, the title struck us, at first, rather like the alleged product of politics: strange bedfellows. Could two words so different in their connotations coexist on the same title page? Politics has traditionally been a man's game; beauty, a woman's, and we view with suspicion anyone who crosses over, whether Bella Abzug or Liberace, in either direction. Politics is perceived as active: men engage in politics, they act, they make deals, they manipulate, they arrange. Beauty, like women, is stereotypically passive; it is created by the beholder, it is appreciated, it is an adornment to someone else. Beauty merely *is*, it does not *do*.

Politics, as is politic, eludes definitions: the word has an untrustworthy feel to it, the ultimate reality that at heart is all symbol, getting something for a hinted-at promise. Basically, the game of politics is the exchange of power, the quest for power, the sense of what can be accomplished with one's own power, or by utilizing the power of someone else. Power, to press further, is 'the capacity to take autonomous action,' according to the *Encyclopedia of the Social Sciences*, 'the ability to pursue one's will effectively.' Power is getting what you want done, done, whether by your own strength or by influencing someone else's actions. Politics is the determination of where this power resides, how much there is, and how to get things done using it. But beauty is not autonomous, anything but: it is, platitudinously, in the eye of the beholder, not in the forms of the beheld (who is, therefore, beholden). Beauty is not itself politics, but it is deeply involved in the horse-trade that politics is.

For beauty is closely intertwined with power: the myth that married the Sleeping Beauty to Prince Charming solidifies that image. To have power, one needs to possess something that someone else wants, or needs. For a man, it can be wealth or influence or knowledge; for a woman, it has always been beauty (or someone else's accumulated wealth or strength, of which she is merely the receptacle, to allow it to be put into someone else's hands). A woman's beauty is of no intrinsic use to herself, but is of value only in that it enables her to attract to herself someone in possession of the things that will be useful or pleasurable to her; so she trades her beauty for his wealth, influence, charm, strength. But it is not really a comfortable trade.

'Uneasy lies the head that wears the crown,' said Shakespeare. The possession of *any* kind of power is problematic. Others may envy it, and someone with more power may therefore appropriate yours, or make yours seem worthless by comparison. This is as true of beauty as of any other source of power. If you have used your power in the political game, once you no longer are seen to possess it, you lose – everything.

All human acquisitions and properties that create power are subject to this danger, but at least most of them involve judgment by objective and external standards. If I can get your head cut off, I demonstrably have power. If my bankbook truthfully lists several million dollars in my account, I am powerful. Moreover, with these kinds of influence, my powerfulness is apt to increase over time. Power creates more power, as one grows older and cannier and acquires more secrets, cronies, whatever is useful in the game. Money is well known to make more money.

Beauty is different in every way. It is not objectively demonstrable. One cannot count it, or objectively demonstrate for the satisfaction of all that A has it, B doesn't. A and B certainly don't know, because the decision isn't up to them. Their beauty isn't *theirs*, but is the result of the judgments of others. Those judgments may change with the season, as fashion necessarily is fickle. And they inevitably will change with time – certainly in a youth-worshipping culture like ours.

A woman can spend her youth learning to be beautiful, and her maturity learning how it feels to be treated as beautiful, becoming used to the privileges that power confers. But at the same time, she is, of course, becoming dependent upon it – just as anyone with power from any source comes to need it. But where possessors of other sources of power can look forward, with cleverness and luck, to holding onto that power until death, the beauty has to be aware that she will lose it, through no misdeed of her own, but absolutely certainly. And, like a witch's curse in a fairy tale, the loss is particularly terrifying because one never knows when it will strike, whether, indeed it has already struck. How can you play politics when your commodity may at the very moment you need to call on it already have vanished?

Thus, beauty is political in that it figures in the exchange of power and influence. But it is also political in that the prospect of being considered beautiful is a political instrument held over women: a promise, a threat. The little girl is signaled, subtly or not: if you do this, say this, act like this, you will be beautiful; if you do otherwise, you give up your one chance of worldly success. As we all are controlled, our actions and even thoughts governed by political power, the power of those in command, women in particular are controlled by the tyranny of looks, by the threat of having approval, and with it power, withheld. And as we shall see, we have been warned that the judgment of beauty goes not to the assertive, the strong, the autonomous. The power of beauty is the power of the weak. It is a paradox, and a dangerous one for women. But women have been controlled and governed by the strength of that paradox, having no other options.

Women have, then, given up much of their potential true power to compete in the beauty game, and have gained less by it than they have been led to believe. Fairy tale, cautionary tale, romance – all lure us into the beauty-is-power paradox. We have to understand the force of that myth over all of us in order to free ourselves from it, to become politically effective in a true way. It is for this – to understand why beauty is political, and why women must learn the pitfalls of that form of political exchange, that we have written this book.

# Chapter 2
# The Problem of Beauty: Myth and Reality

Picture the scene.

A royal wedding, celebrating the marriage of Thetis, the daughter of a sea-god, immortal in her own right, to a mortal hero, Peleus. All the Olympian gods are there. The guests are having a divinely good time, wishing the couple well. Then, suddenly Eris, the goddess of discord, for obvious reasons uninvited, materializes, only long enough to fling into the assemblage a golden apple inscribed, 'For the Fairest.'

Chaos erupts. You might think the serene Olympian deities immune to such petty competition, but by no means. Each of the three principal goddesses demands the prize: Hera, queen of the gods, sister and consort of Zeus, goddess of marriage and childbirth; Pallas Athene, patron of wisdom, poetry, and invention; foam-born Aphrodite, goddess of love and beauty. Each in her own way is supremely fair. Who is the rightful recipient of the golden apple? The assembled guests are unable or unwilling to make the decision. They suggest arbitration: bring the dispute to an impartial judge. The Trojan prince Paris is selected for this role.

Paris' task might be difficult enough in itself, for political as well as aesthetic reasons. But to complicate the situation further, each of the deities offered a bribe: Hera, power and wealth; Athene, honor and glory, and renown in war. These were tempting offers indeed, but Aphrodite's was still more so: the most beautiful mortal woman on earth for his wife. Paris hardly hesitated. Paris' choice, whatever its later disastrous repercussions, seemed perfectly reasonable to the Greeks who devised, told, and heard this story.

Aphrodite certainly intended to make good on her promise. The only problem was the prize was already married. This was

21

Helen, daughter of Leda – a famous beauty in her own right and wife of Tyndareus. Helen had been wooed by many of the most powerful princes of Greece; Tyndareus, realizing the peril her successful suitor was certainly exposing himself to, exacted an oath from all the suitors before the choice was made that they would protect her husband and their marriage with their lives. Menelaus, ruler of Sparta, was chosen.

Paris made his way to Sparta and was received hospitably by Menelaus and Helen. In Menelaus' absence, he seduced Helen and convinced her to go back with him to Troy. Menelaus returned, discovered his loss, and reminded his fellow-rulers of their oath. The Greeks gathered their armies, eagerly or reluctantly, and made war on Troy – a deadly ten-year struggle, won at hideous cost, over the possession of a woman.

The Trojans were finally vanquished, and Helen taken by Menelaus back to Sparta, where she grew gracefully old and lived happily ever after, with no further whisper of scandal attached to her. There is, in fact, a later legend exculpating Helen: that the woman Paris abducted was but a phantom, a copy – Helen herself was taken by Aphrodite to Egypt where she lived for the whole of the ten-year war. The real Helen, unscathed by infidelity, was returned to Menelaus later.

The story still has power and meaning for us today. Neither the Greeks nor we find its premises absurd. Three powerful goddesses disrupt a wedding, throw tantrums, spitefully attempt the corruption of a mortal, interfere most deleteriously with the course of world history, purely in order to ascertain who is 'the fairest'? Why not? A prince of a strong city-state, who has all or most of the perquisites a man of his time could desire, requiring an oath of loyalty from his peers – some under duress – for fear of losing a mere woman? Yes, of course. These same chieftains leaving the comfort and safety of home, engaging in human sacrifice, ten years of terrible bloodshed – for the selfsame woman? No problem. It is plausible, it is powerful. If Menelaus' fear were of losing political power, or money, we would consider the issue petty and the story implausible. We do not, as the Greeks did not.

The legend, with its eternal credibility and power, rests on the implicit assumption that beauty is of paramount importance, that its possession – whether by a woman herself or for a man, through the possession of such a woman – is of more value than anything else, worth more than power, wealth or fame. Yet at least partly for this reason it is deadly: women's beauty lures men to their own damnation and destruction. Not powerful men like Agamemnon, not intelligent men like Odysseus, not courageous men like Achilles are immune. Beauty is worth the sacrifice of life itself – but for that very reason it is baneful to its possessor and those who fall beneath her spell.

We need not confine ourselves to the Greeks. Parts and variations of this legend occur in the legends and fairy tales of all cultures. In one such tale, *Snow White*, the stepmother's wickedness derives from her vanity, from the terror that her one source of power, her beauty, will be eclipsed by that of her stepdaughter. She checks the mirror daily and sure enough, one day the mirror gives her the news she has feared. There is only one course of action. Or think of Rapunzel, whose beauty drove her jealous foster-mother to imprison her in a tower surrounded by thorns, and for whose beauty the prince gave up his eyesight. Again and again we find the dual theme: for a woman, beauty is a precious, in fact crucial, resource; for a man, a beautiful woman is worth undergoing every risk to possess, and the possession of such a woman is deserved only by the truly valiant, indeed a badge of manhood. But possession for both sexes is inextricably bound up with destruction, pain, or deprivation.

How are we to make sense of all this? Do the legends arise from realistic observation? Or do we construe reality to conform to the myth, because we *need* to believe in it? For the majority of us who are not great beauties, or do not have an intimate connection with a mythically beautiful woman, does the myth represent 'sour grapes'? If you cannot have the blessing, is it easiest to turn it into a curse? Or, if beauty is, intrinsically, a curse, do the legends represent timely warning of real dangers?

The legends surrounding beauty and those who possess it are manifold and contradictory. Virtually every myth has its opposite – odd, if proverb and parable are supposed to reflect a culture's received wisdom. Clearly we have not sorted out our collective opinion about beauty. As we examine these legends, we find some truth hidden in many of them, but others seem utterly without substance, and would appear to have risen from nothing – rather unusual for stereotypes, which typically have in them, as Walter Lippmann has argued, 'a grain of truth.' Then we must ask, as we examine some of our prevailing assumptions, Why do they exist – when their opposites also exist, and even when there is no reality to back them up? There are the myths, and the realities.

For instance, we have mentioned one familiar debate: is true beauty bestowed by nature or by artifice? To reach a conclusion we must sift through myth, countermyth, and reality.

## The myth

Beauty is God-given. It cannot be acquired by deliberate effort. Certainly we recognize that natural endowments often are, and must be, enhanced, but we do not give credit to the artist. 'Natural beauty,' like 'natural blond,' is high and unambiguous praise, in a way that 'natural artist,' or 'natural actor,' is not: the latter carry with them the hint that it comes too easily, a bit unfairly. And we can compliment a writer, or an architect, by telling him or her how hard the work must have been to produce. But we would never dream, short of really exemplary cattiness, of complimenting a woman by saying, 'It must have taken you *hours* to create that face!' Or, 'Your hairdresser must have spent *days* on your hair!' We can appreciate unqualifiedly the time and effort involved in making the Sistine Chapel a feast for the eyes, but not a comparable amount of labor on the person. To learn that a noted model or movie star spends hours primping prior to going before the cameras distinctly diminishes her luster for us. And indeed, for certain aspects of the beautification process, any labor expended is wisely concealed, and learning of the trouble taken is tantamount to espionage: we may inquire about a haircut, but not a face-lift, or electrolysis.

## The countermyth

'We must labor to be beautiful,' says Yeats, a sentiment particularly in evidence in books of advice to women, but not unknown, as we see, to poetry. This piece of general wisdom hovers on the border between platitude and well-kept secret. If beauty is natural, why the plethora of instructional texts – from at least the Roman poet Ovid's *Ars Amatoria* of the first century AD to the latest cosmetological manual? Go to the bookstore: shelves overflow with advice, from getting more from your hair to having the world's most beautiful feet; how to become blond – thin – bosomy – pimple-free – and so forth. And while misogynists rail at the feminine vanity that keeps women in front of their mirrors perfecting themselves for hours, women know full well that if they don't seem interested enough to show evidence of working at how they look, they will be considered undesirable and unfeminine. Indeed, many kinds of looks are thought to be beautiful precisely because they are unnatural, and clearly must be the result of artifice and application: blond hair, suntans in winter, long spiky eyelashes, eye shadow, opalescent lipstick, and much, much more. In part this has to do with the polarization between human and animal that is, as Robert Brain (1979) has pointed out, a significant force behind judgments of beauty. Humans are the unnatural animal, and the more we underscore that fact, the more beautiful we are. Of course, there are limits to this, and the provocatively unnatural is a dangerous toy to play with.

Because the myth and the countermyth exist side by side, we find cultures trying to deal with them, reconcile them or decide between them, in sometimes rather bizarre ways. What, for instance, are we to make of the ladies-in-waiting at the court of Marie-Antoinette playing at being milkmaids and shepherdesses? What they were attempting to suggest, of course, was the pure unspoiled natural and unsophisticated beauty of country maids; but it had to be accomplished by monumental labors, and presumably the most successful court lady was the one who obviously expended the most effort and expense in the camouflage. (One suspects an *actual* milkmaid would be ignored or derided at Versailles.) Sometimes the artifice is justified by the argument that beauty gives pleasure to those seeing it, and therefore it is an act of consideration to labor so as to afford those others as much delight as possible. But there is still an irony in the idea of making oneself beautiful by techniques that, ideally, will not be discovered. Standards change regarding how much make-up and so forth is 'too much'; but every culture has some notion of too much, and when the limit is exceeded the result and its wearer will be deemed tawdry. W. S. Gilbert, in *The Mikado*, succinctly expressed the balance between the two ideals:

Braid the raven hair, weave the supple tress,
Deck the maiden fair in her loveliness.
Paint the pretty cheek, dye the coral lip,
Emphasize the grade of her ladyship.
Art and nature thus allied
Go to make a pretty bride.

Although the most prevalent assumption is that the best beautifying technique is the least conspicuous – 'the greatest art is in the concealment of art,' as Ovid put it – sometimes, as if bursting out of a particularly confining straitjacket, fashion openly turns her back on 'naturalness' as desirable. A current example is the punk-rock movement, whose practitioners vie with one another to create the most outrageous, infuriating effect on the rest of the populace. Various means are used to create the effect, all stressing unnaturalness and violation of convention in dress and deportment. Even names are created to appal: Sid Vicious, Johnny Rotten. Styles range from the merely visually shocking – hair dyed pink or green, arranged in spikes or crests; clothing deliberately tattered or heavily metallic; exaggerated make-up on both male and female faces – to the virtually pornographic: razor blades and safety pins through nose and ears; bracelets with metal projecting spikes. Behavior goes with appearance: unprovoked aggression is at the milder end; and spitting and vomiting at will and upon others at the other.

What is interesting about the punks is precisely their attempt to be as unnatural, as remote from their 'God-given' forms as possible. Asked about their choices, punk-rockers will say that to them, they are beautiful. In almost the same breath, they will say that their choice of apparel and behavior is a comment on the unnaturalness of everything in our world: the heavy emphasis on dress and cosmetics, water and air pollution, the threat of atomic holocaust, our media-induced isolation from one another, man's inhumanity to man. Then the style is both a primary choice – this is beautiful – and a secondary comment – this represents the hateful world we find ourselves in.

The punks' argument that their appearance represents beauty is in keeping with Brain's discussion of beauty as unanimal and unnatural. But the outside world's judgment of punk fashion as disgusting and provocatively ugly argues against this thesis. Why do we draw so firm a line between blood-red nails and green ones? Teased hair, dyed platinum, and pink, in spikes? While the first may in some periods be judged tasteless or overdone, it is not considered a deliberate attempt to insult or disgust the viewer, as punk is – a reason for the hostility with which it is viewed.

Although the punks present themselves as an ultra-modern response to late-twentieth-century problems, they were not the first to court lurid artificiality as an ideal. The Decadent movement, a small group of artists in France a century ago, exalted the unnatural, the lurid, and the exaggerated and received in return from the public at large little but opprobrium for their daring, a response similar to that which greets today's punks: people tend to be very suspicious of and recalcitrant to any attempt to effect sudden violent changes in current aesthetic standards. And despite our having more than a century in which to have assimilated and become comfortable with the promulgations of the Decadent movement, descriptions of its values, such as this encomium to the poetry of Baudelaire by its self-appointed chief publicist Théophile Gautier, still send a barely-repressed shudder along the contemporary spine:

the morbidly rich tints of decomposition, the tones of mother-of-pearl which freeze stagnant waters, the roses of consumption, the pallor of chlorosis, the hateful bilious yellows, the leaden grey of pestilential fogs, the metallic greens smelling of sulphide of arsenic. . . the bitumens blacked and browned in the depths of hell, and all that gamut of intensified colors, correspondent to autumn, and the setting of the sun, to overripe fruit, and the last hours of civilization.[1]

We find the same shifts of allegiance in more pragmatic cosmetological circles as well. Over the years – as advertisements for cosmetics and their intended effects, as well as make-up and costuming traditions in the movies, indicate – assumptions about the proper role of make-up have shifted dramatically. Sometimes it is intended to be striking, shocking, dramatic. Cosmetics promise to create the vamp, the *femme fatale*, with blood-red lips and nails and heavily lacquered hair; or their colors are sun-drenched, natural, outdoorsy, reminiscent of honey, of fruits, of the earth. When fashion dictates dramatic and striking make-up, last year's bronzes look drab, mousy, and washed-out; but by the next year, to be still wearing blood-red nails or heavy black mascara is to invite comparison of an ungracious kind. There is, incessantly, a shift between the assumption that beauty is something that comes from heaven, and hence cannot be acquired by human efforts, and the notion that one who wishes to be truly beautiful must work hard for it.

## The reality

As usual, the reality is somewhere in between the polar opposites. There is a general physical configuration that, in a particular time at a particular place, has the potential to be beautiful. Regularity of features – though not too regular – figures in this, as well as – at present, in our society – luxuriance of tresses and slimness of figure. Given those – which are at any rate equivalent to prettiness – a determined woman can, with diligence and perhaps some suffering, make a beauty of herself. This creative venture is equivalent in time and energy to inventing a novel out of a bare plot synopsis, but hardly receives the same recognition – at least in part because, as we have said, it is impolite to comment on the labor and energy expended on beautification. But we do tacitly recognize the contribution to nature made by artifice. Cinderella is described early in the tale as beautiful, as befits her virtuousness. But later, when the Prince comes around with the slipper, and Cinderella is sitting by the hearth in rags, smeared with ashes, he doesn't recognize her as the ethereal vision of the night before – not until he has, as a sort of joke, tried the slipper on her. Cinderella is not 'princess material' in her natural state, nor is any of us, alas.

There is a second area of controversy: is personal beauty universally recognized, or culturally-relative? Again, several positions have been advanced.

## The myth

There is such a thing as 'the most beautiful woman in the world,' and that standard holds across time and space. We could recognize it anywhere, Helen is beautiful forever, for everyone, Greeks and Trojans alike, and presumably Americans too. Beauty is an absolute, and as intrinsically recognizable and definable as any other virtue – say, goodness or wisdom. And just as those are unchanging, at least in broad outline, so must beauty be. Since there is a natural basis of beauty, and nature is unchanging, at least some aspect of beauty is invariable.

## The countermyth

Beauty is fashion. It is determined to meet people's specific needs at a particular time and place. Beauty is defined by those in power, and as the possession of power shifts, beauty will vary with it. Since what is beautiful at any time and place is determined by the vagaries of fashion, it is unpredictable and not based on any sort of universal aesthetic. (This is true of personal beauty, while natural beauty, say of a mountain range or a sunset, is universally appreciated.) This argument is particularly salient when we look at 'artificial' beauty in other cultures: the disfigurement that many cultures consider beautiful appals us. Or if we look (as we shall in the next chapter) at representations of ideal beauty in Western culture over time, it is almost inconceivable to us that these portraits are intended to capture any sort of feminine ideal.

## The reality

Again, we must draw a line somewhere near the middle, though perhaps more to the side of the countermyth. Both the natural basis, and the desired artifices, change over time and space. Further, while many of us may agree on a specific woman's beauty or lack of it, there is as often wide disagreement, which would not exist if there were a universally recognizable prototype. Even though an American Caucasian can, with some training, learn to recognize some Asian or Black types as 'beautiful,' and will accept their representation in middle-American beauty pageants, on closer inspection these 'exotic' beauties will be found to approximate more closely to the Caucasian type than to the norm of their own race. This argues against a universal standard, since we are obviously appealing to the ideals of a specific racial group, in terms of its own singular traits. Beauty is not instantly and instinctively recognizable: we must be trained from childhood to make those discriminations. Nor can we assume an objective and quantifiable standard of beauty against which everyone could be judged with equal fairness, a 'BQ' parallel to the ideal – not, of course, the reality – of the IQ.

But we still recognize certain changeless verities, more abstract than concrete. For one thing, the most ancient statues of the Greeks, or even those of more exotic cultures, still have the power to move us – not always, but frequently enough that we can assert with some confidence that some aspects of beauty evoke the same response everywhere, at least in the great majority of people. The Knidian Aphrodite and the Mona Lisa still appeal to us. And at a symbolic level, beauty is still intelligible to us in terms of polarization: the features that set us apart from animals – flowing hair, full lips, sculptured nose – are those that recur again and again, in culture after culture, as exemplifications of ideal beauty. As we shall see, the proportions of the ideal female figure change radically from time to time, but the idea of *some* recognizable proportion, some kind of symmetry of face or figure, recurs again and again.

Then there is another source of disagreement: is beauty an unqualified good, an intrinsic evil, or something in between?

Here we are confronting several myths at once. First, whether beauty is, for the world at large, beneficial or harmful: is a beautiful woman to be desired or reviled? And second, what does the possession of beauty do for its possessor? Does it enrich her life and make it happier? Or are great beauties doomed to lives of tragedy and pain, as if in recompense for being dealt a greater gift than others to begin with?

## The myth: beauty is good for us

Often in myth, beauty is allied with innocence and virtue. The beautiful woman is the good one: you can tell a book by its cover. Further, goodness itself creates beauty: beauty comes from within, handsome is as handsome does. Hence the Greeks, ever sensitive to aesthetics, found it necessary to embellish the Helen myth with the abduction to Egypt, to protect the perfect virtue of the perfect beauty. This addition marred the unity and perfection of the literary creation, but this was a necessary loss, to protect a more significant aesthetic unity – the oneness of beauty and virtue. Helen must remain unblemished.

Additionally, it seems axiomatic to us, very often, that beauty is good to have. A great beauty *should* be happy, *must* be happy – how otherwise? A great beauty must be secure in her beauty and confident of being loved. And, since beauty is allied with virtue, a beauty deserves love and gets it – all she can handle.

## The countermyth: beauty is evil and destructive

The opposite occurs in myth just as often. Too often, a beauty's allure drives men to their doom: Pandora, the Sirens, Delilah, and Eve, along with Helen, are examples. The woman herself need not necessarily be a conscious conspirator (like Delilah), but may be only a dupe of her beauty, as was Helen. But because beauty is so powerful, and arouses in its observer that most peremptory and inexplicable of impulses, sexual desire, it evokes fear. Because great personal beauty comes close to what Burke called the 'sublime' – phenomena that seem transcendent, arising not by human intervention, and thus creating awe and even dread – and because we cannot understand it, much less understand the effect it has on us, we may fear it. Thus, we perceive beauty as dangerous, and as pleasurably titillating as it may be, we are forewarned to be on guard against its effects – the myths are to that end.

Perhaps also contributing to the awe and fear is the fact that beauty is intangible, non-objective. This concept of beauty is in one sense liberating: a *tabula rasa* on which men write their fantasies. It is often pointed out that no description exists of Helen. If it did, it would evoke intellectual argumentation and individual tastes ('No, Helen can't be blond. Blonds are less beautiful than redheads.') rather than emotional fantasy and universal concurrence. Even in a photograph, a true beauty leaves something tantalizingly ineffable. We go feature by feature: this is too large, that is crooked, that an odd color. . . but still overall, it is beauty gazing out at us from the page. This is mysterious, perhaps discomfiting: we cannot analyze nor classify this phenomenon – it clearly has transcendent power. Beauty does not always announce its presence, but hints. Great beauties in fact often photograph disappointingly, what in life is irresistible seemingly flat and lusterless on paper, and a model dazzling in photographs is unnoticed in person. We cannot control beauty, not at its source, and not in our minds. That is to be feared. What we cannot control is out of control, and may destroy us.

## The myth: great beauty brings its possessor misery

Great beauties themselves seem to have more trouble than pleasure. The poet Yeats, who was obsessed with feminine beauty, reflects on its dangers to its possessor in 'A Prayer for My Daughter':

May she be granted beauty and yet not
Beauty to make a stranger's eye distraught,
Or hers before a looking-glass, for such,
Being made beautiful overmuch,
Consider beauty a sufficient end,
Lose natural kindness and maybe
The heart-revealing intimacy
That chooses right, and never find a friend.

Helen being chosen found life flat and dull,
And later had much trouble from a fool,
While that great Queen, that rose out of the spray,
Being fatherless could have her way
Yet chose a bandy-legged smith for man.
It's certain that fine women eat

A crazy salad with their meat
Whereby the Horn of Plenty is undone.

Legend obliges us, as too often does reality. Just as Helen functions to exemplify one aspect of our feelings about beauty, so Marilyn Monroe (and, to a lesser extent, other famous beauties of stage, screen, photograph, and society who lived or died painfully) serves us in another. The woman who seems to have been given everything a woman could want ungratefully refuses to be content. We feel at first a dull incomprehension, even a moment's anger, then pity – perhaps even with a pang of empathic yearning.

## The reality

There is no logical link between the possession of beauty and happiness, or success, or virtue – or their opposites. There is, however, a difference in the way we treat attractive and unattractive people, from earliest childhood. And if we believe that our childhood experiences are reflected in our mature personalities, we will not be surprised to find certain correlations. Moreover, all of us are capable of being moved by aesthetics alone. Who would not rather hear music than a jackhammer? See a sunset, rather than a slaughterhouse? Then it is not unlikely that we respond differently to an attractive person standing before us, or displaying her work to us, than to someone less happily endowed. Perhaps this makes a difference in character – it is a truism that people are different depending on whether things have come hard or easily to them. There is evidence that we respond more positively to the productions of an attractive person than to the identical work when it is allegedly produced by someone less gratifying to our senses.[2] Then, if people with great beauty can gain their desires more readily, what does this do to their characters? Theoretically, it could go either way. The beauty, to whom things come so easily, might be less insecure than the rest of us, more gracious, more generous. Or, since things have come only too easily, she has no sense of the struggles of others, lacks compassion, becomes unwilling to make the compromises the rest of us learn to make. Or, because things come so easily to her through beauty – for which she has had to do nothing active – she does not need to learn what the rest of us have had to learn – intellectual and social skills, the full development of talents. She becomes an empty shell, vain, narcissistic, useless. Or – worst of all – she ends up hostage to her beauty. Because she has learned that it is the only thing she is valued for, she comes to despise it and herself, and at the same time depend on it too much. This is not too different from the way the wealthy often regard themselves and their money. Beauty becomes, like money, externalized, a possession, one that, like money, can be lost. But it is different from money, for it *must* be lost, sooner or later. And the beauty's life becomes a terrible parody of feminine vanity: endless peering into mirrors waiting for the ineluctable sign that it's all over, repeated trips to the fat farm, the operating table, only to see the results, real or imagined, fall away in time, leaving only despair. A life predicated on beauty alone is not a life worth living. Snow White's stepmother, looking into her magic mirror every day, waiting for the inevitable sign of the end, neatly captures the link between this 'vanity,' which is fear at heart, and evil.

It is unquestionable that beauty affects others' perceptions of, and behavior toward, its possessor. But the possessor may make various uses of this special treatment: it may, and does sometimes, make her into a kinder and nobler person, like Snow White in the fairy tale. Or, conversely, it can make her into an empty, frightened, and depraved creature, like Snow White's stepmother. Of course, we also have to bear in mind that Snow White was (presumably) younger than her stepmother, and we have no testimony about Snow White's impeccable character at age forty.

This set of myths sometimes combines with the first set, and artificially-created beauty – the kind that involves looking in mirrors – is equated with evil, and natural beauty with virtue. The latter, then, is the beauty that arises from goodness, while the former arises out of vanity and selfishness. We should note, though, that this treatment of the myth puts the cart before the horse, if psychology is right: in the myth it is not beauty that makes you good, but goodness that makes you beautiful, while in reality, alas, if anything, it's the other way around. Handsome does as handsome is.

Then there are other equations and comparisons, involving the relation between beauty and intelligence, or sanity, or sense.

Here we have a couple of intertwined assumptions whose root is the rationalization we all use to console ourselves for our shortcomings: nobody's perfect. Therefore, if I lack beauty, I am compensated by virtue (brains, money); and if someone is extraordinarily attractive, that person must have some deficiency, perhaps hidden from view.

## Myth: beauty goes with stupidity

This is a recurrent stereotype in many cultures, most familiar in ours perhaps in the form of the dumb blond. Actually, this is not merely sour-grapes theorizing, but a more complex orchestration of desires. For one thing, blondness is, for us, the quintessence of the utterly feminine. Therefore, the perfect blond should capture in herself all that is stereotypically desirable in a woman. Blondness is itself a sort of passivity: the fairness of the hair, eyes, and skin of the perfect blond is parchment, the proverbial *tabula rasa* to be written upon, to absorb and reflect the ideals and illusions of those who look upon her. In that sense the blond is the embodiment of innocence, where innocence is the absence of any possible intent. This symbolization – fair is innocent, good, and pure, dark is knowing, perhaps evil – recurs not only in myth, but in more sophisticated literature into our time. Even in the movies, the heroine has a tendency to be blond, the villainess (or sidekick, just for variety) to be brunette: Marilyn Monroe and Jane Russell, for instance. Or contrast the roles that Doris Day and Elizabeth Taylor typically play. The blond in literature, is often insipid, but seldom *bad*: Amelia Sibley, Amy March, Rowena, and Rosamond Vincy come to mind: generally none too smart, but well-meaning if destructive through their combined beauty and stupidity. Contrast them with the brunettes: Becky Sharp, Jo March, Rebecca, and Dorothea Brooke, all more fully delineated characters, not necessarily bad, but certainly striving toward autonomy. For blondness is, physically, imprecise: especially in portraits, but in reality too, blond hair merges with the atmosphere to create a sort of haze, an aureole, which both symbolically beatifies and at the same time obscures its bearer. The blond, as *tabula rasa*, is someone who does not make a clear, bright mark upon her environment. And this is, too, the mark of a virtuous woman: she is not meant to be clearly perceived, but to be (in so many ways) in the background.

Hence, blond is the most beautiful, and the best blond is the one who is the most passive, has the least direct influence on her environment. And that is the 'dumb blond', who has no ideas, no ambitions other than to use her beauty to find a man to support her and, more importantly, to give her the definition she cannot achieve on her own. Hence, too, blonds are more sought-after than brunettes. This phenomenon is otherwise difficult to account for. Sociobiological explanations,[3] based on blond hair being a recessive genetic trait which must be preserved and is therefore more highly valued for reproductive purposes, sound scientific, but overlook an important hitch: if the preservation of the genes for blondness were of paramount importance, then blond men and blond women would be equally valued. But in fact, while blond men are considered perfectly all right (although the stereotypically handsome man is, of course, 'tall, dark and handsome,'), they have none of the mystique of blond women. And this is true in very many cultures, including those where blondness is a rarity, an exotic feature. When the Romans first encountered the blond barbarians from the North, it was the women who took to wearing blond wigs in emulation – not the men.

Additionally, beauty almost naturally seems to ally itself with passivity of mind, for beauty is itself a passive characteristic – it is in the eye of the beholder. If beauty is not derived from activity, it is apt to be stereotypically associated with mental passivity.

## Countermyth: beauty goes with brains

There is not too much evidence for this in popular mythology, only a recurrent bit of public-relations fluff which probably is the exception that proves the myth itself. More often than can be attributable to mere coincidence, and not directly referable to any observable reality, screen sex goddesses (Jill St John and Jayne Mansfield are prominent examples) are claimed by their publicity to have extraordinarily high IQs – not in the merely 'gifted' (120–40) category, but in the range above 160 – well above 'genius' level. We may wonder what we are to make of this phenomenon. It is not really important whether or not the claim is true (especially given the uncertainty as to what an IQ means in any case). Even if true, if it were considered irrelevant or negative, it would not appear in the entertainer's biography. But this information seems to be used principally for its shock value, the startling contrast to our expectations. Actresses who are undeniably attractive, even blond, but not renowned for voluptuousness, seldom have high IQs made a part of their public legend. Rather, the IQ is attached to precisely those 'blond bombshells' we would least expect it of. And its function seems similar to that of another sort of unlikely juxtaposition. Very often, it is the most beautiful women who wear the most outlandish, ungraceful, outrageous and downright ugly fashions. And since this get-up, which would make any ordinary woman look ludicrous, enhances this woman's glamour, observers can only conclude that the outlandish garb functions as a sort of advertisement of the true beauty it purportedly masks: the contrast, the shock, enhances the beauty – like Cinderella's through the rags and ashes. Similarly, high intelligence, or rough mannish garb, hardly enticing or alluring in a woman, exaggerates and enhances the 'bombshell' image. In fact, then, the 'brilliant bombshell' of public relations does not contradict the 'dumb blond' stereotype, it lives off it and strengthens it.

## The reality

There are, in fact, some interesting correlations between beauty and brains. We might argue that in the many cases brought to public notice where the inverse relation seems to hold (the 'dumb blond' phenomenon), we are really seeing true intelligence at work. That is, until recently and perhaps still too often, a woman who wanted the sort of success society unambivalently allowed women – success in love, 'catching' a successful man – had to play dumb. And the more intelligent someone is, the quicker she is to learn important lessons. If there were indications that men preferred women who were beautiful but dumb, why, she'd not only figure out how to be more beautiful than anyone, but more dumb as well. And if the prevalence of the stereotype is any indication, it works – often enough. But the price, in lack of respect and loss of self-esteem, is tragically high – another reason for the beauties-are-doomed myth perhaps. The victory too often is pyrrhic.

## Myth: beauty is mentally unsettling

A variant of this myth is the one alluded to in the Yeats poem quoted earlier: that great beauty is often linked to madness, 'a crazy salad,' and thence to tragedy. Yeats gives a clue to the origin of the myth: 'Whereby the horn of plenty is undone.' This is, then, our old sour-grapes comforter back again. There is a persistent thread running through our legend and litera-ture concerning the link between *any* great blessing and madness. To be blessed by the gods is to invite their envy; and 'whom the gods would destroy they first make mad.' Besides, the beauty is only too aware that she has a special providence, and is in some sense set above other mortals, who have had to work for what they get. This realization could easily lead to paranoia; or, given the fear of the inevitable ultimate fall from favor, to despondency. There is also, perhaps, a link to reality here as elsewhere. If the beauty learns to depend too much upon her beauty, she will never acquire the psycho-logical depth and social skills that will get her through the kinds of adversities that strike the beautiful and non-beautiful alike. She will depend on her beauty too much, and miss it too much when it fades.

There is another connection, more subtle. Beauty creates a sort of exculpatory 'diminished capacity' defense – someone so beautiful *cannot* receive full blame for whatever damage she does – just as madness does. Beauty in some mysterious way lessens the beauty's responsibility for what she does. The Helen myth is an example of this, with its image of the old men of Troy, watching the course of battle from the walls, and seeing Helen, the cause of so much destruction for them, and of no direct benefit to any of them. Yet they say, as she walks by, 'Truly, she is passing fair.' Her beauty both excuses and explains her destructiveness, as madness would. Hence we are not surprised – in fiction or reality – when a beautiful woman turns out to be deadly. As paradoxical as it seems – for the beautiful is, as we have been led to expect, good – we expected it. The only wonder is that the hero – the dummy – didn't see it as soon as we did. But he was dazzled, which is also inevitable. We need only think of Brigid O'Shaughnessy in *The Maltese Falcon* as an obvious case of this kind.

## Countermyth: beauty is serenity is sanity

There seems to be no countermyth – for example, that beautiful women are cleverer than others, or that they lead more orderly lives. Such a myth would have no function, symbolically or otherwise. None the less, a possible example of such an emergent countermyth are the heroines of the popular romance novels, who tend to be just this – utterly ravishing, but organized, efficient, and generally marvelous and lovable human beings. They have, for example, a nearly miraculous eye for detail of certain kinds – they can spot a Gucci at a thousand paces. But it's too soon to tell whether the type is pervasive and meaningful enough for us to ascribe to it true mythic status.

## The reality

There may be certain tentative connections between beauty and sanity – the reverse of the prevalent image. The psychoanalyst Erik Erikson (1962) quotes 'a master in our field' as saying that a child who is loved becomes more beautiful. If there is in fact this correlation between feeling loved and being beautiful, and if feeling loved as a child is a significant contributor (as most psychological theorists would agree) to a healthy psyche as an adult, then we might expect there to be a greater-than-chance correlation between beauty and mental health. (Of course, we can also point to women who have determined to become and have become beauties because they were unloved as children.) But, as analysts love to remind us, their theories are not intended as predictions or certainties, only general probabilities, and everyone surely knows stories of famous beauties who lead disorganized or miserable lives – whether because of or despite their looks. Whether beauty in these cases *causes* unhappiness, or is merely a chance association, brought into prominence by the notoriety of the beautiful woman, we cannot say.

Finally, we have differing opinions on the relation between beauty and power.

## Myth: beauty is powerful

As the Helen story shows, a beautiful woman can be perceived as affecting destiny, whether for good or evil. She makes things happen, because she is adept at manipulating men – who themselves hold the real power to make things happen. Beautiful women, then, are in a doubly enviable position – not only do they get what they want, but they don't even have to do the work or take the responsibility. This is truly omnipotence. The beautiful woman, the myth continues, has the world on a string, men at her feet, women visibly envious, but all eager to befriend her because she is desirability incarnate, and her presence enhances the luster of anyone she accompanies. She therefore can count on being loved and protected, whatever she does; and whatever she does will seem to others better, more successful or less vicious than it would if done by someone less easy on the eyes. Her beauty *is* power – she can and does use it to get others to do her bidding. It is as potent as a loaded pistol – and as dangerous, and compelling – if more attractive.

This myth is exemplified in legend after legend, and all through literature. Perhaps its most striking recent appearance was during the 1920s, the heyday of the 'vamp' in movies, with her dark and mysterious looks, her kohl-rimmed eyes, her serpentine grace, and her deadly intention. (The derivation of 'vamp' from 'vampire' is sometimes forgotten.) It is not a wholly-new model, of course: from Cleopatra to Shakespeare's 'dark lady' we have examples in fact and fiction of the seductive exotic whose joy is to lure innocent males to their doom. In light of what we have said about the blond myth, it is instructive that when it is the (destructive) *power* of beauty that is being stressed, we tend to think in terms of brunettes.

## Countermyth: beauty is worse than powerless

The power of the beautiful woman, being only usable through another, is in fact no real power at all. Beauty, being transitory, is weak and ineffectual:

Since brass, nor stone, nor earth, nor boundless sea,
But sad mortality o'ersways their power,
How with this rage shall beauty hold a plea,
Whose action is no stronger than a flower?[4]

## Reality

Again there is truth on both sides, depending on the perspective. Certainly a beautiful woman can get things done, whether through her own efforts or (more typically) by others, more easily than can someone less attractive. 'The ability to get things done,' it will be recalled, is a standard definition of 'power.' Moreover, accomplishments of this sort are often viewed by such women as tests of their beauty: power *is* a test of beauty. When doors stop opening at your smile, you know you've lost your looks. But in this definition resides the weakness of beauty and the weakness of the beauty-is-power theory. Beauty's power depends on its possessor being considered beautiful by others – a passive accomplishment – and power is not, of necessity, passive. Power that depends on manipulativeness – through beauty or otherwise – is always suspect and always capable of overthrow, tending to create resentment in the hearts of those who seem so eager to serve. Moreover, as we shall see in detail later, the very physical features that tend, in age after age and society after society, to be equated with feminine beauty, arise from or are suggestive of weakness and dependency. Hence beauty, deriving as it does from a base of uselessness, cannot by nature be powerful in itself. Beauty *per se* does not have the power to get things done; but someone with beauty does indeed – for a short time, if she is skillful in other ways – have the power to accomplish what she wishes done through others, but at considerable risk. The power of beauty is shorn of responsibility, and in that way may seem to some the most desirable of all kinds of control; but by this very fact, it leaves itself open to resentment on the part of others, with the beauty herself eventually losing self-esteem as she sees that she is not being taken seriously, only her beauty is, and that it is treated as if it were not a part of her.

We begin to understand, finally, the complexity of our thoughts and feelings about beauty. For every myth there is an equal and opposite countermyth, and both of these typically have some relation to a reality, but not always much of one. The distortions in the myths are interesting; still more interesting, the very prevalence of mythology involving and explaining beauty, the behavior of beautiful women, and our responses to it. To understand the existence and form of these myths, we need to look deeper into our perceptions and classification of beauty, the basis of the myths. In what ways do the standards we use to determine beauty change – across time and space? How do these changing standards reflect other differences in the way people live and think? What, if anything is unchanging?

The myths tell us a great deal about how we want beauty to function symbolically for us. By keeping our eyes on a mythic ideal, we can come to understand constancy and fluctuation in the ideal. And one good focal point is that embodiment of feminine perfection first realized by the Greeks four thousand years ago in the goddess Aphrodite, the Roman Venus. Since that time she has served artists as an abstraction – divine, perfect beauty – which they could literally flesh out according to their individual dreams and the ideals of their own societies. Where portraits of existing women – though they too are often idealized – must involve compromises with the artist's internal ideal, his depiction of Venus will represent all that is for him as a creature of his time hauntingly desirable, painfully unrealizable, ultimately beautiful.

In our own time, classical mythology as a scaffold on which to construct ideals has lost a good deal of its power, so that from the turn of our century onward pictorial representations of Venus become rather scarce, and when Venus is invoked in art at all, the effect tends to be either intentionally or unintentionally ironic:

Venus, if you will,
Please send a little girl for me to thrill.

and we must perforce look elsewhere for the idealizations that speak to us. The women who give form to our fantasies are less apt to be found in temple statuary now, and more on the covers of glossy fashion magazines. So we can follow the succession of changes and constancies in the next two chapters by progressing from Venus to *Vogue*.

Chapter 3

# The Representation of Venus: An Ideal in Search of a Definition

If we want to know what beauty is, there are a couple of ways we can go about finding out. We can hunt for definitions, examine the ways in which experts in one field or another have talked about the subject and hope for some consensus we can take away with us. Or we can see how the abstraction, Beauty, is given fleshly form in art: how, at various times, a society or its individual artists have idealized the perfectly beautiful woman. At the outset of our search, we might hope for a rather simple conclusion: general agreement on a clear and precise definition, words that call a specific and common image to mind; and representations by artists in every epoch, in all civilizations, that have a common thread running through them. We would hope for something easy to spot, with no serious disagreement possible about whether the attribute was or was not there, was or was not crucial.

Why is the definition of beauty important to us? We are a science-worshiping society, and science entails definition and precision about what is being talked about. If we are going to attempt to come to an understanding of beauty, it should be, we have come to feel, a 'scientific' understanding. We have come to suspect claims to understanding of any phenomenon that are not based on empirical evidence, tests, experiments, the spotless laboratory, the running rats. We study the butterfly by skewering it to the dissecting-board, not observing it impressionistically in mid-flight. That is the business of the poet, and that does not tell us the truth. Plato spoke for all of us when he excluded poets from his republic because they lied. We don't really think they lie – just that their opinions are based on emotion, and therefore can't be trusted.

We bring these same hopes and prejudices to the task of

understanding beauty. We would like a simple, universal, and all-encompassing definition, clear as a chemical analysis of a compound, or a medical diagnosis of a disease. We would like precise instructions: if a woman has characteristic A, and not B, we can say she is beautiful, otherwise not. If we insist on 'scientific' certainty in our work, we are certain only of frustration.

That is not to say that the attempt has not been made. But if we want the truth about beauty, whom do we turn to? A great many experts in many fields have pondered the problem of finding a definition of beauty, or an understanding of it, and there is little agreement among them. If we want a definition of a meteor, we will ask an astronomer; a metaphor, a literary critic; DNA, a geneticist. But many kinds of specialists have tried to understand beauty: philosophers of aesthetics, psychologists, cosmetologists, and, of course, in their own way, writers and artists. Perhaps rather than selecting one, we can look briefly at each of their attempts, in the hope that, like the blind men with the elephant, each will provide a glimmer of the truth, and put together the glimmers will add up to a satisfying whole. Let us look at the definitions proposed by aestheticians, then at one discussion influential in psychology. Only then, having touched on the resources of science, let us look to art, the ways in which poets and artists have made the abstraction of beauty concretely meaningful for us.

Perhaps because beauty is so impermeable to clear scientific once-and-for-all definition, attempts seem often to be freighted with verbal complexity that only makes a difficult topic more cumbersome. At the same time, while much has been written over the millennia by theorists on aesthetics, the writing tends, rather understandably, to veer away from dealing with human, and more specifically feminine, beauty, and toward the more serene and less emotionally disturbing attractions of nature. Beauty, then, is often contrasted in such writing not with what might strike us as its most relevant antithesis – e.g., prettiness, or handsomeness – but with the sublime. Beauty tends to be confined to the emotionally manageable. While we may feel a thrill viewing both an ocean and a mountain, the first is active, unpredictable, passionate, and hence a candidate not for the beautiful, but the sublime. The second, being more quiescent, can be beautiful. Edmund Burke, in 1757, attempted a definition of beauty which is still influential.

On the whole, the qualities of beauty, as they are merely sensible qualities, are the following: First, to be comparatively small. Secondly, to be smooth. Thirdly, to have a variety in the direction of the parts; but, fourthly, to have those parts not angular, but melted as it were into each other. Fifthly, to be of a delicate frame, without any remarkable appearance of strength. Sixthly, to have its colours clear and bright, but not very strong and glaring. Seventhly, or if it should have any glaring colour, to have it diversified with others. These are, I believe, the properties on which beauty depends; properties that operate by nature, and are less liable to be altered by caprice, or confounded by a diversity of tastes, than any other.

This attempt at definition is unusually precise and specific for the field, for all its hedging ('*comparatively* small,' or 'melted *as it were* into each other,' for instance). Here, as elsewhere, Burke refutes the arguments of earlier writers, for instance Aristotle and Thomas Aquinas, that beauty is dependent on symmetry, 'fitness,' or proportion of parts alone.

Burke's definition is only in part applicable to personal beauty, and in each point subject to refutation by counterexample, but none the less is very valuable as an unusually clear basis for beginning a discussion of the nature of personal beauty. One thing that is striking in this definition is the continual reference to qualities that entail helplessness or non-assertiveness – even here where Burke is certainly thinking principally of natural or artistic objects. When we look closely at personal beauty, we will of course first be struck by the fact that the word applies almost exclusively to feminine attractiveness; when, in contemporary English, it is applied literally to male looks, the imputation of effeminacy is virtually always present. Many of the characteristics Burke ascribes to these more general forms of beauty are at the same time those that we use in determining feminine beauty – precisely those aspects of appearance that suggest passivity and helplessness: smallness, smoothness, non-assertiveness in shape and color, delicacy and so forth. In this sense, we can speak of a landscape of towering and rough mountain crags, or the ocean in a storm, as impressive, or overpowering, or perhaps even as sublime – but probably not as beautiful.

Beauty, then, involves a lack of threat, a lack of aggressiveness or even assertiveness. Concepts like symmetry, fitness, and unity recur, as in this definition by Barry, in 1784, cited in the *Oxford English Dictionary*:

According to the definition generally given, Beauty consists of unity and gradual variety; or unity, variety, and harmony. Our rule for judging of the mode and degree of this combination of variety and unity seems to be no other than of its fitness and conformity to the designation of each species.

Here, as with Burke's definition, there is a problem: if symmetry and unity are characteristic of beauty, then the purest beauty should be found in the most typical and ordinary type of anything. But this is not the case: we know variety – unexpectedness, unlikely juxtaposition – is often a part of our judgment. Yet the garish and the outrageous are not beautiful, *per se*. Where do we draw the line? We judge, Barry says, according to some internalized notion of the 'fitness and conformity' of the judged object to its species. But how do we determine that? How do we abstract an idealized model of a species from the many imperfect specimens that pass before our eyes, and how, in any particular case, do we determine how close one representative comes to this never-actually-encountered ideal?

Beauty may also be defined subjectively, that is, in terms of the impression it produces on the mind of the beholder: if you feel this way, beauty is what you're experiencing. St Thomas Aquinas, in the *Summa Theologica*, makes use of this sort of definition in developing a conception of beauty:

Beauty and goodness in a thing are identical fundamentally; for they are based upon the same thing, namely, the form, and consequently goodness is praised as beauty. But they differ logically, for goodness properly relates to the appetite (goodness being what all things desire); and therefore it has the aspect of an end (the appetite being a kind of movement towards a thing). On the other hand, beauty relates to the cognitive faculty; for beautiful things are those which please when seen. Hence beauty consists in due proportion; for the senses delight in things duly proportioned, as in what is after their own kind – because even sense is a sort of reason, as is every cognitive faculty.[1]

We must have respect for St Thomas's courage in confronting

several thorny issues about beauty at once. What other virtues is it related to? Is the good the beautiful (an unresolved question going back to Plato)? Is beauty an end in itself? No to both, says St Thomas. But we may quibble with his brave attempt, noting that he draws the line on the basis of beauty being 'cognitive,' where goodness is more or less emotive (or appetitive, much the same thing). Yet he implicitly defines cognition in terms of emotion ('*please* when seen'). We would want a sharper distinction. But there is something right about the very confusion. Beauty is not, we should say, merely cognitive or merely emotive. It inspires in us certain emotional responses, based on the beautiful object's calling to our minds, perhaps, earlier pleasant experiences. But at the same time, the pleasure is based on learned intellectual judgments, a sense of symmetry, expectedness, and proportion, as St Thomas and Burke (and others) have argued. These are cognitive considerations, based on reasoned judgment and evaluation. It will be fruitless to try to separate the two, and the love of beauty, perhaps more than any other human psychological attribute, shows the futility of trying to separate the thinking and feeling aspects of the mind.

In fact, the thrill of encountering the beautiful – a thrill unique, it would seem, in the world of virtues, since (alas) we are not thrilled by truth, or goodness, or even courage or wisdom, not the breath-catching moment that the glimpse of beauty carries in its train – is the excitement of encountering opposites that unite into a seamless whole, and the beautiful object itself is made of the mixture of opposing, even paradoxical, qualities. Beauty kindles excitement in the viewer's mind, but at the same time invites repose; offers the comfort of the familiar, coupled with the shock of the unexpected. Often there is involved in a judgment that someone, or something, is beautiful, the titillation, just below the surface of consciousness, of a scintilla of pain – an emotional response to the visual shock of a clash – at the same time augmenting a sense of pleasure and health. There is refinement and vulgarity at once in the truly beautiful, organization and chaos, uniqueness and sameness, wildness and placidity. In one particular representation of the ideal, one of the opposites will, naturally, predominate

– but there will always, somehow, be a hint of the other member of the pair.

Therefore, beauty can only be distinguished in terms of a union between physical realities present in the object, and a complex of associations and emotions these realities create in the observer. There is no beauty without observation, as a tree falling in a forest without anything to hear it cannot be said to make a sound. While 'beauty is in the eye of the beholder,' the beholder must have plausible material to work with.

If aesthetic theory will not provide us with a satisfactory all-inclusive and explanatory definition of beauty, if it will still less tell us why beauty is so important yet so elusive, perhaps we should look to other fields for enlightenment. If the idea of beauty is not to be found in qualities intrinsic to the object itself, we must locate the responsibility for determining beauty with the beholder. What makes one thing beautiful and another less so is our psychological attraction, probably unconscious, to some quality in the former that is absent from the latter, combined of course with equally-implicit cultural biases. Hence we have difficulty in arriving at a generally-acceptable definition. If beauty resides in the object, we ought to be able to agree on what it is; but if it is ascribed to the object by the perceiver, and all perceivers have had different experiences, and different psychological needs, then it makes sense that what one person considers beautiful, another may find insipid, grotesque, or revolting. We might hope to find our answers in a discipline that attempts to account for the differences in human judgments in terms of individual needs arising out of idiosyncratic prior experiences – that is, psychoanalytic theory.

Here we are faced with something of a mystery. Sigmund Freud, whose writings go into illuminating detail about such a great deal of the human experience – emotional, intellectual and physical – has virtually nothing to say on the subject of beauty. Perhaps his clearest, and certainly one of his very few, remarks on the topic is to be found in this passage from *Civilization and its Discontents*:

The enjoyment of beauty has a peculiar, mildly intoxicating quality of feeling. Beauty has no obvious use; nor is there any clear cultural necessity for it. Yet civilization could not do without it. The science of aesthetics investigates the conditions under which things are felt as beautiful, but it has been unable to give any explanation of the nature and origin of beauty, and, as usually happens, lack of success is concealed beneath a flood of resounding and empty words. Psychoanalysis, unfortunately, has scarcely anything to say about beauty either. All that seems certain is its derivation from the field of sexual feeling. The love of beauty seems a perfect example of an impulse inhibited in its aim. 'Beauty' and 'attraction' are originally attributes of the sexual object. It is worth remarking that the genitals themselves, the sight of which is always exciting, are nevertheless hardly ever judged to be beautiful; the quality of beauty seems, instead, to attach to certain secondary sexual characteristics.[2]

Two points are especially significant, as well as characteristically Freudian, in this passage. First, there is the reduction of what aesthetics has considered a specifically human motive – the love of beauty – to a basic animal instinct, sexuality. Second, there is the argument that those physical attributes that we consider beautiful are so by virtue of their capacity, as secondary sexual traits, to function as displacements of the primary sexual organs – beauty is sexuality defended against, that is, once removed. In this formulation, the love of beauty is an 'aim-inhibited impulse,' that is, a sublimation of the sexual drive. The object of the drive remains conscious and is consciously striven towards, but the aim of the drive stops short of its true goal, sexual union, so that the underlying erotic impulse is transformed into the quest for purely visual gratification. If aesthetic theory stops with the attempt to classify what sorts of objects we consider beautiful, psychoanalytic theory goes beyond it in attempting – however sketchily – to provide at least the opening wedge for an explanatory theory: why these particular sorts of objects, these shapes or colors, might tend to be considered beautiful. There is nothing intrinsic to the objects themselves, Freud implies, that makes them 'beautiful' in our eyes; rather, our own instinctual needs endow these objects with power, which we call 'beauty.' It is their underlying relationship to our sexual drives, on the one hand, and their removal from the sphere of *direct* genital sexual gratification, on the other, that make certain objects 'beautiful' to us. Beauty is in the gonads of the beholder.

We may wince at this reduction of higher spirituality to base animal need (and Freud would be happy to tell us why we are wincing). In fact, it is easy enough to argue with his formulation – at least to suggest points that are not accounted for by the theory of beauty as aim-inhibited sexuality. It seems true that, in our culture at least, genitals are not considered beautiful. Or rather, more accurately speaking, in our culture, they are not taken into consideration in making aesthetic judgments. Breasts may or may not enhance a woman's beauty, depending on their form; but genitals are never judged as contributing to a woman's beauty or otherwise. At least in public discourse, they are not part of the checklist of items on the basis of which judges award or subtract points at beauty contests. (More privately, of course, genitals are subjected to comparison, although beauty is not the point; something close to 'utility' – i.e., size or shape – is the relevant criterion.)

An apparent problem with the aesthetic theory sketched by Freud is that there are so many aspects of personal beauty that are not obviously related to secondary sexual characteristics: eye size, hair color, whiteness of teeth, and so on. Freud might rejoin that these are in turn displacements from the secondary sexual organs, that each of these characteristics is symbolically related to some sort of sexually-relevant function. But the skeptic could object, in turn, that under this argument anything in the universe could be construed as sexual. The question then remains unanswered, why these parts, in this form, not others? Further, if sexuality itself remains the same for all time, and throughout the human race, why does the idealization exemplified in art differ from one period to another? Suppose, then, that Freud's hypothesis is correct as it stands; and suppose further that both the rounded stomach of one period and the large bosom of another represent secondary sexual attributes (involving pregnancy and nurturing). Why does one represent an ideal at one point in human history, the other in another? And perhaps more curiously still, why are there periods where the ideal seems to be represented by the absence of reference to secondary sexual differentiation – in the 1920s, for example, where slenderness and a 'boyish' figure were in vogue? (The psychoanalyst might cry here, 'Aha! Denial!' or, 'Reversal!' – that is, the absence of interest in sexual attributes is evidence for a very deep interest indeed, or that boyish slenderness replaces the feared womanly curvaceousness – but such argumentation tends to reduce Freud's essentially interesting and challenging claim to unfalsifiable triviality.)

In any case, what we have seen in comparing two types of attempts at the definition of beauty – one taxonomic, the other explanatory – is how very hard it is to create a definition that makes sense, which covers all the cases, and answers all our questions.

All of these attempts are guidelines rather than hard-and-fast definitions, for they do not tell us, if we see someone for the first time, on what basis we determine if that person is beautiful. It may be that aesthetic and psychological theory, dealing as it does in generalities, cannot help us to understand what rules we bring to bear in judging particulars. For this perhaps we must turn to others, who demonstrate through the particular our universal feelings – poets and artists. Certainly they have in their several ways been chiefly preoccupied with beauty and with expressing their notion of it so that others could share it. Perhaps if we look to them, they will deepen our understanding.

While the poets accurately guide the emotive and subjective side of the understanding of beauty, they provide rather little for our cognitive needs. We are helped to experience the thrill, the intake of breath, the wonder of the encounter; but we are seldom told clearly and succinctly, as the scientist would like, precisely what impression on the retina occasioned that psycho-physiological aberration. Even the emotional response can involve a dizzying set of possibilities, from exhilaration to despair. Of course, the poet will argue, and rightly, that this is the very essence of the poetic experience: to suggest, evoke associations in the reader, rather than doing what the scientist does, telling the reader what to perceive. So we plug our own more or less vaguely recalled perceptions into the emotion the poet invites us to experience. Poets can go from the gauzily ecstatic to the vituperative in their expressed feelings about beauty and its possessors, but in every case leave us pretty well in the dark about exactly what physical characteristics of the subject of their admiration created the surge of ungovernable emotion. Shakespeare, for instance, can go from rhapsodic to ironic in making comparisons without giving the reader a clear sense of their basis:

Shall I compare thee to a summer's day?
Thou art more lovely and more temperate:
Rough winds do shake the darling buds of May,
And summer's lease hath all too short a date

Or, on the other hand:

My mistress' eyes are nothing like the sun;
Coral is far more red than her lips' red;
If snow be white, why then her breasts are dun;
If hairs be wires, black wires grow on her head.[3]

And, in terms of the emotions evoked in the poem by the power of beauty, we can go from Byron's serenely rapturous:

She walks in beauty, like the night
Of cloudless climes and starry skies;
All that is best of love and light
Meet in her aspect and her eyes:
Thus mellowed to that tender light
Which heaven to gaudy day denies.[4]

to something quite different from Chaucer:

Merciles Beaute

I. Captivity
Your yen two wol slee me sodenly,
I may the beaute of hem not sustene,
So woundeth hit through-out my herte kene.

And but your word wol helen hastily
My hertes wounde, whyl that hit is grene,
Your yen two wol slee me sodenly,
I may the beaute of hem not sustene.[5]

Since the poets have had a good deal to say about beauty over the millennia, we could explore their feelings on the subject at considerable length; but that would in all probability shed no more light. The poets, as we have seen, prefer to remain tantalizingly evasive about the source of their ecstasies and anguish. We are given no real guidance about what physical attributes to look for – perhaps we are more likely, in fact, to discover what *not* to look for. But mostly we are instructed in how to respond to an appropriate stimulus, and the presupposition is that we naturally know how to recognize that stimulus.

So we can hope for no clarifications or definitions of beauty from the poets, explicit or implicit.

One more approach remains. For artists, like poets, have always availed themselves of feminine beauty as the lodestone of their efforts, the justification for their genius. And unlike the poet, an artist must produce a physical expression of his inspiration. What we see on the canvas will represent, to some degree or other, the artist's idealization of feminine beauty.

It is fortunate for us, of course, that we are considering, among all possible indefinable abstractions, the ideal of beauty. For the poets devote equal space to many ideals, all of them worthy of inspection: beauty, love, friendship, courage, and so on. But of all of these, beauty most lends itself to ready depiction in a graphic medium. An artist can – and many have done so – allegorize any of the other abstract virtues; but beauty he can paint directly on canvas, and leave unambiguously clear what he is representing, and why he has chosen a particular physical form for it.

But when we look for a clear point of view from artists' representations of ideal beauty over the centuries, we are faced with confusions. Over time, innumerable portraits have been made of women in stone or on canvas. Which of these are we to consider representations of an abstract ideal, beauty, and which merely portraits, allegorical representations of other virtues, faces and forms chosen by the artist for reasons other than the depiction of his ideal? We see, as we range over time and space, an almost infinite variety of types that have been selected to be depicted: how are we to thread our way among the multiplicity of types, how are we to make any sense of the myriad choices we see? Can we abstract from the confusion a single type that is, and always will be, ideal beauty? Or are there other ways to understand what we are confronted with? And finally, we may be at a loss because one man's vision of beauty is greeted by another with revulsion – or, still more perplexingly, utter indifference. Even if we, the viewers, are touched by a portrait's beauty, how can we have any guarantee that the artist intended us to perceive his creation this way? How dare we claim to interpret the artist's statement with certainty?

If a culture has created and generally recognizes a symbolic figure standing for all that is womanly, beautiful and desirable, then an artist, in giving physical shape to that idealization, will at the same time be giving physical shape to his abstract conceptualization of Beauty – influenced of course by the preferences, explicit and otherwise, of the period and place where he lives. In a portrait of an actual woman, an artist must incorporate her features into his representation, and therefore must almost necessarily deviate from his mental ideal. But in painting Venus, or Aphrodite, the classical goddess of love and beauty (and therefore, since the time of the Greeks, the symbol of all that is lovely and desirable in a woman), he can give his own, purely abstract ideal physical reality. Then by looking at how Venus/Aphrodite has been depicted over the centuries, we will get a sense of what has been considered the ideal of feminine pulchritude: what remains constant, and what changes in time, according to changes in people's tastes. The artist will not have to contaminate his ideal with the less-than-perfect image of any actual women that he might be asked to paint; but he would, of course, be influenced by his own and his society's preferences. Then a tour of Venuses through the ages will be, effectively, a tour of beauty and its vicissitudes across time and space. (We will, of course, have to confine our examination to Western culture, since Venus/Aphrodite has meaning only there.) And since the symbolic figure of Venus (or Aphrodite) has been with us for some three thousand years, we will be able to trace changes or consistencies in her representation over that long period of time. Similarly, since Greek and Roman mythology has had, in practically every period from its inception, a profound influence over European art and literature, we will find images of the kind we are looking for at practically every time and practically every place in the Western world. We say practically, since during one period, the Middle Ages, pagan goddesses were not in favor for symbolic or other artistic purposes, and artists had to make a choice between the temptress Eve, and the woman of radiant inner soul, the Virgin Mary. In the Classical period, and later in the Renaissance, the two could unite in the satisfying and harmonious whole that we view as true beauty; but during the medieval period, the artist could depict only one or the other in one image. Compare, for instance, the Eve in the *Adam and Eve* triptych (3.1) with any number of Madonnas, for example the *Wilton Diptych* (3.2), of the French School, which might be compared with an analogous theme, Bronzino's *Venus, Cupid, Folly and Time* (3.3), another mother-and-child, but with quite a difference. This strict distribution of permissible feminine properties has curious effects on the aesthetic sensibilities of the Middle Ages (and, we might argue, our culture has never fully, in its collective psyche, repaired the split; or we might say that the split has always been with us – the Virgin and the Whore – but only during the Middle Ages was it unavoidable).

To begin our search for 'beauty' by assuming any universality in its representation is to court disillusionment. A choice made by one artist at one time bears no necessary relation to that of another artist, at another. Today's essential ingredient is yesterday's irrelevancy; another culture's necessity, our superfluity. And at least, even as we are smarting from our failure to uncover comforting all-time truths or generalizations about the nature of feminine beauty, we will see that this failure in itself is a worthwhile discovery: that beauty is not located in any specific physical attribute, but rather in the aggregate of physical and less tangible traits that a particular time esteems. An invocation of a feeling carries further than a concrete representation: while we might not admire the cellulite of a Rubens Venus, there is still some indefinable charm about her that is ineffably attractive.

We might hope to resolve, or take steps toward resolving, an ancient argument: does beauty reside in the beauty's physical form, or in some more intangible aspect of her person? Is beauty to be located in some attribute – hair, eyes, face, skin, figure, whatever – or must we resort to the hoariest of platitudes, and assume beauty resides in the soul? And if the latter, how do we identify it? It is often argued (and quite persuasively) that beauty consists in the beauty's own exquisite self-consciousness – her communication to the artist, or the camera, that she exists, is desirable, and desires. An opposite view is that beauty consists in a luminosity of intelligence, goodness, sweetness – unselfconscious virtues that emanate from a clear and autonomous sense of self.

But even if we conclude that beauty has more to do with

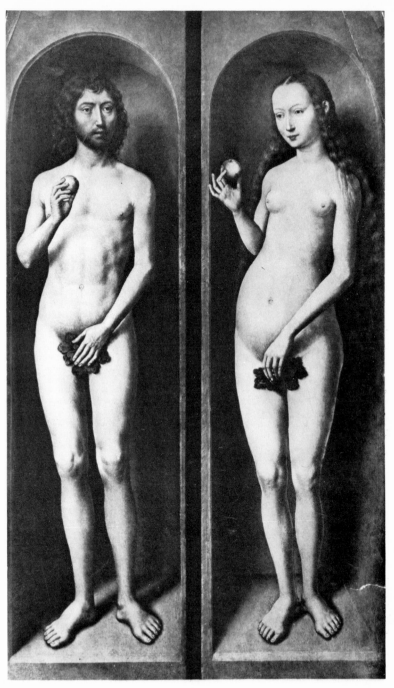

3.1 *Adam and Eve,* triptych detail, Memlinc

3.2 Madonna from the *Wilton Diptych*, French School

3.3  *Venus, Cupid, Folly and Time,* Bronzino

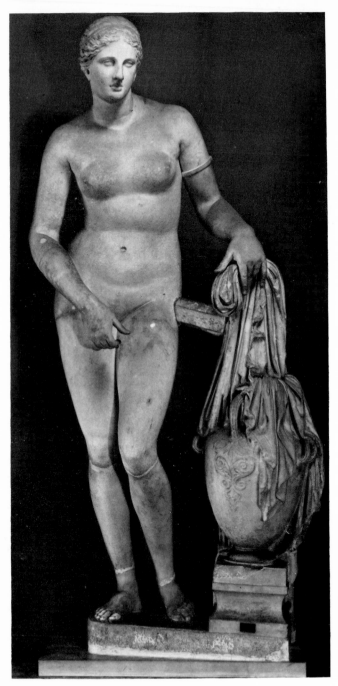

3.4 *Knidian Aphrodite*

3.5  *Venus de Milo*

3.6 *Sleeping Venus*, Giorgione

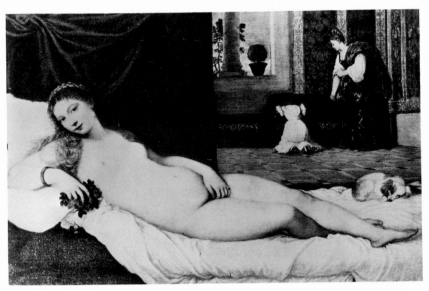

3.7 *Venus of Urbino*, Titian

3.8 *Venus, Bacchus and Areia,* Rubens

3.9 *Venus*, Cranach the Elder

3.10 *Venus*, Costa

3.11 *The School of Love*, Correggio

3.12 *Venus Anadyomene*, Ingres

3.13 *The Toilet of Venus,* Velázquez

3.14 *Venus with the Organist,* Titian

3.15 *Adam and Eve,* Van der Goes

3.16 *Adam and Eve*, Cranach

3.17 *Diana*, Rembrandt

3.18 Mirror with representation of Aphrodite, second century BC

the beauty's own psychological needs and powers than with physical traits, we still have to admit that the most desirous, or the most soulfully radiant, of women will not be accounted beautiful, or be anyone's model of Venus (or Eve, or the Virgin Mary) if she does not also have certain basic attributes of physical attractiveness. The aesthetic philosophers have mentioned some of these: symmetry; proportion; predictability; regularity. Thus, a nose must fit the face: it must not be large, or hooked, nor, for true beauty, very small and snub. The mouth must not seem to cover too much area, nor too little (but here we have already crossed into subjectivity: what is 'too'?). The figure must not be ridiculously obese, nor painfully thin, nor must any part of it be out of proportion (subjectivity intrudes again!). But how often we see a portrait of a beauty – and we respond to her as such – whose every feature, even whose face as a whole, has something lacking in terms of the harmony, symmetry, or normality we have been instructed to require. And finally, there is no universal agreement. Any ten people, asked about any movie-star sensation of the moment, will cover the spectrum of responses, from 'nothing special' to 'spectacular,' with everything in between. It is not at all surprising if we despair of proving the arguments of aesthetics by actual example.

More often than not the aestheticists' definitions of beauty in terms of symmetry, expectedness and harmony are explicitly violated. More often than we would think possible, if we confined ourselves to theory, a Venus is somehow out of proportion, beyond symmetry. Things don't fit – they are bigger than life, they don't go together. Yet our attention is riveted. In fact, we are tempted to suggest that what aesthetics defines as 'beautiful,' when applied to personal, feminine, beauty comes closer to the standard we use for 'prettiness' than for 'beauty' which perhaps requires – or at least is accentuated by – something out of proportion, not expected – a bit dangerous, and therefore the more titillating.

If we doubt that we derive excitement from the oppositions we create in our feelings about beauty, we need only think back to the myths we looked at in the last chapter, the tendency for every myth to carry along with it an opposite of equal potency. It might at first seem that the existence of these opposites was more or less by chance, or in any case merely arose out of the fact that we are confused about the role of beauty in our lives. But another case could be made: we *need* the oppositions in and of themselves. What makes the idea – as well as the actuality – of beauty psychologically exciting is the tension of the dualities with which we endow it. Beauty *is* by definition not harmony, symmetry, proportion – but the sense that a perceived harmony, symmetry, proportion is teetering on the edge of breaking down. Implicit and irreconcilable opposition is an intrinsic part of our concept of beauty.

In fact, many of the metaphors we create and recreate to concretize our psychic experience of beauty suggest the danger with which the experience is charged. What is beautiful is 'stunning,' 'dazzling,' 'a knock-out.' We use these terms for both personal and natural beauty. Serenity may be a part of the experience – but not the whole. We are tempted to conflate what we find about feminine 'beauty' with the aesthetic definition of the 'sublime' – which covers phenomena that are vaguely threatening, always exciting, often dangerous – and the aesthetic antithesis of 'beautiful.' Feminine beauty often is viewed as somehow dangerous as well, for strong, unique looks also presuppose a danger – of too much autonomy, or of self-definition. The merely pretty woman poses no such risk. We do encounter the innocent, pure beauty, who is no threat. But it is impressive how often a woman sure of her own looks chooses to be publicly seen and photographed in clothing, make-up or hair style that is shockingly unexpected – garish, bizarre. Non-beauties, looking at the punk hairstyle, the cornrows, the exaggerated mascara or the military uniform, know perfectly well that they wouldn't in their lives dare to appear like that in public. Yet the true beauty somehow gets away with it – and the fact that she does makes it all the more clear how very beautiful she is and how different from other women. It is not so much, perhaps, that the ravishing beauty is made more beautiful by the garish *per se*, as that the contrast created in the observer's mind between how anyone else would look in that bizarre get-up, and how she does – still achingly desirable – sends the message: here is a true beauty. The Cinderella story – the girl whose very rags cannot keep her beauty hidden – is another evocation of this gut knowledge.

In any event, we can see the manifold ways in which people have envisioned ideal beauty by contrasting Venuses that have been sculptured and painted over the last two thousand or so years, keeping in mind some of the commonest oppositions that we can find:

## 1 The 'neat' beauty vs the 'wild' beauty

Is beauty chaotic or controlled? Should we expect a neat cap of hair, short, close to the face but off it, sleek or tightly curled; pale eyes, porcelain skin; clothing simple, efficient, fitting close but not overly revealing, not flying in the wind? Or tendrils of hair whipping across the brow, into the eyes, untrammeled – nature's triumph over art; dark snapping eyes, blood-red lips, generously wide; a 'hectic flush' on the cheeks; clothing clinging in places, or perhaps flying in the breeze, not in any rapport with the body, but as free as its wearer? At different times, these have been feminine ideals, as well as everything in between. The 'neat' beauty is suggestive of demure femininity, unobtrusive womanliness, or on the other hand efficiency in movement, independence of spirit (in the sense that the woman has nature, including her own, under control). The 'wild' beauty perhaps links femininity and nature by playing on the uncontrollability of each, their alluring hint of danger; but also suggest woman's dependence on the elements, her domination by nature and thus, like nature, her capacity to be brought to submission by 'scientific' and 'efficient' man. Each of these, it will be noted, can be interpreted in terms of conflicting stereotypes of femininity. Which will have meaning at any given time will depend on the currently favorite way of symbolizing the eternal feminine.

The 'neat' beauty was a favorite of the Greeks, and recurs in period after period, into the present day. Examples are the *Knidian Aphrodite* (3.4) and the *Venus de Milo* (3.5), from the Classical period; Giorgione's *Venus* (3.6) and Titian's *Venus of Urbino* (3.7), from the Renaissance; and Ruben's *Venus, Bacchus and Areia* (3.8). These Venuses, of course, are in many ways as different from one another as women could be; but they share a neat, disciplined coiffure, whether through the hair being cut short, or artfully braided and tightly wound.

We are drawn to the face, especially the eyes, since the hair has been pushed out of our central vision. Yet, there is something gratifying to the eye about the hair itself; the effort at control, the elaborate work to render the 'crowning glory' as inconspicuous as possible – an early form of throwaway chic. A recent version is Bo Derek's cornrowed coiffure, and her repeated preference for being photographed wet, her hair clinging to her head (and of course, her clothes clinging elsewhere on her body).

On the other hand, there is the romantic version, hair flying, with a life of its own. The most famous of all these representations is undoubtedly the Botticelli *Birth of Venus*. Related is Raphael's drawing *Venus*, with locks flowing over her back; a Titian *Venus* with thick, long hair (though under control in her hands). All depict the woman at the mercy of the elements, borne by a force beyond control. (The open sexual energy in such representations is quite unlike the demureness of the 'neat' Venus.) This type, too, is as popular at present. The famous Marilyn Monroe photograph of the actress posed over a subway grating, her skirt flying into the air, is representative. Or we might think of Farrah Fawcett's hair – apparently wild, actually meticulously arranged – instantly famous and interminably imitated.

There seems, looking back on the various changes in fashion over the last quarter-century, to be a delicate balance maintained: neat coif with voluptuous figure during the 1950s, on one extreme, and during the 1970s romantic flying manes coupled with spare figures. We would not claim, of course, on evidence this flimsy, that any such pairing is intrinsically necessary; but if beauty is based in part on harmony and proportion, this balance between efficiency and chaotic romance is one kind of symmetry that could be attained. Just as experts in fashion have pointed out that, for instance, as heels get lower, skirts get shorter, to keep a proportion in the amount of legginess on view, so there is an ideal balance of all parts in the determination of beauty, and as one aspect shifts in favor over time, others will necessarily go along with it.

## 2 The temptress vs the innocent beauty

While sexual innuendo plays an indisputable role in the determination of beauty, there is a wide range of sexual fantasies
– conscious and otherwise – and tastes. What we think we are
responding to purely intellectually may be triggering quite
different impulses elsewhere in the mind, the true source of
our attraction. And so it should not be surprising that beauty
is sometimes represented in terms of raw sexual fantasy – the
temptress – and sometimes as the opposite but not so very
different fantasy, the innocent virgin. Here we focus less on
hair, and more on face itself, less on the actual features, more
on their expression and their relation to the painter (or
photographer). Is the smile demure, secret – or suggestive?
Are the eyes downcast, or inviting? If the beauty wears no
clothes, is she nude and conscious of her effect on the seer (in
Kenneth Clark's perceptive distinction), or naked and
unaware? Does the drapery of clothing hint – or promise?

The viewer can expect to be swept up by different emotions
in the two cases. The nude, provocative beauty arouses lust in
the male viewer if successful – however sublimated (for we
are not speaking of pornography); in a woman the effect is
more like an identification with her favorite erotic fantasies.
The virginal beauty, on the other hand, engenders in a man
feelings of protectiveness, at least some of the time, and in a
woman, recollections of youth, tenderness, the hope of being
protected and precious. Consider on the one hand, many of
Cranach the Elder's works – for instance his *Venus* (3.9);
Lorenzo Costa's suggestive *Venus* (3.10), Bronzino's *Venus,
Cupid, Folly and Time* (3.3), in which Cupid and Venus are
engaged in some very provocative interplay, strongly tele-
graphed to the viewer; Venus in Correggio's *The School of
Love* (3.11). In all of these, we are drawn hypnotically into a
relationship with Venus: she is playing with our emotions, our
needs; there is clearly a message being sent, from object to
painter to viewer. We look hungrily, perhaps after a moment
turn our eyes away, almost embarrassed that our desires have
been guessed at so accurately by the woman looking back at
us. Who is the voyeur?

On the other hand, the demure, virginal Venuses are safe

for us in the passivity. We can absorb their beauty as much
as we like: they will not flirt with us, look back out at us, or
indicate that they know what we want. There is less electri-
city, but more serenity, for the object, the viewer, or both.
Giorgione's *Venus* (3.6) sleeping like a child, totally unaware
and uninvolved, exemplifies one image of innocence. More
debatably in this category is Ingres's *Venus Anadyomene*
(3.12) looking full at the viewer, but seemingly unaware that
her rounded nakedness could produce any prurient effect. (Yet
her hands, in her luxuriant hair, beckon the viewer.) If it is
hard to see any of these this simply, it is probably because,
in a fully successful painting, the enticing and the innocent
are really mixed. Even the most demure beauty has a sense
of self-possession, even asleep, a sense of her own attractiveness, a sense that she need not really invite, there will be
viewers enough; she is aware of being seen, or at least open
to the possibility. Even the most lasciviously-posed have at
the same time a kind of inner-directedness, a coolness, less
than a total need to be admired. Yes, they can make love to
the artist, but they do not need the adulation – not all that
much. We might say that this duality is a requisite of a truly
desirable woman, a real Venus – that she know about her
desirability and be aware of its potential, but at the same
time be comfortable enough in her body and her mind that a
radiance emanates from within – the vaunted beauty of the
soul.

### 3 The thin, childlike figure vs the matronly, buxom, womanly body

Perhaps body type, of all the possible attributes of beauty, has
fluctuated the most from time to time, and in each period has
occasioned the strongest feelings. While at a particular time
we may agree that 'gentlemen prefer blonds,' or that tall
women are more elegant than short, or dark eyes more interesting than blue, we are not, in general, utterly convinced of
the rightness, the justification, of this aesthetic – rather, we
tend to see it as a preference we are free to argue about. Thus
in *A Midsummer Night's Dream*, Shakespeare created two
female characters, Helena and Hermia, one fair and tall, one

dark and short; and while we get the impression that the former has the advantage, we also have a sense that this is not absolutely an open-and-shut case; the short, dark Hermia is certainly potentially as desirable as Helena, and the fact that her charms are slighted in favor of the fairer and taller Helena's seems to be but a quirk of momentary taste. But we do not find similar contrasts contemporaneously between thin and plump women. It is plain to us that a desirable woman must be girlish – even childlike – in body shape; figures that a generation ago were approvingly labelled 'curvaceous' are seen presently as simply fat. Even if we have in our hearts a preference for blond beauty, we can appreciate a drawing of a dark-haired temptress, or understand the attraction of a brunette actress: Jane Russell not only serves as a foil for Marilyn Monroe's blondness, but is voluptuously attractive herself. But looking at a Rubens today, we cannot see past the cellulite; we quiver on the edge of disgust. If Rubens could have seen Twiggy, we can be pretty certain his response would have been equally squeamish.

Thin and plump are but two of the several body types that have been considered ideal at one time or another. So, for instance, a woman in a given period might be expected to be thin and 'boyishly' shapeless; plump, and 'motherly' shapeless; 'curvaceous' that is, thin-waisted, but with large hips and bosom; thin, willowy, but large-stomached; and thin, but muscular, with no visible body fat, but muscular definition suggesting strength. Currently, we are poised between the thin, childlike and the thin, muscular ideals, and have almost forgotten the curvaceous paragon of barely a generation ago, as well as the plump, womanly type which was in fashion around the turn of the century.

Why are different types in vogue at different times? Is the choice governed by larger social forces? It has been pointed out that in periods when starvation is a real threat, and only the wealthy can look plump and well-fed, large women tend to be idealized; in a period when the Madonna represents the feminine ideal, the large-bellied look of pregnancy – whether or not the woman is in fact pregnant – is most desirable; and at a time when it is easier to be sedentary, and food, especially of a calorific kind, is readily available to almost everyone, only the wealthy can afford the time and money required to be slim and/or athletic, and therefore these looks will be 'in.' It can also be argued that the current girlish look, the popularity of teenage models with children's bodies, but very adult and sexually knowing faces, suggests confusion of the times in which we live: our desperation for youth, coupled with our thirst for sophistication; men's wish that women should be innocent, like children (or the Virgin Mary), so that men may initiate them sexually, yet in fact already knowing (like Eve), promising forbidden thrills and not really able to be harmed, like an experienced woman: the Lolita myth. With the possible exception of the current athletic look, all images of feminine desirability over the ages share certain characteristics: they stress, from one angle or another, feminine helplessness and passivity, however this is to be achieved, whether because the woman is pregnant, or weak, dependent and sickly, or fat and slowed by her girth. Male beauty, as depicted in art, seldom if ever suggests weakness or dependency; idealized women almost always do.

It will be hard to find examples of Venuses of all these types, since not all were popular over the periods in which Venuses were painted. During the Renaissance, we find one or the other of the 'womanly' types in the south of Europe, and the large-bellied types in the north. We have many versions of the voluptuous ideal (slender-waisted, large breast and hips); in fact a favorite convention during several of these periods was to paint Venus from the back, with generous buttocks. Veláz-quez's *The Toilet of Venus* (3.13) is one typical example. Titian's *Venus with the Organist* (3.14) is an example of the plump Venus, as is the Venus of Ruben's *Venus, Bacchus and Areia* (3.8). All of these are difficult for us to comprehend today as idealizations of beauty – we can understand, intellectually, that Rubens and Titian may have thought them so, but we cannot. The large-stomached type of the north (e.g. Van der Goes's Eve in his *Adam and Eve* (3.15), or Cranach's *Eve* (3.16)) is equally incomprehensible to us. With all the lip-service we give to the radiance of pregnancy, maternity clothing still is designed to camouflage (leaving aside T-shirts with an arrow pointing down to BABY). We certainly cannot comprehend representing a non-pregnant woman as if she were, as the embodiment of beauty. Particularly strange to us in this regard, although not a Venus, is a painting of Rembrandt's, *Diana* (3.17), large-bellied, with sagging flesh. The thin, willowy types that we *do* understand are scarcely found anywhere during this whole period. They occur millennia earlier, for instance in a second century B.C. Greek mirror handle representing Aphrodite (3.18).

We began this chapter in the hope of finding a definition of beauty that was as concise as it was universal. We have gone to the authorities – the psychologists, poets, philosophers, and painters – and each in turn has disappointed us. Maybe, after all, we have been attempting the impossible. Perhaps precise definition is not compatible with understanding beauty. The very transitoriness of styles of beauty, the indefinability of the concept, are inherent aspects of something rooted at once in the intellect and the emotions. When we speak of beauty, of standards and gradations of beauty, we are necessarily speaking metaphorically rather than precisely – and metaphor resists definition, is in a sense its antithesis. The moon is not, after all *definable* as a ghostly galleon, and if beauty is best understood in terms of emotion – what an encounter with it evokes in our mental and emotional association of pleasure and even pain – we are foolish in trying to pin it down.

But then, someone will object, we do, after all, attempt to be scientific about beauty today, even if we didn't in the past. For example, that American curiosity, the beauty contest, treats beauty like a concrete object that can be judged like apple pies at a county fair; lately, even given a computerized, quantitative score. In many beauty contests, contestants are rated against each other on a scale of one to ten, by hundredths of a point, and there is at least the pretense that the contestant with the composite score closest to ten will, deservedly, be declared the winner. Actually, this only sometimes appears to happen, probably no more often than chance. In practice, that indefinable thrill of delight triggered in the judges' minds for an instant creates a winner. But it is significant that we think we not only can, but should, quantify beauty, that we can allocate its components into degrees by hundredths of a point, as we can weight, or height, or speed. But this seems to be a confusion, not well resolved, between the modern passionate

desire for quantification, and scientization, and the age-old
pleasure in something for reasons the intellect cannot say:
'The heart has its reasons,' as Pascal said, 'which reason does
not know.'

In fact, unlike height, or speed, beauty cannot realistically
be objectified and quantified. In part this is because, as we
have seen, beauty is only partly physical or objectively observable. The tremor of a smile, the twinkle in an eye – these
cannot be measured and weighed against someone else's, as
we can determine the bluer eye, the tinier waist. Beauty is a
combination of too many different kinds of subjective decisions
to let us think we could reach a definition, much less general
agreement about who, or what combinations of characteristics
meet that criterion. Even other relative terms – like 'tall'
– can be specifically defined, and a standard of comparison
established that is unambiguous and satisfactory to everyone.
Negotiation is possible, on intellectual grounds. But beauty is
not like that. For instance, if we know only that Mary is 5'7",
on that information alone we can form no valid judgment
about whether she is 'tall': but if we are told that the average
American woman is 5'5", then we can confidently call Mary
'tall'. But if we hear that Mary is beautiful, we are dealing
with several levels of relativity, as well as value-judgments
that make any decision dubious. What could be used as an
objective standard? Relative to whom, or what, is Mary 'beautiful'? We will agree that someone 5'7" tall is taller than
someone who is 5'5" but is any blond more beautiful than any
brunette? Is someone with large eyes (whatever 'large' might
mean objectively) more beautiful than someone with small
eyes? On what basis can we make any such claim? Yet, impressionistically or not, we make it, all the time and generally
with little concern for validation. What could it possibly mean
– logically – to say that Helen was 'the most beautiful woman
in the world'? We could understand 'tallest' or even 'darkest-
haired' in terms of objective measurement, but 'most beautiful'
is an abstraction, pure poetry. And even if there were in
Homeric times a Helen who was accounted by her contemporaries the 'fairest' in the world, suppose she returned to earth
today: would she get past the semifinals in the Miss Universe
contest?

It's true that someone who, in Homeric times, was 'tall' would probably not be today. But that is because the objective standard against which he or she would be measured has changed – people in general are taller than they were. But if Helen would no longer be considered a beauty, that is probably not because the average of human pulchritude has objectively risen over the millennia. Rather, it is more likely due to the fact that subjective standards have changed. We have altered our aesthetic perceptions and judgments, so that someone who, as a contemporary of Helen's, might not have been considered worth a second glance, might well today be considered beaut-iful – and the reverse might be true for Helen. (We are tempted to argue that a contemporary of Helen's considered *pretty* would still be so today, that prettiness is not subject to the same sorts of fluctuations over time as is beauty. But we will take up these questions later.)

Judgments about beauty, being subjective rather than objec-tive, differ from person to person and one person's judgment cannot be 'proved' right or wrong. If one person says Mary is tall and another refutes that, the issue can be resolved by bringing Mary into the room, measuring her, and having recourse to a table of average female heights. But if two people differ over Mary's beauty, no reasonable argument is possible. You cannot objectively arbitrate a beauty contest. The winner merely attracts the largest number of subjective preferences.

For these reasons, beauty remains in the realm of the poets and painters, where it probably belongs, and out of the labora-tory, which destroys all the joy of it. What we can observe with precision is its very imprecision – how it changes even as we look at it, how it defies being pinned down for all time, or even for any time. We have seen how the definition of beauty slips through our fingers in part because, across time, the ideal vision of feminine beauty changes so radically and unpredictably – there are fashions in beauty as in its adornments. We have seen that the Venus of the pre-Christian era is not the Venus of the Renaissance, and if we had Venuses today, they would not much resemble any of their forebears.

In fact, Venus, the artist's convenient fiction for repre-senting a model of perfect beauty, is no longer viable for us in our time, when Classical mythology has lost its evocative meaning for most of us. Can we still think in terms of this culture's idealization of beauty? And if we can, how will this ideal be given flesh? In what form, so that it is instantly recognized by anyone seeing it – as the vision to fantasize, to strive to attain? Where do we look to find today's Venus?

# Chapter 4
# **Beauty in Our Time**

Hotheads of the beauty business have spelled out possibilities almost as heartening as 'Yes, Virginia, there is a Santa Claus.' And to anyone who clings relentlessly to the Puritan whimsey that looks don't matter, we wish to say, 'Face facts, they do. If you haven't quite got all you need, go out and buy them.' *Vogue*, 15 Sept., 1960.

The countless faces on the covers of books and magazines that stare out at us from the racks of drugstore and supermarket counters provide clues about our culture's perception of beauty. The cover-girl has become the modern Venus. Her face provides the contours of all we aspire to be. On the cover we confront both our desires and frustrations, our fantasies and reality. In that momentary confrontation we are forced to recognize our imperfections, to feel our physical flaws, to experience psychological turmoil. Somehow the Venuses of today remind us of what we are not, while they make us feel by the human color of their eyes, the warmth of their flesh, even their names, that we might be not unlike them if only we bought this cosmetic, that face-lift. We are told it is possible but we know it is impossible as we compare the airbrushed figure of the new Venus with our less-than-perfect bodies. The pictures on these covers are radically illusory yet they are sold to us as reality.

In the beginning the borders between illusion and reality were distinct. Artists' conceptions of the beautiful woman represented an unrealizable, intangible ideal: the distillation of everything desirable about all women, and therefore possible for no one woman. With photography this changed: the image caught in the lens was not filtered through an artist's eye. She *was* a real woman, and if she was flawless, then any of us could, and had better, aspire to a like state. The modern Venus is not born of foam, but through the lens of the camera.

The new century marked a turn in the mode of visual reproduction. The camera – conceived in 1839 by Louis Daguerre, and later made more accessible and appealing through George Eastman's Kodak camera – was not only to change the way we look at the world but also the way the world looks at each of us.

But it was not until the 1920s that both still and movie camera burst onto the American scene with their full revolutionary effect on our vision and imagination. For some time after its invention in 1895, the movie camera pretty much limited itself to the literal translation of vaudeville skits. The still camera, on the other hand, imitated portrait painters in its attempt to capture the beauties of the day and of high society drama. It was a time when skirts still swept the streets and the corseted bodices of dresses molded bodies into stiff hourglass shapes. The round bodies and plump rosy-cheeked faces of the beauties of the day (such as stage actresses Lily Langtry and Lillian Russell (4.1)) set the style and photographers made sure to catch in their shots the static, immobile, frozen, remote faces of their beautiful sitters, a legacy of the painful hours of sitting required by the portrait artist. Beauty was still the prerogative of society belles or 'legitimate' stage actresses. By and large the early female movie stars, because of their lack of social status, did not have legitimate access to the realm of beauty. But the world was changing. Women appeared in bathing suits – sometimes defying the law; suffragists marched; war was declared; the movies changed, too.

Ironically, prohibition brought in its train an increase of social freedom and physical mobility. Sales of automobiles soared. Women had gained the vote, shortened their skirts, bobbed their hair, and taken up smoking in public. Harlem night-spots, jazz, and the Charleston set the tone and the pace of the time. Men and women were on the move and the camera not only recorded this but helped to give movement a new status. At the time, it must almost have seemed that the line between illusion and reality was erased – at least blurred. Technology had irrevocably altered the way we engaged in and recorded movement, the technological changes themselves as fantastic as the vision they allowed the camera to capture. Spurred by the irritant of Prohibition the young developed a boundless appetite for novelty. Female beauty, too (always a reflection of the taste of a period), put on a new face.

This new face appeared both on screen and in the still photos in society magazines such as *Vogue*. These media were instrumental in developing trends, defining new ways of looking at women and creating new illusions. But movies at first had less influence on viewer judgments of beauty than the fashion magazines which were to have a more powerful hold on their beauty-seeking audience not only because of the intimacy they established with the reader but also because they, unlike the movies of this period, were developing a new standard of beauty, singularly appropriate for modern fashion, visible only through the eye of the still camera. The aim of fashion magazines is simple: to sell clothing through the association of fashionable dress with beautiful women. The intention of the movies, however, is more complex (and therefore, it took their audience time to learn how to respond): movies show us reality through the gauzy lens of artifice. The movies, a uniquely American contribution to culture, brought this country to the attention of the rest of the world.

The camera showed large segments of the population, for the first time, how they looked to others, creating a new concern about 'seeing' and 'being seen.' Then, in a further step, the camera linked this to credibility. Where the artist's conception was a dream, the photographer's image was real. It compelled belief. Heretofore we had not been accustomed to let images control our judgments. It was once not unpopular to have faith in things that could not be observed with the naked eye. Milton said that a mark of true faith was the ability to believe in things unseen. Two millennia earlier Plato taught that observable reality is deceptive and that true reality lies somewhere else, unobserved. This was all part of our cultural baggage. Indeed, the deceptive nature of outward appearances made even female beauty suspect. Beautiful women have often been used in the arts to warn men against falling prey to fair appearances, for they can be deceptive, illusory, and even fatal.

But science and technology speak a different language, one that relies on proof and replication, clarity and reason. Appearances can be deceiving but a picture is still worth a thousand words. We are not unlike José Arcadio Buendía, a character in Gabriel García Márquez's novel *One Hundred Years of Solitude*, who refuses to believe in the existence of God unless his camera can prove it by revealing His image. The camera never lies, we are told. But this is not really so. It is not like the naked eye that randomly skims what surrounds it. The mind behind the hand that aims the lens and presses the button makes the difference, for it selects its subjects and their context. The camera sees 'reality' in a studio where artificial lights can make shadows look as if cast by a hot Caribbean sun, where backdrops make space recede endlessly into the sand dunes of the Sahara, where props create an environment that outdoes nature in its very 'naturalness.' The camera can make artifice look more real than reality. It can put in and take out what the naked eye has to make do with. It can switch illusion and reality before the viewer's eye. By its apparent direct lines to reality, the camera can con.

The camera catches us in a terrible and exciting paradox. It can innocently capture reality with a blink of its eye by not tampering with what it sees, or it can rearrange, distort, embellish its subject and engage us in its make-believe, its fabrication, its lies. The problem for us, the observers, is that it becomes difficult to distinguish the degree of fabrication. Our susceptibility can be dangerous; the camera's perspective offers us a way out of a drab existence, an escape into a world of adventure, or sumptuous leisure, or delicious decadence, and not show us the falseness behind the glitter.

Surely, you say, this is nothing new. Literature has always had the power to fuel imaginations, to take us, at least momentarily, on flights of fantasy. But there is a crucial difference between the verbal and the visual mode of presentation. Literature lets us know that it is creating fictions, sometimes even pointing to the artifice, revealing the mask. This is not to say that we cannot be or have not been conned by the printed word, but rather that it is more difficult. Verbal media operate through the filter of the reader's intellect: the reader has time to withdraw, judge, test the apparent reality presented on the page. But the visual medium grabs and involves the emotions, circumventing all evaluative skills. We read and think. We see and feel.

Like those who have been momentarily trapped in the mazelike delights of Disney's world, unable to shake the grip of that fantasy and to distinguish between Fantasyland, Tomorrowland, and the land of freeways and billboards, we are caught in a world where the boundaries between illusion and reality have become blurred. But our world is sometimes not as benign as popcorn and cotton-candy on a sunny day with Mickey and Donald. Instead, what we see and what we get are a proliferation of images that somehow have the power to belittle us, and yet – and therefore – to make us pay homage to and believe in them.

The camera has taught us new ways of looking at beauty and for beauty, and taught beauty new ways of making itself known. For beauty has always had to advertise. One must be 'seen' to have a beautiful face.

Great beauties [writes Roy Strong,[1] an observer of beauty] are of necessity public figures. They are never the *belle* of the village, the nymph who unrecognized bears her pitcher to the well. To be a great beauty one has to be seen which means that all such beings move in spheres where media can acclaim and record their triumph.

Before the advent of the camera the notice of a woman's beauty was spread only by word of mouth, and more widely in print or a portrait. So beauty was the prerogative of those who could patronize writers and artists – smart society's seal of approval. The key, of course, was recognition. A woman's beauty was judged directly by human eyes which, seeing with human sensibility through the beguiling garb, knew the artifice involved in the beauty's creation. The inanimate camera, of course, all-seeing but knowing nothing, changed all that. It began to advertise beauty in a new way. Artifice no longer counted as such. The camera glossed over it.

Thanks to the camera, now for the first time a new technology, rather than the whim of an artist or aristocracy, imposed an ideal form on female beauty. The rigor of this technology revised our aesthetic ideals, feeding our culture's obsession with beauty by making beauty possible for anyone of whom the camera approved. For the camera, female beauty was not limited to a certain social setting. While the society beauty (especially at the beginning when the camera did not yet know what it was looking for) has always received special attention because she is in the public eye, the camera has never really been class-bound and has become less so as its popularity has spread and its techniques have been refined. This has not only made the selection of beauties more democratic but it also has opened the way for the 'professional beauty' who can be made to look good (by other professionals) in front of the camera, no matter what she looks like by the light of day.

'Photogeneity' is the camera's contribution to the language of beauty. Suddenly, beauty begins to be judged on new terms. This means that the figures and faces that had been considered beautiful until the turn of the century were to become a thing of the past. The camera desires motion. Not only the motion picture camera but the still camera as well likes its images caught in the midst of purposeful movement. The pliable body, the body that bends and seems to move gracefully even when in repose is what attracts the eye of the camera. The whalebone corset had to go to satisfy the camera's demand for movement; the female body was let out of its prison so it could learn the acrobatics necessary to please the camera. But there is more. A lithe body can coil easily in front of the camera, assuming pose after unlikely pose at the photographer's whim. A tall lithe body is even better because height suggests slenderness. Ideally the face should be as mobile as the body. High cheekbones and hollow cheeks, irregular features lend a note of drama to the face with their interplay of shadow and light. Emaciation on the move – this is what the camera would claim as its ideal, the essentials of photogeneity. And photogeneity, these days, is what the professional beauty is all about.

The camera has found its ideal of feminine beauty in an emaciated image that is unnatural and unhealthy. There have been other periods in history, such as the early nineteenth century, when slimness was in fashion, but this was another time, when illness, in the form of tuberculosis, was romanticized as an expression of an exalted spirit in a starved body. Thinness was seen as alluringly 'fatal' (the look of the new *femme fatale*) and tuberculosis, indeed, was fatal.

The association of beauty and emaciation, of course, was by no means immediate. The camera had to take time to define its ideal, and discard what it didn't like. With the professionalization of beauty, the camera, too, became more professional. Special photographers (now known as fashion photographers) were called upon to photograph women. But this was all part of a growing realization that beauty could become big business, that it could be sold for a profit – and a beautiful one at that!

Photographic reproduction helped to make beauty big business. Suddenly, one woman could be admired simultaneously by millions of observers. The new beauty became public property. With time, money, and dedication her 'look' could be copied by anyone. The success of photographically reproduced beauty depended primarily on its popular consumption. Beauty became a collective experience. And consumerism and the camera became bedfellows.

Magazines and movies felt the immediate benefits of photographic reproduction. Audiences were captivated by what they saw. Perhaps the immediacy of visual representations was the strongest lure, opening up new worlds. Suddenly, places, objects, people, situations that had once seemed inaccessible became familiar. But at the core remained a paradox which would with time become troublesome. Photographic reproduction seemed to make things familiar, yet they remained remote. It promised intimacy, yet kept the images themselves untouchable, impersonal. In short, it offered the impossible under the guise of the possible. And so it was with beauty which, now turned professional, found these media as its new arena, the place where it could best advertise itself.

But, in the beginning, there were two extremes of photographic representation, each appealing to vastly different audiences. On the one extreme were society magazines, best exemplified by *Vogue*, which directed themselves to an exclusive and limited audience. On the other were motion pictures which brought delight to millions of Americans. Both professionalized beauty. *Vogue* fashioned it to appeal to its select audiences. Originally, it drew its models from the ranks of high society. The movies exploded with scenes and images targeted for mass audiences with tastes yet undefined, but with a thirst for pleasure, titillation, escape. Both contributed to this century's notion of beauty, taking their cues from the worlds they had set out to represent.

Of the two, *Vogue* presents the most complete, concise, and consistent history of female beauty in this century, in part because it is primarily dedicated to the idealization of beauty, its display and its pursuit, and in the course of its history has paid tribute to all the modern Venuses of the age, whether society beauties, film stars, stage actresses, or models. It has the power to create Venuses, making it the final judge of who's who among beauties. *Vogue* has helped to intensify the importance of beauty in modern society, not only by giving it visibility, but also by showing that the way we see beauty is as much a reflection of social, political, and economic events of the real world as it is of our fantasies.

'Do you read any fashion magazines?' we asked a young woman who was majoring in Women's Studies. 'Yes, I read *Vogue*,' she responded. 'What in the magazine entices you?' 'The fantasy,' she said. 'It allows me to fantasize.' *Vogue*, at least in the beginning, was rooted in reality. One might argue that fashion is, at its core, fantasy. But in 1909, when Condé Nast bought the publication (which was little more than a society newsletter founded in 1893), and for a couple of decades after that the principal objective of *Vogue* was to show how women dressed, to photograph the way the well-heeled moved, socialized, worked, and played. *Vogue*'s was a world peopled by the likes of the Duchess of Marlborough, Lady Paget, the Duchess of Kent, Mrs William Astor, Lady Abdy, Mrs William Grosvenor, Eleonora Duse, and Isadora Duncan. Some of the people in *Vogue* included royalty, nobility, the otherwise well-born, and the talented among them (4.2). These women appear in *Vogue* wearing their own clothes, setting a standard for fashion and beauty. *Vogue* gave them a stage on which to be seen. At the same time it made photography an important, and eventually essential, vehicle for society news.

Photography, a voyeuristic medium, gains its power by giving the viewer a peek into private places. *Vogue* is voyeurism refined. Early on, the magazine put photography in league with gossip. It showed members of polite society, what they wore, where they went, to whom they spoke, how they looked. 'The Duchesse d'Albe winds a chain of large emeralds surrounded by diamonds around her wrist. . . Madam Muñoz makes use of a black enamel pin to catch a drapery of her gown for dancing,' *Vogue* writes in 1928. It gave socially intimate details of parties such as the one given for Cole Porter on his birthday in 1926 at the beach at Lido, which was attended by the famous Lady Abdy, who, *Vogue* writes proudly, was 'discovered by the Americans and who now sets fashions. She is both beautiful and extremely natural. . . She is the Lily Langtry of her age.' *Vogue* clicked the camera and chattered as it advertised the behavior and whereabouts of the well-to-do, expanding their influence. 'To be much discussed,' *Vogue* writes in 1926 'is to become immortal.'

*Vogue*, at first, did not dictate trends, or define beauty, it merely recorded what was already there. Of course, the genius of *Vogue* was that it knew how to make social events and society beauties newsworthy. Society women existed to be admired and *Vogue* knew how to admire them. Early *Vogue* photographers, such as Baron Adolphe de Meyer, Cecil Beaton and Edward Steichen, helped to fashion an ideal of feminine beauty that fit the tastes of its readers. Their photographs of women were composed to give an aura of elegance, luxury, and refinement. In their photographic portraits the women look comfortable in their luxurious world, and at the same time, remote, emotionless, inaccessible. Their beauty is not ready-made for the camera; nor a perfection of feature and figure. It is not typically a beauty of high cheekbones and ghostly thinness but rather a beauty born of poise and refinement. It divides the 'haves' from the 'have nots.'

Photographic portraits often clashed with candid photos that caught women on the move – horseback riding, playing tennis, swimming, or simply walking. *Vogue*'s photographs document the new respectability of an active life and active looks for women. The magazine hints at its new role, one which would be not only to record newsworthy events, but to help create them as well. Money, movement, modernity were key words for the *Vogue* set. Ads for travel abounded and it was taken for granted that, as a Rolls Royce ad suggests, for the magazine's readers the world was limitless. One of the 1928 issues dedicates itself to defining those indefinable boundaries.

Clothes changed to accommodate this movement (4.3). Looks changed to show that, yes, one was a participant in this leisured world. In the summer of 1928, *Vogue* describes the new look:

The short skirt is first of all practical. But it is also the opposite of that muffling and voluminous garment that once shrouded the feminine form. . . In the short skirt, the beauty of a free and swinging walk, of graceful length of limb is evident. And the bobbed or semi-bobbed coiffure reveals the beauty of the head.

*Vogue* tells us that to be beautiful is to be long of limb (and to show it!), to have a close-cropped head. Elsewhere in the same issue in an article entitled 'The Judgment of Paris as to Sea, Sun, and Sands,' we learn that 'narrow hips' are '*de rigueur*', and that to 'tan is fashionable.' Even though the magazine admits that 'to burn or not to burn is still a warmly debated question,' and that the 'burners' are often referred to as 'rebels,' it speaks of the 'sunburn craze.' It was beginning to develop more clearly an aesthetic of female beauty which showed the confluence of many forces. Beauty was associated with leisure and the leisured class (the tan look spoke of vacations in exotic places); beauty accommodated the demands of the camera (the long legs, the thin, hipless body); beauty reflected the times (the boyish look). Finally, beauty was what *Vogue* saw as beautiful. Beauty was now *Vogue*'s primary concern, for as the magazine put it, in its February 16 1929 issue, 'we are living to-day in a modern world where beauty is demanded on every side – the sound underlying reason for comforts and luxuries.'

Above all, *Vogue* was a commercial venture. While it knew that it was speaking primarily to converts, it was also busy converting. The twin prods of gossip and voyeurism were used to advantage. The lives of the wealthy seemed to have a dramatic dimension that only Hollywood could equal. They seemed happily caught in the heady movement of their times, riding in chauffeured limousines, traveling to all those distant places, dining, dancing, daring to appear in bathing suits and short skirts and to hold cigarettes in public. The rich broke rules and *Vogue* recorded it with style, all the while allowing glimpses into a glittering, spectacular world of beauty and titillating those who could afford, if only barely, to buy more and join the ranks.

But *Vogue* was in a curious, if not untenable, position. While its readership expanded it still had to hold tight to exclusivity. No, the masses were not invited to Vogueland, at least that is the position the magazine took toward the end of the 1920s. On 1 January 1928 *Vogue*'s editor describes the magazine's reader as

a lady for whom clouds need have no silver lining, for she never walks below them. She leaps lightly through the skies in full blaze of popularity, gaiety, and a reputation for the chic. . ., she will never neglect her exercise.

Although the magazine admits in May of the same year to 'the breakdown of caste barriers,' the conspicuous 'mingling of the aristocratic and mercantile classes' a year later, almost as if caught by the same fear and paranoia that crashed upon the wealthy when the stocks fell, *Vogue* in a bout of wishful thinking holds tight to the notion that the masses, otherwise known as 'the class nobody knows,' are not the 'People that Really Rule.' In an article of the same name *Vogue* notes that

the effect of the masses on all kinds of taste is worse than deplorable – so we are told – and what we constantly ask is whether they are going to keep on influencing the trade market till it finally becomes all quantity and no quality. . . *Vogue* knows that the princesses have not webbed feet and don't make a practice of wearing white velvet shoes. . . just as it knows a thousand details about the habits and customs of its world, which are in direct contradiction to those claimed by the commerçants.

*Vogue* also knew that it was at the hub of that trade market, that to keep going it had to keep moving, to change. Change it did but it still hung on hard to Vogueland magic. It reflected the painful economic realities but clung to the notion that life could still be lived with dignity and elegance, that fabulous wealth still existed if only in dreams. Its pages still carried pictures of the wealthy and well-born, still gave the illusion that its fashions were 'approved by Paris' (even though American buyers were not to visit Paris again until 1933), still created a geography that was boundless and that invited endless seasons of sun and sand.

The Depression brought about a change in lifestyle, and a modification in the notion of beauty. The look of flight and freedom was trimmed down. To counteract the reality of retrenchment, *Vogue* took subliminal refuge in extravagant fantasy. Skirts got longer and often flaring at the bottom. Hair, too, was longer and more elaborately coiffed. On the surface, however, the ads and editorials spoke of a different reality. 'Smart Fashions for a Limited Income,' *Vogue* announced in the subtitle of one issue and features ranged from an article detailing how to keep house without a maid to do-it-yourself tips on how to 'Perk up your Home,' how to achieve 'Beauty for less than a Dollar,' on 'Outwitting the Cost of Chic.' While the magazine still offered readers the fantasy of exotic travels, it became a little more realistic in its 'Guide to Gaiety,' where it spoke of the pleasures to be had in New York and other places near home. 'Shop-hound: Tips on the Shop Market' became a regular feature. The faces that appeared in *Vogue* with more frequency were faces that the camera chose. *Vogue*'s main objective was no longer to show how the wealthy dressed and looked, but rather to sell the dresses and the look. Beauty was not just a product of wealth, but a commodity in and of itself. In other words, it was no longer a matter of looking to wealth to find beauty, but of looking to beauty to find status. Now beauty could give the illusion of wealth. *Vogue* looked to its photographers and professional models to create that illusion.

Photographers, of course, knew that modern beauty was something that the camera could create. Edward Steichen, a *Vogue* photographer of the 1920s and 1930s, was one of the first to see photogeneity as a new definition of beauty and the magical transformation created by the momentary but intimate confrontation between the model and the camera. He wrote of his favorite model, Marion Morehouse. 'She was no more interested in fashion than I was, but when she put on the clothes that were to be photographed she transformed herself into a woman who really could wear that gown.'[2] Transformations. The stuff that fairy-tales are made of. Now it was possible for a woman without great means to be transformed, if only momentarily, into the image of elegance and beauty.

Models, or mannequins as they were initially called, were once considered objects on which to hang clothes. They were poorly paid, and like the early film actresses, were not respected by polite society. Originally, they were allowed in the pages of *Vogue* only to sell products. But, in the 1930s, in collaboration with the photographers, they began to gain a new status, one which acknowledged the value of their photogenic beauty and their central role in building the make-believe of elegance that *Vogue* featured. As early as 1928, *Vogue* predicted that 'titled mannequins will soon. . . be the rule rather than the exception' in the circles where the aristocracy and the mercantile classes begin to mix. By the 1930s *Vogue* realized that fashion and beauty need no longer be 'approved by Paris,' and that beauty and elegance could be found at home, as long as there was a photographer to complete the transformation from street urchin to sequined seductress (indeed, American designers in Hollywood and Hollywood stars were setting trends in beauty and fashion). Photographers were the magicians who could transform ducklings into swans. 'The gist of every modern photographer,' writes Alexander Liberman, former art director of *Vogue* and later editorial director of Condé Nast publications, 'is the ability to transform every child of the street into a momentary goddess and object of envy and desire.' (*VB*, 7).

No doubt this was *Vogue*'s new goal: to promise the reader the possibility of beauty. Wealth at the moment seemed out of reach, but not beauty. 'A lovely girl is an accident; a beautiful woman is an achievement,' *Vogue* declares in 1935 (*VB*, 121). Perhaps taking its hint from photography, from its models, it begins to dedicate itself to the 'how-to' approach to beauty, promising transformation if only you bought this product or did this exercise, or ate that food. In a 1935 article provocatively entitled 'There are no Beauties,' *Vogue* argues that the 'beauty of today. . . earns it one-half by personality, one-fourth by Nature, and one-fourth by the modern miracle of make-up.' *Vogue* then instructs the reader to 'analyze' the photographs of five women, and to notice the irregularity of their features. 'Yet,' it explains, 'their radiant irregularity is the beauty of today.' No doubt, after years of photographing it, of being able to see trends outside its limited social enclave, *Vogue* is defining the modern ideal of beauty, pretending all the while that with a little bit of effort it is within everyone's reach:

It all ties together very neatly. This is a tense, nervous, explosive age. An age that has not time for classic serenity in anything, not even in the faces of its women. An age that demands motion, change, even chaos. Perfection is an alarming thing to modern man, because perfection implies a static state, and that is the last thing he wants.

There exists undoubtedly, women whose faces approach the classic ideal. But they are not the women who make heads turn in a restaurant, who are worshipped by movie fans, whose names dot the columns of every paper, and whose features decorate the pages of luxurious magazines the world over. They are not 'the beauties.'

*Vogue* captures the spirit of the times with its description of beauty. The modern face of beauty was one that, above all, was eminently photogenic, that could move for the camera. It fitted *Vogue*'s new philosophy of ready-to-wear beauty well, for with its imperfections it tantalized the reader's imagination, creating the desire that she, too, be transformed. But what the magazine was really describing, and selling, was its own look: one that required much more than make-up, that needed the camera above all to achieve perfection. We see this philosophy clearly articulated in an article entitled 'The Strange Face of Beauty,' written in 1939. The article focuses on the face that is structured to delight the eye of the camera.

This is the type that combines, in one woman, a disturbing set of paradoxes. A specific picture of her is impossible. A general portrait would be of a woman, a little curved, but still meagre; her cheeks a little hollow; her skin white; her hair not too much dressed; her clothes, perhaps, too Gothic; her eyes too spectral and her perfume too monstrous. Again, her veins may be too blue, her movements too sinuous, nails too long, voice too sepulchral, appearance too arresting. But for all her apparent unearthliness, she is the indubitable enchantress of a new and recognized order.

Meager, hollow, Gothic, spectral, monstrous, sepulchral, unearthly. This. . . the vocabulary of beauty? But we must remember that, during the nineteenth century in England, this was the preferred terminology for the description of beauty, inspired by the Gothic tradition of literature. The Gothicism of the Romantic poets purveyed an unnatural, perverse sexuality. Beauty was fashioned by artists who believed that the unusual, strange and exotic were expressions of freedom and fantasy; the boundaries between illusion and reality were blurred. Normal associations were turned upside down and the unearthly, sepulchral, meager (all words which connoted life of the spirit), even monstrous, became signs of beauty. It was a time that made the *femme fatale*, 'La Belle Dame sans Merci' – whose unearthly beauty could be spiritually enhancing but nevertheless destructive – popular. Again, female beauty and asymmetry are linked.

The modern enchantress of the 1930s looks not unlike this enchantress of old. But the new beauty also had been made recognizable by having her features flashed across a multitude of magazine covers and movie screens, titillating the fantasy of thousands of admirers with her 'strange' looks, and strange, remote behavior. Greta Garbo, more than any other well-known face, became the epitome of the strange look and remote behavior that *Vogue* treated as beauty for its 'irregularity' of feature. If she did not bring it into style she captured the mood of the moment:

It is true that she moves magically, that her skin is white and of a perfect grain; that her face is a mobile mask under which two enormous eyes first sleep and then burn like fiery beacons; that there is extraordinary mobility in her features; and that her forehead is unmatched among the women in the world. But as opposed to all that, her teeth are irregular, her cheekbones are too clearly defined, her mouth too wide, her figure too boyish, and nostrils too quivering; while the furrow that descends from her nose to her lips is so deep that one would swear it had been incised by a surgeon's knife. (1 November 1939)

Of course, by the 1930s the image of Garbo was not new. She was already on her way to becoming legendary with her enigmatic face that seemed made for the camera, and her enigmatic ways that seemed to capture the fantasy of the fantasy-seeking even beyond the limits of the screen (4.4).

Bracketed on the one side by the Depression, and on the other side by World War II, the 1930s found in beauty both a reflection of the chaos of the 'tense, nervous, explosive age,' and an escape from the anxiety it generated. Dresses were long and elegant, evoking either romanticism or exoticism. Hair announced its wearer's readiness for romance with cascades of curls or was pulled back severely to show off her newly fashionable angular features. Surrealism and romance, both the stuff that dreams are made of, were also the stuff that dominated the art and fashion of the time. Surrealism was a powerful force in the 1930s, especially after the Surrealist exhibition of 1936 in New York and London. The art of Dali, Miró, Magritte, Tanguy, and Ernst expresses the power of dream and fantasy by building compositions that are strange and irregular, not unlike the face of beauty that was praised so much at the time. Fashion did not ignore these trends. For example, Elsa Schiaparelli, the first French fashion designer who opened her own boutique in 1935 (a boutique which, by the way, was decorated by Dali), featured daring fashions which bore the indelible stamp of Surrealism. Dali and Cocteau as well as other artists of the time designed her fabrics, thus making the simple act of wearing clothes a venture into art and fantasy. Many of the fashion photographers of the time took their cue from these artists' new way of looking at reality, and with the use of elaborate backdrops against which they posed their models, the photographers created pictorial fantasies which with their strange, unrelated shapes gave a view of the underside of dream.

But there were those who preferred to represent escapism by the romantic style. Cecil Beaton, for instance, preferred to create an aura of romance in his photos like those 'taken in the early photographers' old master style,' rather than borrowing from the fantastic forms of the Surrealists. Yet he recognized the artifice of this position as well. 'I never got in a tizz about doing fashion pictures,' Beaton writes, 'but I enjoyed them tremendously. The complete falsehood, the artifice intrigued me.' (*VB* 122) And he, like other photographers, considered unusual or irregular features to be an essential ingredient of female beauty.

At the same time, the new hand-held camera allowed photographers the flexibility to move outdoors with their models and to use natural surroundings as a background. But even so, they produced, in the words of *Vogue* writer Polly Devlin, only 'a new assembly of illusions – the illusion of spontaneity, the illusion of movement, the illusion of reality.' (*VB* 199) While this could be construed as an attempt by *Vogue* to catch women in the simple act of wearing clothes, it was not so simple any more. 'Turn the page,' *Vogue* advises its readers in the last lines of its article 'There are no Beauties,' 'look at these women. . . . Say what you will, analyze how you may, they still give the illusion of beauty. And is not illusion enough for this transient age?'

Unlike the illusion of the still camera, playing with mere

instants of time, the fantasy involved in movie-making stretches beyond any one scene, set or movie. Hollywood became fantasyland, built to house the fantasies of movie-makers and their stars. It was both a product and a creator of myth. Hollywood was Hollywood. It boasted its own geography, its own morality, its own laws. By the 1930s even *Vogue*, which had in its early days shunned Hollywood beauty, had to acknowledge it.

Cecil Beaton captures the mood of an outsider looking in, in a 1930 article for *Vogue*. 'This is a town,' he writes, 'inhabited almost entirely by gods and goddesses of beauty. The girl shutting the window is Venus disguised as a most exquisite Madonna. The newspaper boy is a young Apollo.'

These gods and goddesses of beauty in Hollywood were revered by huge audiences. The aura of splendor radiated out into the everyday life of these divinities. Their houses, their cars, their clothes all became part of the elaborate paraphernalia of beauty and glamour. Never before could a beautiful face be an object of worship for so many people at once. For the first time, universal standards of beauty became conceivable. The goddesses of the screen wielded an unprecedented influence on the idea of feminine beauty. Styles and looks circumvented the influence of fashion designers. From the garments, hairstyles, and faces the screen showed, the audiences picked their favorites. Hollywood created trends, from the square-shouldered, rather mannish look made popular by Joan Crawford, to the bleached blond sultriness of Jean Harlow (4.5).

By 1936, reassessing its cultural role, *Vogue* can write:

Future historians of our times will have no Phidias or Leonardo to study, but if they want to sum up what the twentieth century thought of feminine beauty, they may dig up the native art, the advertising photographs, the magazine covers.... They are done by the spokesman for the masses. They show the aesthetic opinion of the masses, manipulated by them.... For the world sees – as against one gallery painting – twenty movies, fifty magazine covers, a hundred travel posters, a thousand newspaper advertisements.

It may seem strange that the masses, which had been so roundly denounced in its pages just a few years before, were now given credit for setting trends. But *Vogue* has never been stupid. Economic and political realities had changed, so *Vogue* changed too. Its readership soared, a result of its lower cost, practical advice about fashion and beauty, its more appealing layout, and its increased use of professional beauties. In the 1930s cover pictures of models began to replace drawings. While never gaining the status of a movie star, by the 1940s some 'cover girls' such as Lisa Fonssagrives, Lud, Jean Patchett, and Dorian Leigh were at least popularly recognized.

The claim that magazines such as *Vogue* were influenced by the masses is only partly true. While *Vogue*'s beauties took their cue from the Hollywood of the 1930s and 1940s, the magazine at first picked only those stars who represented the refinement, sophistication, and elegance with which the magazine had become identified. Garbo, of course, is the most obvious, but there were others, such as Crawford, Dietrich, and Hepburn, whose beauty approximated the magazine's ideal. *Vogue* had retreated from Paris because of the war, which had shut down its Paris offices and the French beauty business, and was finding new faces in Hollywood.

The pendulum of beauty swings along with the pendulum of politics. Fashions in beauty have always provided a gauge to political fashion and the war was no exception. At the end of the 1930s beauty became patriotic.

Not for nothing [writes *Vogue*] is the American Beauty Rose as emblematic of America as the Stars and Stripes, for in no country in the world is feminine beauty more firmly entrenched as a national ideal. We talk about American good looks with the same unaffected pride as we do our American highways or school systems. And every girl in her teens taking her first serious appraisal of herself in her mirror and determining that she, too, can become a glamour girl, advances the credo just that much further. (*VB* 119)

Beauty's patriotic stance, of course, anticipated the United States' entrance into the war. But beauty was wearing the Stars and Stripes not because of premonitions, but because Europe's troubles were allowing the American beauty industry to explode (4.6).

In its November 1 1939 issue *Vogue* reports on how the war had changed fashion in Paris where 'gas masks are worn nonchalantly, snoods are almost uniform, knickers are possible, boots ideal,' and how in Britain women wear 'a spate of white accessories' in order 'to avoid head-on collisions while going through. . . blackouts'; low-heeled shoes because with gas rationing 'people have to walk'; and 'special dresses called A.R.P. (Air Raid Precaution) for nocturnal diving into air raid shelters.' American beauty was on its own for the first time in history.

The resurgence of American patriotism before and during World War II included, of course, the beauty and fashion industries. In these, perhaps, the war played an even more pivotal role, since by forcing the shutdown of Paris's fashion industry, it greatly encouraged the development of indigenous standards, and the industry itself, in this country. But the war, as war will, influenced the look of fashion more directly.

Rationing of fabric and the development of nylon by the government induced *Vogue* to put a new look together. Following Britain's example, *Vogue* made bobbysox a fashion item, along with practical short-skirted dresses or skirts with squared-off tops or jackets. By day the American beauty donned her uniform-inspired dress; by night, as the January 1942 issue shows us, she wore flowery and frilly dresses with long, full skirts to deny the hardships of the war. *Vogue*, by now the arbiter of American beauty, was divided between a daytime and nighttime existence, between the casual and the chic, between the fuller-bodied look of pin-up girls and corset ads and the ghostly thinness of the emerging 'model-type,' between a 'natural' all-American look and one that still remembered Paris, between the people, its new audience, and the 'smart set,' its old, between reality and illusion (4.7).

When the war was over and American men had packed up their pin-ups and come home, *Vogue* was still uncertain. But by 1947 *Vogue*'s constituency found out that the American 'look' had lost. With a single stroke Christian Dior had won back for Paris its leadership in the world of fashion. He had stunned the post-war fashion-hungry world with an impractical look that idealized the female form. Vaguely reminiscent of the Gibson Girl hourglass look of the turn of the century, the Dior look nipped the waist, padded the hips, softened the shoulders, lengthened skirts, and made pointed toes and stiletto heels mandatory. Dior picked up where designers of the late 1930s had left off. 'Paris puts you back in laced corsets. . . to cinch your waist and round your hips by stringent cut and boning,' announced *Vogue* in its September 15 1939 issue. Almost ten years later Dior made his intentions explicit. 'I design clothes for flowerlike women, with rounded shoulders, full, feminine busts, and handspan waists above enormous spreading skirts,' he said, adding triumphantly, 'I brought back the art of pleasing.' (*VB* 134) Once again, feminine beauty was corseted and bound (4.8).

By 1950 the Dior look was everywhere in the United States. Through the pervasive influence of *Vogue*, women committed themselves to the uncomfortably corseted fashions. The 1950s were a curious period. After being active and taking part in crucial work during the war, women seemed to be packaging themselves in constricting dresses and tight skirts. Politically, it was an age of constraint as well: conservatism and anti-communism, when political oppression passed for patriotism, when conformity and conspicuous consumption ruled.

Practicality seemed *passé*. And why not? New affluence and technological innovation almost made movement obsolete. Cars took women shopping with the simple push of a pedal, television brought entertainment into the home, fast and frozen foods made homemaking simple, telephones made socializing as easy as dialing a number. It was a time when people saw the American Dream come true. A time of wealth, a baby boom, a lust for acquisition, all worked to redefine the notion of the beauty as a woman, homebound or carbound, beguilingly dressed in clothes in which she could hardly move. 'Buy it,' a Foundettes ad for Munsingwear advises in 1951, 'see how it brings rebellious curves into line for that well-put-together look.' This ad sums up the mood of the 1950s. From under-clothes to undercover agents everything conspired to bring rebellion 'into line' and to show that America had a disciplined look.

The *Vogue* model represented this new ideal of American beauty and elegance. The age of the cover girl had arrived. Cover girls became the beauty stars of the magazines. Advertisements in *Vogue* began to give cover girls special billing. Candy Jones, a 1951 *Vogue* ad for hair coloring tells us, is a 'favorite magazine cover girl' (though in the advertisement she is certainly in the good company of Princess Obolensky

4.1 Lillian Russell and Lily Langtry

4.2 Mme Chanel and
Lady Abdy, 1929

4.3 Leisure looks lithesome,
unfettered, unconcerned

4.4  The faces of Garbo

4.5 The goddesses that Hollywood creates: Joan Crawford and Jean Harlow

4.6 Marlene Dietrich

4.7 Pin-up dresses up:
Betty Grable

4.8 The flower-like, cinched-waist Dior look becomes popular

4.9 Teen rocks fashion taboos

4.10 Jackie: the first lady as trendsetter

4.11 Verushka, Twiggy and Penelope Tree: a 1960s trinity of freaky goddesses

4.12 The Farrah phenomenon

and Mrs Igor Cassini). But it was not only in ads that cover girls made special appearances. Readers were given glimpses of their home lives. Typically they were photographed with their children, at home with their husbands, or hopping in and out of cars. This 'intimate' view of America's beauty professional seemed to contrast sharply with the inaccessibility and icy aloofness of the beauties on the cover. *Vogue* knew that readers liked to identify with the women who were featured in its pages. In the early days there was no distinction between its readers and its high society trend-setting models. Consciously or not, *Vogue* was trying to establish a similar identification, except now professional rather than society beauties were offered to the public to emulate by consuming. *Vogue*'s covers titillated the reader to buy, and its pages gave directions on how and what to buy.

But consumers are fickle and tastes variable and *Vogue* was no longer dealing with a narrow readership. While the magazine throughout the years kept revising its notion of beauty and fashion to fit an ever-broader range of tastes, the widespread affluence of the 1950s presented a special challenge.

[A]lmost overnight, as it seemed, [writes Polly Devlin] the 1950s became the decade of the affluent young. The discreet, allusive signals of wealth, good taste, and international chic meant nothing to them. Overall effect was more important than detail. Dress became an idiosyncratic affair, revealing the interests and allegiances of the wearer. Fashion taboos were broken with relish. (*VB* 136)

It has been said that the 1950s invented the teenager. The teenage phenomenon could only emerge in a culture of mass affluence and leisure. We now think of the teenage years as marking a transition between childhood and adulthood. But the very stuff of adolescence is leisure, the ability to prolong childhood and play. Before the 1950s most young people were forced to pass quickly from childhood to adulthood, to ensure their own and their families' economic survival. In the 1950s, the same youth, with general prosperity and mandatory education through tenth grade, worked hard to define its leisure. The new youth labored to learn not how to make money but how to spend its money and its time.

Fashion magazines were caught off guard. For *Vogue* and

its readers, little girls still grew up into ladies. This did not appeal to the current generation who felt there were more interesting things to do with their lives than be ladylike. As much as glamour, propriety, and leisure were central to beauty during this period, the old notions of aristocratic, drawing-room elegance, which *Vogue* still promoted, were becoming obsolete in the age of middle-class rule. It was no longer simply a matter of trying to imagine the refinement of the Vander-bilts, but of trying to keep up with the Joneses.

Movies and TV portrayed a multiplicity of images of beauty, generally more accessible than the cover-girl look. Teenagers, especially, found in movies a special language, a special dress, and a special notion of beauty, whose stereotypes were easy to emulate: they could choose among Marilyn Monroe's child-like sexy look, Audrey Hepburn's elegance, Natalie Wood's innocent pretty-teen-next-door, and Sandra Dee's nubile *ingénue* in trouble for allowing the teen in her to momentarily take over. The American movie industry offered the young the adventure, excitement and safe titillation that was lacking in their suburban homes, but the proffered adventures were always rooted in middle-class morality.

The 1950s, more than any other period in the movie indus-try's history, marketed cuteness. The Mary Pickfords of the age included a number of American starlets such as Sandra Dee, Hayley Mills, Annette Funicello, and the older Debbie Reynolds and Doris Day, whose doll-like looks diluted the threat of sex and mature womanhood. Not only did they lack the angularity of features, the exotic face, so much admired a couple of decades earlier, but they also offered the innocence of a Mouseketeer. They presented a safe and fun-loving image to America's youth, who quickly adopted rolled-up jeans and ponytails as trademarks of cuteness, immortalized in those forgettable lyrics: 'Ponytail, she's got the cutest little ponytail. . . how it wiggles when she walks and she talks,' or another song which spoke of the new 'Venus in blue jeans' who looked like 'Mona Lisa with a turned up nose.'

Others seemingly cast in the mold of Garbo and Hepburn, with their self-assurance and cool sophistication, appealed to more adult audiences. But the cool beauties of the 1950s like Grace Kelly were not provocative or powerful, sexually or

otherwise. Their beauty was pure and restrained. They represented the beautiful and untouchable 'lady' that *Vogue* talked
about with so much pride, the young woman who was destined
for, and educated for, a fairytale wedding. '[R]emote as a Snow
Queen. . . Gold-flecked, graceful, and unbending,' wrote *Vogue*
in 1955 about Grace Kelly, who had, 'in the course of her
two years as Hollywood idol, caused countless writers infinite
uncomfortable moments hunting for variations of the one word
that describes her – "lady." ' It was as if the audiences of the
1950s, still suffering from the shell-shock of a decade earlier,
were bent on wiping out any element of danger from the social
and political fabric of the country. It was a time when 'making
things safe for democracy' and the American way meant homo-
genizing everything, making it antiseptic. So, too, the sting
had to be removed from beauty.

Unlike those of earlier decades, even American sex symbols
such as Marilyn Monroe projected a look of beauty that might
be titillating but was really harmless. There was a childish,
vulnerable, innocent, playful air about her which was missing,
for example, in the vamps of the 1920s. 'Sex kitten' became a
popular term during the decade, describing the mixture of
innocence and playful sexuality of the new sex symbols of the
screen. Other terms, such as 'sexpot,' that made their way into
the vocabulary during the 1950s also lacked the connotations
of aggressiveness or power that made the 'sex goddesses,'
'queens,' or even 'bombshell' catchwords of an earlier time. A
'sexpot,' like a teapot, was an article to be used – passive.

The few foreign beauties, like Brigitte Bardot or Sophia
Loren, who captured the attention of Hollywood with their
explosive sexuality, could be largely ignored as un-American.
It was hard to tell if they were dangerous because they were
foreign or sexy, but Hollywood managed to exploit all three –
danger, foreignness and sexiness – by uncovering their scanda-
lous private lives. Indeed, sexual scandal was not tolerated
on US turf, nor was the mixture of beauty, intelligence, and
independence. Not only was Ingrid Bergman's love affair in
1949 publicly denounced in the US Senate but it was treated
like a real threat to national security. In the 1950s, beauty
was not admissible except as cuteness and dependency.

But some daring teenagers chose to imitate Brigitte Bardot,

whose beauty showed an unrestrained and wholly natural sexiness. Teens were learning to speak an idiom which expressed their lifestyle and helped give form to their subculture. It was a language of the streets rather than mainstream society, fads not fashion. To these young people beauty was not the sophisticated stare of the *Vogue* model, but rather the insolent glare that knew the freedom of the streets. Teen beauty had an energy, an urgency, a knowing innocence, and an active stance that made the cool, elegant, ladylike, passive adult look of *Vogue*'s covers seem foreign and fettered (4.9).

However irrelevant the *Vogue* look was for the teen audience of the 1950s, its covers still uttered the platitudes of the times. The American look was in fashion – at least *Vogue* said it was. *Vogue*, now, saw itself as representing the American Dream. On the one hand, the magazine retained the old aura of inaccessibility, on the other, it promised mainstream America that all this was within their reach.

The 'how-to' approach to beauty which it made popular in the 1930s became a dominant feature of the magazine in the 1950s.

I used to look at the magazines my mother's older sister had around the house [said a woman we talked to who was coming of age in the late 1950s]. I would flip through the pages to see how it was done. I developed all the traits that would make me a beautiful youth and I spent so much time on it that I didn't really consider any other ideas.

When asked what traits she meant, she mentioned the influence of *Vogue*'s and other magazine's 'how-to' approach. For years she followed the magazine's directions faithfully. *Vogue* began to feature a beauty section, which offered a 'Progress report on American Beauty'; gave an 'eye-view of the revolution in beauty'; reported on 'The beauty shake-up; new looks; new ways to get them'; and told 'the Story of a plain woman who is considered a beauty,' all in an attempt to assure the reader that any woman could 'develop the traits' that would make her beautiful.

She's a beauty, you say [writes *Vogue* in one of its 'Discoveries of Beauty']. But often, you are wrong. Perhaps she is only very clever, very knowing about her assets, liabilities – and, most especially, about her make-up. Some women have a talent for beauty make-believe. Others need to be shown.

True to 1950s form, *Vogue* spoke of a woman's face in words that are vaguely reminiscent of investment manuals. Women were directed to assess their assets and liabilities and to play the beauty market accordingly. The overt message was that beauty could make money. 'Beauty means security. Economic security. Money, position, status,' reflected a woman in her early fifties to whom we talked. 'Women of my era did that. It was blatant, open. That's what the men were for and that's what the women were for. I'll give you this and you give me that. It was an economic exchange.' It is no wonder, then, that *Vogue*'s promise to turn every duckling into a swan, a 'gold-flecked' beauty, was perhaps its strongest selling point (for those who could afford the dream but not the clothes). In the 1950s beauty became big business.

By the mid-1950s, as models became essential props to the glamour industry, their salaries soared. They gained status and became, along with the photographers, the stars of the beauty business. In the intimate tangle of creation and technique, the photographer and his model began to dictate taste in beauty. As a medium, photography was no longer innocent. Images of photogenic women, however stunning and unusual, were simply not enough to make an impact. Fashion photography needed new images to get attention. The accretion of images from movies, television, and magazines had inured the senses to the usual, and inventiveness became crucial. The eye needed to be shocked. The look of the untouchable elegant lady needed change.

Already photographers like Irving Penn tried to give their models a touch of 1950s reality by making them look as if they were wholeheartedly engaged in familiar activities. They ate sandwiches and drank Coke as they slouched carelessly in their chairs; they were seen in rumpled beds, waking up to early morning phone calls; or they posed as models trying to be the image of beauty perfected, engaging fully in the make-believe (*VB* 137).

Photographers like William Klein took their cameras steps closer to street culture.

I liked the tough girls from New York and the backstreets, rather than the upper-class socialites [he recalls]. In my photos the girls are always in trouble, always askew, or I play two girls off together.

Helmut Newton's photos come out of mine because I was the first to use hard girls. (*VB* 139)

The lady and the whore, two images of women that were not new but rather clothed in modern dress in a magazine that had always dedicated itself to showing the lady, not the whore. But the times demanded Venus' double face, the earthly and the heavenly. By the end of the 1950s and the beginning of the 1960s *Vogue* had developed a formula with more appeal to its growing audience in an attempt to make the elegant more accessible and the everyday more glamorous.

Times had changed. The United States now felt comfortable in its affluence. The inauguration of the young President Kennedy, accompanied by his stylish young wife, made youth not only respectable, but requisite (4.10). The jet age had arrived and there was talk of journeys beyond the earth. Everyone was on the move, including women, who were beginning to cast off some of the more constraining clothes and opt for shorter skirts, chemise dresses which recalled the look of the 1920s, the A-line, and the sack, and who were now looking for racier, more innovative fashions. Hollywood was getting racier too. Now stars involved in scandals still got star treatment, a few whispers but little of the abuse that the earlier movie sinners had been subjected to. The Taylor-Burton affair, for example, was more like an exciting drama being played off-screen, making even greater stars of them both. The country seemed a bit more relaxed, and out of its corsets, beauty breathed a bit freer.

The American good looks and unaffected pride that *Vogue* had talked about at the beginning of the 1950s seemed finally to make their way onto its covers a decade later. *Vogue* seemed more and more to take its cue from the streets, from the world outside its studios, whether Hollywood, Washington, or New York. In the early 1960s, Jackie Kennedy's rise to stardom as First Lady had *Vogue* offering versions of her famous bouffant hairdo, pillbox hats, and knee-tickling A-line dresses. To rival this girlish, demure look, there was something more exotic. As early as 1960 the magazine began to show off the fruits of its travels to far-off places. 'The quexquemtl find in July' of that year showed to advantage the influence of Mexico in the high fashion business. And in 1962 the magazine adopted the look made popular by Elizabeth Taylor in the movie *Cleopatra*. For months the rage was the Cleopatra look with its imaginative hairstyles and winged eyes which recalled somewhat the kohl-rimmed eyes of the 1920s vamp. The look taxed the imagination of hairstylists, make-up artists, and photographers, who came up with numerous variations on the theme for the pages of *Vogue*. Beauty had now become a major production; the collaborative efforts of designers, art directors, hairstylists, make-up artists, and photographers all became essential to the projection of a 'look.' The Cleopatra look was so extravagant that it would not be matched until the late 1960s. *Vogue* followed the eyes of the world and those eyes in the early part of the decade were on Liz and Jackie.

By now, the influence of teenagers had infiltrated the world of fashion. On 1 August 1960, for example, *Vogue* featured 'Clothes for the young who set the Style,' indicating that finally trendsetting was no longer the prerogative of established society. *Vogue* adopted the tamer styles that showed off those American good looks of which it was so proud, styles that were best interpreted by young models. Suzy Parker, a 1950s veteran, and Jean Shrimpton became the first real superstars of the modeling world. Photographers like Richard Avedon, Helmut Newton, and David Bailey gave these models a form of stardom and *Vogue* finished the transformation by giving them top billing on its covers and pages. 'The paragon figure on these five pages – fit and supple with a luxuriously unhurried kind of tawniness,' announced *Vogue* on 1 May 1964, 'is Suzy Parker.' And a month later it featured a lengthy show-and-tell article entitled 'Suzy Parker Has Her First Short Haircut – the Story Begins Here.' Top models along with their photographers began to move in glamorous circles previously reserved for socialites, film stars, and artists. *Vogue* had finally proved it had the power to take a young girl off the street and make her a household name.

Under the guidance of Diana Vreeland, *Vogue* seemed to be more or less in tune with its times, sometimes even anticipating and legitimizing possible trends. As early as 1963 with the exotic Cleopatra craze going on, *Vogue* focuses on the young and the flowering youth culture. The adjectives which kept popping up emphasized youth, freedom, adventure, and the new look of beauty increasingly does the same. 'Vogue's eye view of fashion adventure,' the magazine announced in August of 1963, 'the new girl who wears what she wants to wear. Vogue's prototype: Françoise Hardy.' And about this singer and heroine of the transistor set, Vogue reports 'She has a sturdy streak of adventure. . . and looks as right as a young animal.' All this the same year as an article on teen tyranny appears! None the less, the magazine admired the adventuresome spirit and look of the young. Dylan and others appeared in Vogue's 'People are Talking About.' Shrimpton and her lookalikes began to shed their clothing to reveal thin, tawny, collapsible-looking bodies. Even the 'Beautiful People,' or BPs, the new term for chic, have a premeditated carelessness and wild look about them. 'Like *belles sauvages*,' Vogue writes in 1963, they 'stretched in the sun − bodies bared, gleaming, taut. . . .' All this anticipating 1965 and Vogue's 'Year of the Body'; all this mere underground rumblings of what Vogue in 1965 would call the 'YouthQuake,' which was to topple once and for all the constraints and structured looks of the 1950s.

What was the YouthQuake? *Vogue's* editor was carefully watching those who were 'tuning in, turning on, and dropping out.' The YouthQuake as pictured in Vogue shared the carefreeness, freakiness, self-indulgence, and lawlessness of the youth movement outside the offices of *Vogue*. Beauty was joining the protest marches; it, too, was rebelling. The YouthQuake was the post-war baby boom come of age.

The street became the stage on which the new face of beauty in its raw, pristine state was to be seen either parading in protest against the war and other injustices or gathering in parks and large strobe-lit dancehalls to catch the psychedelic sounds of popular rock bands. Beauty had to be bizarre, psychedelic, to keep up with the times. Short hair and long dangling earrings and a mini-skirt marched down the street alongside long flowerladen hair and antique store-bought clothes or 'free box' unloadings. Breasts were bared and the body, too, spoke the language of freedom. Among the young it was hard to determine monetary worth. Money wasn't supposed to matter. Youth had been substituted for wealth as coin of the status realm. The Beatles, the Stones, Dylan, Baez, Warhol, and street leaders, among others, were the cultural heroes. The underground, whether the press or movies, culled through and advised on new strategies, let everyone know what was happening.

Youth was in! The young were out to see and be seen. And they knew how to do it in real style. After all, they were the media generation – the first generation raised on TV – and so they knew the drama that 'the tube' required. They could now dress and act accordingly, could delight in the fact that they were on stage in bizarre garb, drawing the attention of the mainstream to their rebellion and announcing, finally, that they had a cause. They even outdid the media at their own game. They made reality seem more fantastic than illusion, fact stranger than fiction. Even if people didn't want to listen, they couldn't help but look.

*Vogue* was paying tribute to youth in its pages, not just the youth of the 1960s, but also the youth of the early nineteenth century who transformed macabre, gothic, and ghostly looks into symbols of beauty, or the youth of the late nineteenth century who wore artifice on their sleeve to boast of their dandyism and decadence; in short, all youth who dared to celebrate their fantasy, freedom, and independence, who dared to counter the culture of the status quo. The 1960s showed itself off by borrowing the slightly decadent, slightly sexually liberated yet intensely innocent look that these and other youth cultures projected.

Most important to the 1960s, beauty was youth, youth beauty. Beauty parted company with adulthood until even sexual boundaries were blurred. Young men let their hair grow long, wore beaded necklaces, earrings, and flowered shirts, and could be called 'beautiful.' Women imitated the Twiggies of the day with close cropped hair, thin curveless bodies and, in general, the unisex look. The androgyne was celebrated. Models were made to look especially young and slightly spoiled in their provocative short little-girl dresses – a true mixture, to use Henry James's words, of audacity and innocence.

*Vogue* had always followed the chic. Now it tuned in and tripped out, picking up on the latest and interpreting it provocatively, outdoing the streets in streetwiseness, still the final arbiter on beauty. Many of the photographers who worked for *Vogue*, like Richard Avedon, David Bailey, Penati, and Helmut Newton, participated in the offbeat world of writers, musicians, artists, and underground moviemakers so much admired by the youth culture (*VB* 140). They gave *Vogue* an 'in,' if not insight, into how to interpret both the street scene and the avant-garde artistic scene. *Vogue*'s favorites were either models turned media stars (Jean Shrimpton, Twiggy, and later, Lauren Hutton), or 'personalities' turned models and media stars (Verushka, Penelope Tree, and Marisa Berenson) (4.11). Other socialites, such as Pilar Crespi, Yasmin Aga Khan, Edie Sedgwick, and Amanda Burden, followed in the footsteps of Tree and Berenson, perhaps hoping that an appearance as a model in the magazine would make them stars. In this media-conscious world, wealth was no longer enough to get one noticed. One had to be seen to be beautiful and preferably seen in the pages of *Vogue*. Indeed, an appearance in *Vogue*, or, better yet, on its cover, was *de rigueur* for any young woman who had hopes for fame through beauty. Catherine Deneuve, Mia Farrow, Candice Bergen, Britt Ekland, Ali MacGraw, all appear on *Vogue* covers.

Putting its old ideals, the elegant and social 'Beautiful People' together with its newly-created elite, the young street people, *Vogue* created a new society of apparently irreconcilable elements. But the America of the 1960s delighted in the paradox and a new elite was born – a fabulous beast, the result of a union of the Beautiful People and the Flower Children.

So *Vogue* engaged in the curious game of pretending to give up what it stood for without giving up the chic. In a sense *Vogue* became a conscious self-parody: creating illusion for illusion's sake – and selling it. Fashion became exotic, extravagant, exaggerated, or fantastic. As early as February 1965, the Beauty Bulletin in *Vogue* predicts that

ornamental make-ups are on; suddenly very much on. The night has come when a few bravura types determine which make-up fantasy they'll wear for a given evening (birds, beasts, butterflies are among the choices as are jewelled faces and authentic Oriental make-ups), and then go on to choose the dress that'll work best with it. One version, which begins with a startling pearl-white face has a future so magnetic that some avant-gardistes are sneaking down to Mott Street this minute to take make-up lessons from a Chinese-theatre make-up specialist.

Here *Vogue* hints at the world of dream and fantasy – and the macabre. There is a none-too-faint glint of decadence. The pearl-white face of beauty suggests the look of death gleaming in darkness as much as it suggests the masked face that would light up a drama and a dark theatre. Make-up is acknowledged as just what it is: a mask. The 'natural look' is mocked by the unnatural presence of birds, beasts, butterflies. Nature is presented as ornament and nothing more – beautiful because artificial, out of context.

And this is not all. *Vogue*'s favorite beauties are featured in all sorts of outlandish garb. Twiggy, 'the Sprig on the Twig,' is featured on July 1967's cover with one eye painted to look like a flower, a tribute clearly to 'flower power.' Responding to the popularity of exotic and ethnic looks, and to the growing awareness of the presence of minorities in the country, black and oriental models became a part of *Vogue* fantasy. Bejewelled and painted bodies, bared breasts, heads of hair turned rainbow-colored fantasies, animal-masked leopard-lean figures, androgynous Greek boys, all helped to give beauty a Felliniesque look. Beauty became bizarre.

'Now beauty is free,' Richard Goldstein claims in a 1968 *Vogue* article. 'Liberated from the hang-ups over form and function, unencumbered by tradition. . . . A freaky goddess surveying her ailanthus realm. Kite-high; moon-pure. Groovy, powerful and weird!' (*VB* 142)

The effect of the overemphasis on youth during the late 1960s was less deleterious than that of the last ten years or so when editorial fashions and advertisers have turned back to realism to create images of beauty. The Verushkas, Twiggies, Trees were meant to be seen, not as 'real' people, but as images, symbols, at most, Beautiful People, who inhabited the freaky fantasy world that *Vogue* had created. 'One could never imagine looking like a Vogue model,' a woman who was in her teens during the late 1960s told us, 'but one could dream about it, dream about being made up to look that way, dream about acting out an image in front of the camera.' Echoing her, the poet and singer Patti Smith speaks about the strength of images that *Vogue* created during those years:

Living in south Jersey, you get connected with the pulse beat of what's going on through what you read in magazines. . . *Vogue* magazine was my whole consciousness. I never saw people. . . . It was all image. In one issue of *Vogue* it was Youthquaker people they were talking about. It had a picture of Edie [Sedgwick] on a bed in a ballet pose. She was like a thin man in black leotards and a sort of boat-necked sweater, white hair, and behind her a little white horse drawn on the wall. She was such a strong image that I thought, 'that's it.' It represented everything to me. . . radiating intelligence, speed, being connected with the moment.[3]

In the 1960s the models were not pretty, the way we think of them today. Rather, they were extraordinary.

But things changed in the 1970s as the pendulum of beauty swung away from the projection of fantasies to the projection of reality, of a look of naturalness. The realities of a severe economic recession, of a cruel war lost, of a US president caught in his own lies and forced to resign, of youth finding out that dropping out often ended in burning out or dosing out, all had a sobering effect on society in general, and the images of beauty in particular. What would remain from the 1960s, however, was the notion that super-models inhabited that glamorous world of beauty, power, money, and make-believe, previously reserved for the very rich. *Vogue* had succeeded in transforming its mystique into mythology. Being beautiful meant being in *Vogue*. 'Every kid wants to be a model,' declares Zoltan Rendessy, owner of Zoli modeling agency, 'whereas it used to be a moviestar.'[4]

True. Models now made the covers even of important news magazines. Lauren Hutton made news when it was revealed that Revlon was negotiating a million dollar contract with her. Hutton was the perfect image of beauty for the times. She was recognizable, real-looking. The gap between her teeth, her self-confessed banana nose made her seem a little more flawed than fantastic and therefore more accessible. There seemed to be no artifice about her; even though she grew out of the 1960s she lacked the strange imposing looks of a Verushka or the decadent innocent look of an Edie Sedgwick or a Penelope Tree. There was something natural, all-American about her.

She recalls the wholesome good looks of a 1950s model. Lauren Hutton looked young, spontaneous, energetic, and modern, the look of the 1960s spilling over into the 1970s.

By 1972, *Vogue* was readjusting its image so that it could remain 'connected with the moment.' In the 1970s women had begun to reassess their social roles and to determine their political future. For some, freedom no longer meant freakiness but feminism, though they are not unconnected; the breaking of one set of social taboos made possible the relaxation of others. After all, if make-up could be seen as a mask then it could be removed. Clearly, this was an untenable position for *Vogue* and its advertisers who relied on women's desire to buy beauty. Women were talking about looking and being natural, throwing off confining clothes and confining ideas, wearing no more masks. The whole notion of beauty had to be downplayed or transformed without destroying women's needs for external reassurance about their looks.

No magazine takes its readers for granted [declares *Vogue* in January of 1972], nor do we. Still, there are things we feel easy. . . in assuming about the woman who reads *Vogue* today. That she likes herself, for one – or she wouldn't give a damn how she looked and wouldn't be here in the first place. On the other hand, as sure as there is more than fashion on these pages, there is more than fashion on her mind.

A woman, *Vogue* suggests, was to look as if she likes herself, as if there are more than looks on her mind, as if she 'works, travels, goes back to school for her Masters. . . is good at some sports.' This, in short, would be the new look. *Vogue* began to announce in its fashion features that 'Ease is the essence,' that there would be a 'new nonchalance in fashion,' and its beauty features also reflected a similar 'too-active-to-care-too-much' attitude. *Vogue* talked about 'real makeup. . . the essence of beauty today,' 'the short cut – the fast moving fashion for shorter hair,' in short, 'ready beauty,' anything that would convey the message that women had too much on their minds and too little time to care about caring too much. It was a paradoxical assignment: teaching women to make up so as not to look made-up, selling artifice as naturalness, selling as alluring a product that wasn't supposed to be seen. *Vogue* knew that it was not just a matter of new kinds of make-up but of selling a new image. Now that women were talking openly about their feelings it was important to take into account how a woman feels and how it feels to be a woman. Lauren Hutton incorporated the new image of a personality peering through a pretty, non-threatening, face, a face that, through make-up, looked both as pretty and as untouched as your kid sister's – well, Lauren Hutton's kid sister's.

When Revlon hired Lauren Hutton they hired a whole image. As the personification of the modern woman she seemed to be everywhere. She seemed to have leaped off the *Vogue* covers to a life of her own, not the life of a Beautiful Person, like some of her contemporaries (Twiggy, Verushka, Berenson, Tree, and the rest) but one more or less like the reader's. Revlon found a safe but stimulating image. They did not have to go through a process of interpreting the New Woman; Lauren Hutton had already been interpreted for them. This new Venus would be equated with their products. The identification was the sell. If you noticed Lauren Hutton, you had to notice Revlon; if you liked her, no doubt you liked Revlon.

Other advertisers quickly picked up the emerging vocabulary of liberation without fully understanding what it meant. One advertiser, for example, concocts images of this new woman whose underlying message now seems laughable if not downright hideous. 'For today's liberated woman,' announces the ad featuring a naked woman posing in a country-side setting. 'Today's woman is a new breed. She has freed herself from the taboos of yesterday. "The mini". . . "the bikini". . ."the see-through". . . "the pill" are all part of what's happening.' Therefore, the ad suggests, she must be in need of 'Cupid's Quiver,' because it both 'mildly yet thoroughly cleanses – *inside*' and it promises to 'eliminate any fear of offending.' Consuming the pill, taking off clothes, paying attention to those 'inner' qualities, suggest freedom but have the ring of cash. Rather than liberating woman for her own pleasure or growth or accomplishment, they 'free' her to be more sexually available and pleasurable for man. Explicitly supporting the gains of the women's movement, cosmetics and fashion advertisers were canny enough to realize that their livelihood depended upon minimizing its influence.

Revlon's formula was cleverer still. Ally one strong image

with a product and the image will sell the product. This Revlon did in its Ultima II ads which showed the different faces of Lauren. Readers could follow her different moods, from natural to romantic to glamorous. The suggestion was that the modern woman was too intelligent to conform to any one look but rather chose her looks to fit her moods. Lauren Hutton looks natural, comfortable, in control of any look she chooses. And this is what her image promises the buyer.

The Hutton-Revlon formula ushered in a new way to talk about beauty. In January of 1976 an article entitled 'Pretty: What it Means,' written by Jill Robinson, set out to redefine beauty – indeed, to take the beauty out of beauty.

What we want now [we are told] is a kind of mental gorgeousness beyond beauty or prettiness. Gorgeousness is Beauty in motion: moving from inside out with a plan. . . . Gorgeousness catches women moving, working, slouching, thinking, and lusting. Gorgeousness is beauty liberated. . . . Gorgeousness is energy.

No doubt in deference to the women's movement we are told further that 'passivity is not beautiful' that the passive beauty 'leaning backward' reflected in the idealized looks and the classic poses of models, is definitely out. According to Alexander Liberman the new ideal is to 'capture women as "modern" – the word that is used today as opposed to "beautiful" – which means to portray women who are part of their time.' (*F* 22) In other words, models should not look like models but should look like real people.

In June 1978 Cleveland Amory writes, in his *Vogue* article 'The Cover "Girl" is a Woman,' that unlike the higher fashion model of old the new model 'no longer scares you. . . . She is probably American. . . has her own new look. . . a look that is perilously close to that of a real person.' *Vogue* engages us in a world where models act, move, and look as if they were in the midst of purposeful action, as if, we are asked to believe, beauty is merely incidental. According to Liberman, fashion photographers act like paparazzi: they emphasize the action, make it look as if the models were caught unaware by the camera in the middle of important, newsworthy events. The illusion that is created is that the camera is in pursuit of these 'gorgeous,' energetic creatures who leap through the air out of sheer joy in going to the office, pose like dancers in street clothes as they reach the corner of a busy street, do somersaults as they accidentally bump into each other, and look contemptuously over their shoulder as if the camera has spied on them and caught them in an intensely private moment.

With the advent of Hutton the American look associated with naturalness became popular, and those who could interpret it with vigor catapulted onto the cover of *Vogue*. By 1977, models were being snatched up with lucrative contracts by major cosmetic, clothing, and cigarette firms. *Vogue* became the go-between of the beauty business. 'Put them on the cover of *Vogue* once,' says Leah Feldon, a stylist for Revlon, Clairol, Avon and other companies, 'and all of a sudden everybody is hiring them.' (*F* 139)

This is because an appearance on *Vogue*'s covers means instant recognizability. The cover girl became, more than a pretty face, a personality in her own right. Her image rubbed off on the product. 'Everyone wants to photograph top models,' says David Leddick, creative director of the Revlon group at Grey Advertising, 'because they are top models. . . . the prestige of their aura carries the project.' (*F* 40) In a strange twist, top models now inspired manufacturers to create products of which the model's personality was the crucial component. This was very much the case with the perfume Babe, which immediately established an identification between the product and newcomer Margaux Hemingway.

Of all the assortment of different looks that were vying to capture the reader and the advertiser, the blond, all-American look was the most successful in translating the Hutton formula of youth, energy, and health. Whereas Karen Graham's sophistication, reserve, and serenity gave Estée Lauder the image of beauty and old wealth, and Renée Russo's appearance for Moondrops mixed sultriness and sophistication, Cheryl Tiegs looked as if she could smoke a pack of cigarettes and still bounce smilingly onto a California tennis court declaring, without a hint that she might be even slightly out of breath, that she had come a long way, and yes, baby, she was going to leap even longer distances.

When Cheryl Tiegs followed Farrah Fawcett in her momentous leap from cover to poster, beauty news was made.

Already Fawcett's poster had been the biggest seller ever. She had revived the World War II pin-up girl tradition and become the object of admiration of millions all over the world. Her formula: the contrived naturalness of her wildly structured blond mane, a hint of nipples casually peeking through her clinging bathing suit, and a wide healthy smile, that, unlike the simpers of the pin-up girls of the 1940s, was too wholesome to have anything to do with sex. Cheryl Tiegs had a similar prettiness, a similar look of glowing health. These new goddesses did not exude feminine mysteriousness. Rather there was something matter-of-fact about their looks, something unthreatening, and surprisingly accessible. *Vogue* eulogized 'Far-ra-out Farrah' in its April 1977 issue and talked about this ' "Sex Goddess of the Seventies' " greatest attraction. . . being her "shot-from-guns" energy. Face it – Fawcett is all about fitness. She breathes it, sleeps it, talks it, and means it.' No Dairy Queen dumbness in this blond. Farrah was running hard to reverse this stereotype. Her energy and naturalness were her selling point. Even her hair, she tells us, has 'a life of its own.' 'The Farrah Phenomenon' had millions of teenagers spending millions of collective hours making their hair look as natural as their heroine's, but they were not alone. Farrah, the goddess of the natural look, Phil Donahue lets us know, 'spent an hour in her dressing room with her hairstylist and makeup artist,' before an appearance on his show, only to come out and tell the audience, 'My hair? Oh, I just sort of toss it around up there, and that's how it comes out.' (4.12)[5]

Universal as the rush to fitness and health may be, it is far from the only current angle on beauty. Sexual seductiveness – the old-fashioned sultry hothouse look – is still a draw; a more recent – and more disturbing – trend is toward sexuality being given a *frisson* with a dollop of sado-masochism: a hint of violence, of whips, chains, maiming, and death. It pleases *Vogue*'s official chroniclers to inform us that fitness is the word of the hour. But much less of their own prose has been devoted to gushing over the decadent and sexually-used look of the mannequins who have been known to grace their pages.

Many of the photographs that have been taken in the past few years show women's beauty in an atmosphere reeking with sexual violence, sometimes as a kinky take-off on women's emerging independence and social strength. Polly Devlin describes the female aggression that appears in a number of *Vogue* pictures:

A stiletto heel pin[s] a man's black slippered instep casually to the floor; a kick from a beautifully shod foot shatter[s] a television screen; models appear to fight over each other tooth and nail; men [are] carried upside down over a woman's shoulder in a faintly humorous show of female power.(*VB* 144)

The suggestion of role reversal no doubt shocked the eye with the unusual associations of women taking power. But the provocation was tolerable only because the viewer knew the scenario was impossible, that beautiful, well-dressed women do not overpower men. There are other pictures where beautifully dressed, chic women show a face of innocence, boredom, decadence, and high-class whorishness. Deborah Turbeville, a leading woman photographer, protests at the misuse of beauty in our times.

I am totally different from photographers like Newton and Bourdin [she says of two masters of eroticism]. Their exciting and brilliant photographs put women down. They look pushed around in a hard way, totally vulnerable. For me there is no sensitivity in that. I don't feel the same way about eroticism and women. . . . it is the psychological tone and the mood that I work for.(*VB* 145).

Despite the number of pictures of women energetically and independently striding through the streets, despite the work of Turbeville and other women photographers, successful models are trained to look sexually provocative.

The good model [writes Alexander Liberman], is. . . involved in provoking the photographer – by her movement, her expression, her attitude – to fall in love momentarily and to capture this fleeting seduction. It is not by accident that cameras have a phallic association; and this teasing relationship between photographer and model – this attempt to show the noncontact rape of a given woman – sometimes brings out the unforgettable, an orgasmic picture. (*VB* 21)

Modern beauty, we are told here, is deeply embedded in sexual politics – the woman acting out male fantasies, engaging in purposeful provocation.

This provocativeness is due in large part to the interplay of unexpected oppositions. The excitement of Helmut Newton's women, for example, lies in the reversing of our expectations, in making blonds hard and brassy. The lure of Fawcett or Tiegs depends on the implied association between their down-to-earth, girl-next-door prettiness, their regularity of features, wholesome and carefree look and the hint of nipples and cleavage, suggesting something very different. Of course this contrast is – as we have seen – as old as art, but the mix of knowledge and vulnerability, of womanliness and childishness, of experience and youth seems to be especially titillating to the camera.

The child-woman opposition is another favorite. In its June 1978 issue, *Vogue* celebrates the beauty of supermodel Roseanne Vela by first asking

How in an era of robust, extroverted models. . . does one explain the superstardom of Roseanne Vela?. . . A child's voice. A child's body. A child's innocent seductiveness. . . with golden, fairy-tale princess ringlets to her shoulders. How. . . does this slight, vulnerable, totally beguiling ringer manage even to survive, much less to triumph?

Photographer Richard Avedon tells *Vogue* that 'The camera loves certain people, Roseanne is one of those. . . . She's different than the others: she doesn't have their overt sexuality. . . . there hasn't been a gentle beauty in our business since Jean Shrimpton.' Irving Penn is a little more explicit about Vela's appeal. 'The little-girl provocativeness, the cuteness, the fantasizing – I can't tell for sure whether I'm dealing with a child or an aware woman.' According to the photographers it is not only her photogeneity that makes her such an exquisite model, but her ability to capture the child-woman dichotomy so well, indeed, to blur the distinction between the one and the other so that what the observer sees is a woman at one moment, a child at another.

Roseanne Vela's star appearance in *Vogue* as a child-woman anticipates by a couple of years the boom in 'pretty babies,' pre-pubescent models who begin appearing on the covers of adult magazines like *Vogue* and engaging in the double fantasy, the make-believe worlds of womanhood and modeldom. The most famous of the young beauties, and the phenomenon after whom the rest have been called, is Brooke Shields, who in 1978 at the age of twelve had sent waves of shocked titillation through the film world with her appearance as a child prostitute in Louis Malle's film *Pretty Baby* and had appeared with a look of sophistication on the cover of *Look* magazine. By 1981 her sophisticated appearance on several covers of *Vogue*, and the naughtiness of her TV commercial for Calvin Klein jeans (a campaign which drew protest, was eventually withdrawn and sold millions), set her up as the prettiest baby in the adult world of beauty and fashion. On February 9 1981, Brooke graced the cover of *Time* magazine making news and announcing 'The '80s Look.'

Today [announces *Time* in its article], Tiegs is still dazzling. . . and it is now OK to be 33. But brunette models, muttering sedition, have come back from outer darkness and onto *Vogue* covers. The natural look that requires an hour and a half at the makeup table to achieve is still in big regard with both editors and advertisers, but the artful windblown disarray that sometimes accompanied it no longer seems as fresh as it once did.[6]

While it may be OK to be thirty-three, we are told, it is in vogue to be brunette and Brookish. A child wearing the sultry and sexually knowledgeable look of a brunette has the same titillating effect as the grown-up blond looking child-like. It was the built-in paradox that fascinated.

According to model agent Casablancas [*Time* magazine tells us], Brooke embodies 'The perfect synthesis of everything that will be successful in the 80's: a little bit of sex and a little bit of innocence; a lot of talent and intelligence but a little cloud of scandal around it; a lot of distinction and yet the warmth of youth.'

We have been told for a long time that the camera loves youth. 'What it is with these young kids,' says photographer Francesco Scavullo about pretty babies, 'is they have beautiful skin. You can use a lot of makeup – that makes them look sophisticated and older. Nothing's better than youth to take a picture of.'[7]

Comparing pictures of Jean Shrimpton and Kristine Oulman, another pretty baby catapulted to modeldom at the age of eleven, Dr H. John Geis, a psychotherapist, observes in the same article that

The Shrimpton photograph evokes all sorts of love fantasies and potentials for sexual arousal [and, he continues,] so does the Oulman photo – but only up to a point, beyond which is forbidden. When some people know, or sense, how young Oulman really is they censor their unconscious erotic fantasies. But then her appeal becomes unconscious and thus even more intense, more dangerous.

Beauty in the 1980s seems to be no longer just a matter of incorporating dichotomies which provoke or shock the eye, but of acting out these dichotomies, of making little girls look all grown up for the covers of *Vogue* or *Cosmopolitan*. It is clearly the case of a cover girl becoming a woman, but not in the sense intended by *Vogue*. Rather, here the camera and the cover lend little girls an aura of authority and adulthood that bespeak the ultimate con.

Even as women were asked to choose between girl-next-door passivity, sexy-siren passivity, masochistic passivity, and pretty-baby passivity, others dared to frame the unaskable question: why passivity? From time immemorial, feminine beauty and muscles did not mix. Muscles were a mark of activity and autonomy. But here were signs of something new. In 1979, the Women's Body Building Championship managed but a handful of entrants; by the next year, there were forty-five. Lisa Lyon, the first World Women's Bodybuilding champion, showed, by appearing in *Playboy*, that bodybuilding was not necessarily 'unfeminine.' Nevertheless, it is still an aesthetic which is viewed with dismay by a majority of men and women who claim that the look of muscularity and strength is not becoming to women. 'I want to be fit,' one woman told us, 'but not to the extent that my muscles bulge out. I still want to look feminine. I still want to feel that men I go out with are stronger than me.' But for the women who are working out the feeling of strength goes beyond surface appearance. 'I can't describe the feeling,' said one woman body builder, 'you feel complete. It is not just for display. Some say it's egotistical, but it's not. It's a matter of caring, of dedication to yourself. If you feel good about yourself it shows.'[8]

In its April 1980 issue *Vogue* paid tribute to the trend by featuring young Mariel Hemingway lifting weights, and maintaining that 'You can do it too. . . . you can take your looks and your health into your own hands and make a significant lasting change.' What started as an underground swell of female activity was now hitting the pages of *Vogue* with some degree of force. Nevertheless, however strong the image, it would take more than Mariel to compete with the faces of the child-women on the other pages. Older models like Lisa Taylor had been seen with Arnold Schwartzenegger in the pages of *Vogue* lifting weights. Bo Derek told the world that Nautilus machines had helped to keep her a 'ten.' By 1982 the fitness boom could no longer be ignored. For about a decade women could be seen engaging in sports which had previously been considered the exclusive domain of men. But now suddenly they were being legitimized by recognized beauties. With bodybuilding, especially, a new aesthetic has been introduced, one not dictated by a majority culture, but by a handful of women. Female bodybuilding has become the first female-identified standard of beauty. Some women actually talk not about losing weight, but about 'building' muscle, about molding their bodies to fit their own image of what is fit and feels good. Women are, finally, challenging the assumption, unquestioned for millennia, that the definition of female beauty is a male prerogative.

In August 1982 (two years after the Brooke Shields cover) *Time* magazine's cover story 'Coming on Strong: The New Ideal of Beauty' analyzes the current fitness craze and women's contributions to it.

As a comely by-product of the fitness phenomenon [the article notes] women have begun literally to reshape themselves, and with themselves, the American notion of female beauty. . . . a new form is emerging. . . . It is a body that speaks assurance, in itself, and in the woman who, through willpower and muscle power, has created it. It is not yet, and may never be for everybody. . . .[9]

Suddenly, the article suggests, sweat is sexy and muscular strength has replaced thinness and the tanned look as status symbols. But while the article seems to praise women's movement towards self-definition, the beauty on the cover belies the written message. Her lean, lithe, leotard-clad body is hardly an image of strength. Fragile in appearance and painfully thin, the model seems to have barely enough stamina to stroll from the cover of *Vogue* to the cover of *Time*.

The prevalent image of beauty is still passive, dependent upon the eye of the beholder. And the beholder still wants to believe that the beauty on the screen or on the cover is just as she seems. We cherish the illusion of reality all the more as the world around us grows ever more illusory. But the camera, which seems to us the stern purveyor of truth, connives with its subject to invent ever more irresistible lies.

A look behind the making of a beauty reveals hours upon hours of collaborative effort to create the effect. Fashion editors, art directors, creative directors, advertising executives, stylists, make-up artists, hairstylists, assistants, among others, are all working to make the meeting between the photographer and his model a moment in which this magic can be worked.

> We are creating illusion [says hairstylist Harry King]. When the makeup is done the transformation has begun. Then I do her hair. . . . If a girl is being shot in profile, it might be brushed a certain way that in reality might look awful. If her head is upside down, then you work so it looks pretty upside down. (*F* 127)

On the surface one might think all the maneuverings pretty ridiculous. No longer is it a simple matter of photographing a society 'beauty' on the run or in the rarefied atmosphere of a salon. The creation of beauty has become an extremely elaborate affair, as everyone who works on creating beauty is aware. As for the model, she is basically an actress who must learn to interpret images, to falsify experience, to effect the final transformation, from the ordinary to the extraordinary, for the demanding eye of the camera.

'I am an optical illusion,' says supermodel Clotilde referring to her magical transformation into the natural-looking beauty whom we have come to know in Ralph Lauren ads.[10] This sentiment is echoed by many other models. 'You create an illusion,' says well-known fashion model Janice Dickinson, 'I have no breasts but by holding my body in a certain way I can create a cleavage. You can create cheekbones or take a bump on your nose and make it disappear with makeup.'[11] And for her part supermodel Patti Hansen – who sees herself as having contributed freckles to the natural look – claims that she grew up from kid to vamp in front of the camera.

> I've learned to play different types of people [she says]. It's wonderful, all these little tricks you can learn. It's too bad you can't walk like that. . . . I became so damn critical of myself. It's frustrating when I wake up and look in the mirror, because I'm so used to seeing myself made up by different people in different photographs. I want to call

them up and say, 'come over and make me look like something else.'
(*F* 99–100)

However realistic the visual message may seem, however
'natural' the beauty may look, artificiality is at the core of the
experience. The final image we see may even be a composite
of different models, the face of one, the hands of another, and
the legs of yet another. Yet we read this as reality, as the
glorious picture of a single beauty, as the model of what we
should all look like. '[T]he illusion or fantasy in pictorial
form. . . is most evident and has the greatest impact on the
covers of fashion magazines, which set the tone for what the
modern person is perceived to be,' writes photographer Robert
Farber (*F* 114). Or better, the covers that, like ads, like
billboards, wield so much power, create expectations of what
the modern person supposes she could be. When we asked
women what the *Vogue* cover girl means to them the answers
were always the same. One woman answered 'She smacks of
money, style, and class.' Another, recalling the young university student's view of *Vogue*, spoke of the image as an invitation to both frustration and fantasy.

She makes me fantasize of warm beaches with a life of ease, yachts,
travel, freedom. For the time I am looking at it I feel it's mine and
that all I have to do is look like that. That's it, look like that! I've
done it and yet it never happens, or you get to the Caribbean islands
and the guy is a shlepp, it's cold, you're bitten by mosquitoes, and
you're asking yourself 'where is the promise?' I'd rather go look at
the pictures than be here. They, at least, ignite my fantasy. They're
a religion. They give you hope, a promise. That is so unfair. That is
the message I have been handed, that that is the way life is, but that
is not the way life is. . . . I am angry at the *Vogue* fantasy and yet
it's nice to retreat in it.

The overwhelming emphasis on external appearance makes
it terribly difficult to feel good about ourselves, especially if
we buy the image of beauty which we are sold, for, however
much we are told it is possible, that look is a virtual impossibility unless we consider the expert use of the surgeon's tools.
It is, in fact, the carefully manipulated product of vast amounts
of researching, marketing, and money.

The emphasis on beauty is escalating as the visual media
gain command over all aspects of our lives and as we, with

our increasing activity and mobility, have to rely on the media for information. The camera already is dictating the direction of social and business interactions. Prospective candidates for jobs now can find themselves facing and even using video themselves as part of their résumé, and video-dating has been providing, for many, a quick way to meet prospective partners.

As television has become predominant in our lives we have reformed our way of seeing the world. As video and related technologies alter our social interactions and limit our news sources, the illusory and edited world of TV substitutes more and more for reality.

All this, of course, is affecting notions of beauty. Camera-wrought beauty must not bore, yet it mustn't be too complicated, too difficult to understand. We are caught in a quandary, for as much as we may know that the visual images with which we are bombarded are without human content, it is sometimes difficult not to see them as real. As a result, the two-dimensional, angular, active-looking, and subliminally enticing face and body that the camera projects increasingly becomes the look that we cannot help but measure ourselves by and want to emulate.

The camera, then, has done more than screen reality for us; it has created a new reality, and with it a new aesthetic that has spilled over to the way we see female beauty. We have come a long way from the days when the camera caught the look of short skirts, bobbed hair, and boyishly trim women, enjoying the heady experience of their new mobility. Since the start of the twentieth century beauties have learned to look beguiling for the camera, bending increasingly to its whims, forcing their bodies to slimness and their faces into unnatural contortions. The camera has increasingly professionalized beauty, making it a vehicle by which the beauty industry sells its wares. Like the Venuses of old, our Venuses reflect our culture. Modern culture is impatient. It demands constant change and begs for newness. The marketplace is its haven and money its passport to a good life. Modern-day Venuses go quickly in and out of fashion. Our Venuses are disposable. They are meant to be tossed away and forgotten lest we should become bored and cease to buy.

'It is difficult to judge beauty,' Dostoevsky once wrote.

'Beauty is a riddle.' The camera in its productive marriage to commerce ironically may have succeeded in sabotaging female beauty by ridding it of the mystery, the power, the awesomeness that has always been associated with it. Today, beauty is pure illusion made to look invitingly common and millions nourished by this fantasy are, if men, off seeking it, and if women, trying to create themselves in its image.

The look of reality into which artifice is translated can only generate a feeling of deep dissatisfaction, even of schizophrenia, among women. The source of fantasy becomes the source of torture. The explosion of the visual media can be lethal for women since it opens up unrealistic expectations. The message we are given daily by the myriad images of beauty is that women must look a certain way to be loved and admired – to be worth anything.

In our time beauty can be tailor-made to fit our ideal and, with money enough, we can surely have 'beauty.' It is not now just the isolated case of a Miss America, a screen star, or a recording artist who may silicone pad breasts or chins or cheeks, or who may restructure a nose, redefine eyes, or reduce lips, but the refashioning of faces and figures, especially among the upwardly mobile, could reach epidemic proportions as men and women struggle to create themselves in the image of media stars. The day may soon be here when upon seeing a beautiful face we will not exclaim 'how beautiful!', but rather ask 'how much?'

Part 2
# The Psychology of Beauty

# Chapter 5

# Attitudes Toward Beauty

She was perhaps the most instantly recognizable movie star of her day, but more importantly the subject of millions of men's fantasies of the utterly desirable woman. Her hair was platinum gossamer, her mouth red, lush and inviting, her figure the ultimate hourglass. She spoke baby-talk in a whispery voice laden with promises; she walked with small, wiggly steps that could stop a weak heart. She was as innocent as a baby, but deadly dangerous as a vamp; and while there had been, and would be, many others who were to the public some of what she was, there was never anyone else like her, no one else who was the stuff of legend and fantasy as she was.

And at the age of thirty-six, Marilyn Monroe killed herself by swallowing forty-seven Nembutals. She was alone when she died.

It doesn't make sense. It didn't then, and it still doesn't. It makes so little sense that rumors crop up continually in the twenty years since her death, that it was no suicide after all – that she was murdered by people in high places, to conceal top secrets, and the murder was hushed up by those who know how. This makes more sense, even if we have to fabricate a whole world of double-dealing by people we had trusted, in order to believe it.

But this is the bare bones of the story. If we look more closely at Marilyn Monroe's whole life, things become clearer – about Marilyn Monroe and about how we used her, and how she used herself. As Helen was the personification of beauty for the Greeks, and her legend was shaped and reshaped to reflect that culture's attitude toward beauty, so Marilyn Monroe, during her life and even more since her death, has become our mental representative of beauty; and we have shaped her to answer to our needs.

In some ways it is a fairy-tale story: the loveless waif, the orphan, who becomes the princess and marries not one, but two authentic princes. What is missing is the happily-ever-after; but perhaps, for us today this is the ending that strikes us as *right*.

She was born on June 1 1926; her name was then Norma Jean Mortensen. But Mr Mortensen – if indeed he was her biological father – had disappeared long before. Her mother, Gladys Baker, worked as a film cutter in Hollywood. She had a history of mental disturbance, as well as a history of liaisons with men who did not stay around very long. A few years after her daughter's birth, Gladys Baker's behavior became increasingly erratic, and she was committed to a mental institution. Until she was nine, Norma Jean was shunted from one foster home to another. Some of these were more or less adequate; in others, she was abused, sexually and otherwise. At the age of nine she was sent to an orphanage. At eleven she went to live with an aunt, and then with a friend of her mother's. At sixteen, in a quest for a home and a stable relationship, she married a policeman, James Dougherty. They separated two years later.

The next year, in 1945, she began her modeling career. When she started, while she was by any standards an attractive young woman, and one who knew how to make herself seductive both to the camera and in life, she was not the Marilyn Monroe we remember. Her hair was light brown, but the modeling agency advised her to bleach it. Over the course of her career, her hair got lighter and lighter; brown to blond and finally to platinum, a color that is unreal yet plausible – the stuff of fantasy. Over the next several years virtually every part of her was remade into an image more in keeping with her fantasy of herself: the Norma Jean that men would love, stay with, and protect – the Norma Jean that, through her childhood and adolescence, she could never be. She thought there was a bump on her nose that made her ugly: she had it removed. Her teeth were put in braces, her jaw reshaped, with implants, to be more assertive; she underwent breast implantation. She tended to wear form-fitting clothes, and over the years they got more and more so, so that she had to be sewn into her movie costumes, and her famous walk developed because her legs were not free to move more than a few inches at a time.

She always projected a curious, somewhat ambivalent image: the childlike blond with the breathy voice, never quite making sense, the quintessential dumb blond but, at the same time, in sexual matters she was sharp, right on the ball: her quips, whether her own or manufactured by public relations experts, were memorable. Asked about a nude calendar illustration she had posed for, what she had 'had on' when she posed for it, she replied, in the demure girlish voice, 'I had the radio on.' Asked later what she slept in, she answered, 'Chanel Number 5.' So here is one image of the totally desirable woman: she is just a child in most aspects of life. But in the bedroom – she is a woman; she hints, but is sophisticated enough not to need to state outright, at impossible and delicious possibilities. She is knowing and wise, but about only one thing.

Controversy continues as to whether, in fact, Marilyn Monroe could 'act.' It is known that she had ambitions to be more than the creature the studios, with her collaboration, had created – to play sophisticated comedy, or Shakespeare. Of course she was never allowed to play serious roles, or roles demanding sharp comedic talent that did not invoke the particular stereotype she played. What we cannot know is whether the studios were wise in that judgment – she could not have played Ophelia, and should not – or whether they were merely wise in the ways of money, and knew that Marilyn-as-Ophelia (or whatever) would not only not sell and not be persuasive, but would ruin her for later returns to the stereotype. In any case she was bitter that she was not taken seriously, either as a person or as an actress. People expected her to be frivolous and irresponsible – the dumb blond – and, perhaps in a spirit of revenge, in real life she played that part better all the time. Her temperament was notorious – she held up shooting for days, weeks, hiding in her dressing-room, pleading illness, being hospitalized with one mysterious ailment after another. It exasperated the studio heads, but was tolerated (as it would have been for few others); not only because she was, financially, so valuable to them, but also because the behavior was true to type, and therefore, when widely reported in the media, as it was, only increased people's eagerness to see her next picture.

When it came time, in the Hollywood scheme of things, for her to marry, there were not too many possibilities. She could not marry just anyone – she had to marry so as to enhance her image, rather than tarnish the fantasy by marrying, say, another movie star, or an ordinary person. If movies were the ultimate feminine occupation – looks were all-important, narcissism and hysterical role-playing the stock in trade – then Marilyn Monroe, as the ultimate movie star, had to be united with an ultimate symbol of masculinity – particularly during the 1950s when (in a backlash against the 1940s, in which women left the home for the assembly line, became the bosses at home in the absence of men and wore pants) sex roles were strongly polarized. What was the masculine symbol equivalent to Marilyn's perfect femininity? The athlete, of course, and in America the player of the all-American sport (as Marilyn was the all-American girl), baseball. And who better symbolized the best that baseball could produce than Joe DiMaggio, the Yankee Clipper – the hitter of home runs, baseball's most masculine activity? So it was inevitable that they would meet and marry. And because symbol married symbol, rather than a woman marrying a man, it was equally inevitable that the marriage would sooner or later fail, which it did sooner, rather than later. They remained fond of each other, but could not live together.

Since the marriage to one sort of virility symbol did not work, the logical thing was to try another. Raw brute strength – that of the baseball star – was one attribute of masculinity; more ambivalent, but still perfectly respectable, was the male as intellectual, the foil of Marilyn's little-girl silliness. And here, again, the symbol obligingly provided himself for the role: Arthur Miller, the playwright, at the time America's symbolic intellectual conscience. And as DiMaggio was Italian, embodying one kind of brawny, dark, masculine stereotype, so Miller was Jewish – another sort of mysterious stranger in the WASP culture. Miller's image was that of the male, powerful because devoted to the intellect, stern where woman was soft, driving where she was yielding. Symbol again married symbol, and failure followed failure.

Not only had she failed in three marriages to find the love and security she had to have, but all the time Marilyn was growing older. The delays on pictures took longer and longer as the star spent more and more time despairingly before the mirror. She was approaching thirty-six, and she knew she could not remain Marilyn Monroe much longer. But she had nowhere else to go. The Nembutals were the only logical way out. Or were they?

The alternative legend: Marilyn was having an affair with Bobby Kennedy (having already had one with Jack, then president of the United States). In fact, Marilyn had met Bobby because he had been sent out to Hollywood by JFK's emissaries to cool things off – there was fear that Jackie would divorce Jack, which would compromise his political career. Bobby had told Marilyn all sorts of state secrets – the Bay of Pigs plans, for instance. She – in order not to appear stupid to him by forgetting the details whenever he quizzed her about them – noted down everything he said in a little red diary. Then he had a change of heart and made himself inaccessible to her. Heartbroken, she announced publicly that if she didn't hear from him at once, she would call a press conference and tell all that was in the diary. That night, she died. No pills were found in her stomach. A needle-mark was found behind her knee. There were other suspicious signs that the death was not self-inflicted. At this writing, the diary is still missing, although those interested in the case claim to know where it is, and when it is found, they hint, all sorts of powerful people dead and alive will be compromised. The incredible story has provoked a rash of newspaper headlines. It is hard, seeing the attention it has been given in the media, to recall that this death occurred twenty years ago.

Whether or not Marilyn Monroe died by her own hand is in one sense important, but in another not so important as the question of why it matters so much to so many people how she died. The proposed manner of death is truly extraordinary – no run-of-the-mill murder here. No less a personage than the attorney general of the United States, acting on behalf of its president, was allegedly responsible. And these were two of the most charismatic, attractive, masculine politicians our country has known – quintessential political figures, as masculine and sexual in their sphere as she was feminine and sexual in hers, a perfect match. Stories about JFK's womanizing are myriad, some of them apparently true – a fact which does not diminish his lustre, but rather increases it. For just as looks make a woman sexually desirable, and proof of her sexual desirability therefore enhances a woman's looks, in the same way power increases a man's sexual attraction, and proof of virility is evidence of his political power. A union between MM and JFK is fairy-tale stuff, even more than her marriages. While athletics and intellect are respectable areas for male achievement, they are, we recognize, only substitutes for real power: the power to make war, to decide who shall live and who shall die. Only the politician has that power. And the president of the United States has more of that particular kind of real power than anyone else currently on earth. JFK and Marilyn Monroe were, symbolically speaking, perfectly matched. DiMaggio and Miller actually were only for practice, and therefore discarded when the real thing came along. In a sense her affair with JFK and his brother is too perfect to be true, though it hardly matters for the legend whether or not it is true. We have to have one or the other, though: *either* MM takes her own life – beauty is ultimately disappointing and deadly – *or* she must be killed because beauty is too close to, and too dangerous to, the source of real (masculine) power. It is a pity we can't have it both ways, but the revisionist (or RFK) version is in many ways emotionally more gratifying than the suicide version, just as Helen-in-Egypt is emotionally superior, in fulfilling a stereotype, to Helen-in-Troy. Although both RFK and Egypt destroy the artistic unity of a story, they both satisfy us by reinforcing a particularly important version of a stereotype and so both have to be created.

While we are fascinated with the problem of who killed Monroe, much less attention is focused on who created her. Where did Marilyn Monroe come from? Who was responsible for her creation from the brow, as it were, of Norma Jean Mortensen Baker? In what sense did Marilyn Monroe actually exist in her own right? And why did Norma Jean Baker expend so much of her energy – her life itself – in MM's creation?

We know that MM physically and psychologically created herself. It has been speculated by many writers that she created an irresistible Marilyn to erase the unloved, unlovable Norma Jean. Only someone coming out of childhood with a desperate need for love and acceptance could have projected that need so forcefully before the camera. And it is to that perceived need – the vulnerability, the dependency, the caring – that the viewer responds viscerally. Certainly no one who did not have such a need – beyond economic survival, beyond ordinary ambition – would have taken the physical pains: plastic surgery, breast implants, continual dieting – and the psychological stress as a necessary part of success. And just as a man with that sort of bitter childhood often makes himself a millionaire, or a political force, so a woman with similar needs knows only one way to assuage them, to put to rest the threat of abandonment: to become infinitely beautiful, and thereby infinitely lovable. No effort is too great for this. The trouble is that in such a position, a woman is never convinced that the faceless *they* out there really do love her, or, if they do, it is for the right reasons; and it is never enough to erase the need. Besides – and here the woman's strategy is much less successful than the man's – she is basing her acceptability on a short-lived commodity, her beauty. When it goes – and it must go – she is forthwith propelled back to the terrors of childhood, still unmitigated in her mind. In fact, they may have gotten worse – fed by years of relentless striving for publicity, relentless criticism as well as adulation. Once a 'sex goddess' reaches a certain age, she is done for. With rare exceptions, she cannot channel her talents into playing the roles mature actresses play. From seeing her name on every marquee and her face on every billboard, such a woman almost overnight becomes a once-was, a 'whatever-became-of.' Marilyn Monroe died at age thirty-six – just the age at which these fears start to acquire an urgent reality.

But Marilyn Monroe would not be of interest to us here, any more than she would remain front-page material twenty years after her death, unless she stirred our imaginations more than ordinary sex-goddess movie stars. Certainly there were many during her life and since who have aspired to her legendary status: Jayne Mansfield, Brigitte Bardot, Raquel Welch, Farrah Fawcett, and Bo Derek come to mind. But none of them catches the mind in the same way, and most of them, after a year or two in the limelight, as the punch-line of every male stand-up comic's jokes, receded into obscurity. Perhaps because her need touched us so deeply, perhaps for other reasons, Marilyn continues to live before our eyes, and to grow in mythic stature over the years. She is more than herself: her life, her looks, the manner of her death make her a symbolic figure for us, one who was more (pardon the phrase) than the sum of her parts. What we know and can guess about her and the public's response to her tells us a great deal about our attitudes toward beauty.

For some mythic purposes, the simple story – she created herself and she killed herself for beauty – makes perfect sense and we are happy to accept it. That story provides support for one of our favorite cautionary beliefs: great beauties are unhappy, great beauty brings misery. The story has a nice completeness to it: the circle closed by the same deliberate means by which it was begun. And the other parts of the tale work for us as well: the uniquely desirable woman marries two of the most desirable types of masculinity, the union of all we idealize in this culture. Stereotype joins stereotype. But such a situation necessarily arouses envy. She has it all. He has it all. How dare they? And therefore, we feel – guiltily or not – a twinge of self-congratulation (they had it coming) when the union does not last. A happy, long-lasting marriage between Mr Male and Miss Female, he puttering in the garage, she baking brownies in the kitchen, the grandchildren clustering around. . . . This does not work. It doesn't work artistically outside of fairy tales (for which adults are too sophisticated) and it doesn't work psychologically – our deeper needs are for a different conclusion. It is not really that we, the public, created the MM story, but just that if she had been another sort of woman, a woman able to have a different sort of life than she did have, she would not have become a myth.

The Kennedy connection is an addendum or afterthought. Nothing was heard of a liaison between MM and JFK during their lifetimes nor for some time thereafter. Of course, we can imagine reasons for this even if the story should prove true. But in a larger sense, it really isn't important whether the tale is true. Freud spoke of the need to distinguish, for the individual psyche, between the 'material' truth (what actually happened) and the 'historical' truth (how the individual, as a small child, constructed his or her version of the events to which s/he was exposed). He also suggested that this distinction could be applied to the religion and myth of whole societies: we make use of actual events in more or less distorted form to satisfy our psychological needs about the way things 'ought to be,' to be symbolically relevant to us. We see that there existed in America at the same time two toweringly charismatic figures (there may never have been two others, male and female, with so powerful a hold on our imagination): America's acknowledged all-time female sex symbol, and a young, vigorous, handsome and clearly sexual president. What would make better 'historical' sense than to unite them – the union so beloved in the mythology of so many peoples between power and beauty? But because we recognize at one and the same time a strong attraction between the powerful and the beautiful, since each displays the paramount virtue of one sex, and a kind of repulsion, since they are so different, one active and doing, the other passive and being, they can, they must, come together, but they equally must part, and with fireworks at that. And since, deep in our hearts, we distrust the possessors of power and figure they came by it by none-too-savory means, and since power is active, beauty passive, the legend works most satisfactorily if the tragic end is brought about by the greed or the ambition of the powerful one, when the beauty threatens his dream of omnipotence. And this, of course, is precisely how the legend works. It is as potent for us, and as deeply satisfying, as Helen of Troy was for our ancestors, and touches many of the same resonant chords.

If we see in the stories, real and fictional, a hint that we are confused by beauty and ambivalent toward it and its possessors, we will not be wrong. For when we look to more 'empirical' evidence than our creation of myth for proof of our attitudes, we see many of the same contradictions embodied.

The Greeks had a word for it: καλοκἀγαθός. The closest English analogue we might create is 'beautiful-n-good,' though the contraction in our language makes the word colloquial, as it did not for the Greeks. The union of two concepts in one word by the Greek philosophers – for this was a technical term of philosophy – indicates that, for the Greeks at any rate, it was natural to think of beauty and goodness together: they belonged together. Keats echoes this assumption (perhaps more self-consciously as he belonged to a culture for which the unity of truth and beauty was by no means so self-evident): 'Beauty is truth, truth beauty – that is all Ye know on earth, and all ye need to know.' We in our turn admire the Greeks for being able to feel that there was a natural link between moral and visual perfection. We would like to believe that, but life is more complicated for us, as is morality, and aesthetics too for that matter, and even as we hope, we are suspicious. It would be too nice a deal. We have become cynical. Besides, even the Greeks were not impervious to cynicism on this score. They created enough legends about women or men, or landscapes, that were beautiful but evil, or at least treacherous and dangerous to suggest that even for them, καλοκἀγαθία was more an ideal than an expectable reality. We have to recall, though, that when the Greeks invoked καλοκἀγαθία, it was most typically with reference to *men*, and referred to political virtue as much as actual physical appearance. There seems to be no evidence that the Greeks applied the concept to women.

We are curious not only about the link between beauty and goodness, but also between beauty and competence, and beauty and happiness. To what extent does being given the head start of beauty guarantee winning the race – however its goal may be construed?

One problem with researching the question in that favorite twentieth-century way, empirically, is that we have no objective standards, as we have already discovered, for 'beauty' – much less for 'goodness' or 'happiness' or even 'competence.' Nor do we have any way of correlating any two of these on a numerical scale in a way that is apt to be meaningful. So in fact it was misleading to suggest that we could determine the answer to these questions objectively or empirically; rather what we *can* do by these means is determine popular beliefs and theories about the relationship between these attributes.

Academic psychologists, not unlike the rest of us, are fascinated with the relationship between physical attractiveness and other aspects of a person's life. A review of the literature by Gerald R. Adams (1977) lists about 120 articles in the psychological literature on the topic, almost all written between 1970 and 1977. A brief overview tells us this much: researchers have discovered that physical attractiveness matters – something we might have suspected without quantitative empirical proof, but it's nice to have it anyway. Adams divides the literature into four salient fields: (1) social stereotyping: our culture's stereotypes about what attractive and unattractive people are like, our subjective assumptions that influence our behavior toward others; (2) social exchange: 'physical attractiveness functions as an elicitor of differential behavior,' which is a poetic way of saying that we behave differently (i.e., better) to attractive than unattractive people; (3) internalized personality patterns: attractive people have different internalized self-concepts than do unattractive people (they feel differently about themselves); and finally, (4) social behavior: attractive people act differently toward others, in social settings, than unattractive people. Finally the article surveys research suggesting that observers are reasonably consistent in distinguishing the two groups, both among themselves and across an individual's life span: someone judged attractive at an early age is, by and large, apt to be judged so throughout life.

While a great many conflicting findings and assumptions emerge from the survey, a surprising amount of agreement – harmonizing in general with our common-sense beliefs and stereotypes – emerges. A brief look over the articles Adams surveys in each of his broad categories will suggest what is known, and what still is not.

Stereotype research is perhaps the area of most active investigation. Researchers in this field typically present subjects with pictures of individuals who have previously been selected (by the investigators) as of either high or low attractiveness. The subject is asked (with no other information about the individual in the photograph supplied) about that person's other characteristics. In many studies, subjects judge attractive individuals as having more positive personality traits in areas apparently unrelated to looks. Teachers judge students' potential classroom performance in this way, and children similarly evaluate their peers: even very young children state that they would prefer to have the attractive child for their friend than the unattractive one. These studies indicate, incidentally, that our notions of what constitutes physical attractiveness are established very early in life – certainly by the age of five. One highly salient factor appears to be obesity: children offered a choice between an obese and a non-obese doll virtually always choose the latter, on the grounds that it is 'nicer.' The same findings exist for other age-groups as well.

Further, families seem to favor attractive over unattractive siblings, in terms of life expectations: the more attractive child is expected to succeed, both in work and in personal relationships, more than an unattractive child. Although research in this area is somewhat inconclusive, there is evidence that attractive children (particularly males) are disciplined differently from unattractive ones – have their infractions explained to them rather than merely being chastised. There also seems to be an assumption that an unattractive child is more apt than an attractive one to repeat the misbehavior.

In the realm of work competence, among adults, the results are a bit cryptic, but some tendencies emerge. In one investigation, college-age male subjects were given essays of either high or low competence written by women (photographs attached) of either high or low attractiveness. While appearance did not seem to matter in the competent essays, subjects tended to rate the incompetent ones written by attractive women higher than those by unattractive writers. This finding suggests that if someone is only marginally competent, attractiveness will help; otherwise not. There is evidence that personnel officers make judgments at least in part based on attractiveness. In this area, though, there are conflicting data: while reasonably attractive women seem to receive job preference, extraordinarily attractive women are sometimes discriminated against, with the rationalization that their presence would be too 'distracting' to office routine. A recent survey suggests that attractive men tend to do less well professionally than unattractive men, although very handsome men do best of all. The reason offered is that the more attractive males expend a larger amount of energy in their youth on sexual activity, while the others exert themselves for work success.

There have been several studies of the influence on a jury of a defendant's attractiveness. One such study finds a difference in jury judgments (simulated) depending on whether the crime is abetted by the perpetrator's attractiveness. In such a crime (e.g., swindling), an attractive defendant is judged more harshly; but in crimes unrelated to appearance (e.g., burglary) the unattractive defendant receives the harsher sentence. In general, though, attractive individuals are convicted less often than unattractive, and receive lighter punishments.

All these findings reinforce several of our stereotypical assumptions: that a beautiful person is morally 'better'; is probably more competent; and is a more worthy person to have as a friend. What these studies cannot discover is whether there is any truth to the stereotypes: they uncover attitudes, not realities. Another thing these studies can't deal with is the question of the self-fulfilling prophecy. Rosenthal's (1966) work in this area is instructive. In one investigation, teachers were given names of students in their classes divided into two sets: potential high achievers and low-achievers. Unbeknownst to the teacher-subjects, however, the names had been randomly assigned to the categories. There was no factual basis for the distinction. Nevertheless, by the end of the school year, the students identified as potential high achievers were doing significantly better than the others. Rosenthal attributed this difference to the likelihood that (unconsciously) the teacher was more encouraging to and spent more time with the group identified as more successful, and as a result they achieved more. These results have been replicated with rats, flatworms, and plants (among others), making it unclear whether judgments of progress really depended upon actual differences in performance, or prejudiced observation by the experimenters. But in human research in any case, there does seem to be a 'Rosenthal effect': and therefore we may legitimately wonder how much attractiveness in fact changes one's character, behavior, and performance. If everyone in the environment is signalling that you are good, nice, and intelligent, there is some reasonable likelihood that you will try to approximate these expectations, and similarly with the opposite. In other words, common-sense logic assigns one cause-and-effect relation between beauty and virtue: goodness leads to beauty, so that it is natural that what superficially appears good will be good inside as well. What glitters is probably gold, and you can tell a book by its cover. (The existence of the contrary proverbs is not a counterexample to this argument, but rather the ends to reinforce it. We need the proverbs to help us deal with real-world occasions, all too frequent, when our stereotypical beliefs have failed us, but they do not induce us to part with these beliefs, nor does the body of actual evidence to the contrary.) But it may well be, given the Rosenthal effect, that beauty creates expectations in others of virtue, and this in turn creates virtue: beauty leads to goodness. We might argue that the prevalence in art of the evil beauty is but another attempt to create artistic effect by paradox and surprise. An evil beauty is more interesting than a good beauty, because she goes counter to our expectations. This makes for interest in art and literature, but in no way affects our stereotypical assumptions about the real people we encounter.

Experiments have also shown that the attractive are treated better than the unattractive. Non-verbal signals in interactions – the smiles, nods, touches, and other marks of interest and favor that are part of our normal interchanges – are different depending on whether we are in conversation with attractive or unattractive individuals – the attractive, of course, receiving more, and more positive, signals. Although we are generally not consciously aware of other people's nonverbal behavior toward us (as we are aware of verbal behavior), nonetheless we are subliminally cognizant of it, and make judgments about our success in an interaction in significant part on that basis. In a way it would be easier for the unattractive if signals of non-interest occurred at the verbal level (say, 'I don't want to talk to you, you're ugly'), since (painful as this would be) people would at least know what the matter was, while non-verbal signals merely leave a sense that things didn't go well. But we are trained from early on not to communicate directly such negative personal judgments; what we overlook when we teach children etiquette ('Never tell Aunt Helen she's fat') is that we do not monitor, nor teach them to monitor, their non-verbal signals, which make the point at least as well. For instance, children stand further away from fatter than thinner children in conversation – thus subtly giving the former a sense of being excluded and unwanted. Even behavior we can't control works differently for the attractive and the unattractive: the pupils of men's eyes dilate at the sight of a pretty female – not others.

If it is true that we have certain expectations of beautiful persons, and behave according to those expectations, it is not surprising that attractive people feel differently about themselves and their lives than do others. It is hardly astonishing, for instance, that the attractive have more self-acceptance and more self-confidence than the unattractive. Our first response to these reports may be disbelief: we all know stories (Marilyn Monroe's being but one) of beauties who hated themselves, were unconvinced of their attractiveness, and had low self-esteem. The research does not, of course, say that all attractive people are laden with self-confidence, only that an attractive person is more apt to display this trait than an unattractive one. No one has ever suggested that the reverse is the case; we are fixated on the Marilyn Monroe type in part because it is the surprising and seemingly inexplicable exception.

The link between beauty and self-acceptance seems self-explanatory, given what we already know. But links between beauty and other positive traits have been adduced which are harder to account for. For example, correlations have been found, in women, between attractiveness, and understanding, achievement and endurance, 'suggesting' says Adams, 'an attractive female is more likely than an unattractive female peer to show cognitive inquisitiveness, achievement needs, and individuality.' It is not entirely clear from the summary here that this is really what is going on. We could argue deeper connections, for instance: attractive women may be more understanding (the word here seems to imply intellectual, rather than emotional understanding), because they have been more consistently rewarded for their intellectual efforts. The same may be true of achievement: they may not have more *need* for achievement, but may feel more optimistic about its possibility. Finally, the relation between 'endurance' and 'individuality' seems the least clear. Again, if attractive women are more 'enduring' this may be less because they are individualistic, but rather because they can see relief or rewards in sight, where to an unattractive person, life may seem one long uphill trudge, and persevering may bring little

additional gain. Indeed, other research shows that – here
conforming again to one popular stereotype – attractive people
are *less* individualist and independent, both more dependent
on the opinion of others about their looks as well as for the
other forms of approval, and more conforming generally. For
males, however, a correlation was found between unattractiveness and 'harm avoidance and defensiveness, or abasement,
aggression, dominance and sentience.' (Sentience?)

We have suggested elsewhere that appearance has one
meaning for women and another for men: specifically, that it
has been for women equivalent to power in men, as well as
the only means by which women may achieve power at all.
Therefore it is not surprising that attractiveness may evoke
different kinds of personality structures in men and women.
Attractiveness correlates with 'positive social-cognitive characteristics for males, but social-evaluative characteristics for
females.' That is, attractive men will tend to be more intelligent, and attractive women, more socially adept, than their
unattractive peers. Further, 'facial attractiveness for males
was associated with internal control, self-acceptance, sensa-
tion-seeking, and resistance to peer pressure to conform,' for
women, with 'self-acceptance, infrequent self-negation,
minimal fear of negative evaluation, and resistance to
conformity pressure.' Some of this, of course, contradicts other
studies. But it does suggest that self-confidence and self-
esteem (which can be said to underlie all the reported characteristics) manifest themselves differently in men and women:
in men, as autonomous behavior, in women, as reduced fear
of what other people will think. Thus, attractive women are
not really *freed* from fear of the opinion of others (as attractive
men seem to be to some degree); they merely feel they have
it under control – for the time being, anyhow. Further, and
perhaps most significantly, while men's self-images as a whole
are derived from many things other than physical appearance,
including 'physical instrumental effectiveness,' that is,
strength and power, women's are almost wholly based upon
'body attractiveness.' So an unattractive male has other qualities to fall back on, while an unattractive woman doesn't.
We might note that one of the favorite adult consolations to
unattractive little girls and adolescents is to tell them about

their intelligence, their niceness, and so on – which are seldom any real comfort. Young men are rarely involved in this kind of conversation – their looks are, if anything, offered as consolation for lack of other abilities, but not often the other way around.

There is evidence that unattractive children are more apt to develop anti-social tendencies. Delinquents in one study were assessed as significantly less attractive than a control group of non-offenders. And lastly and not surprisingly in view of all the above, there is evidence that attractive people find self-disclosure easier and more congenial than do the unattractive – again, presumably because the former feel more likely to receive acceptance and therefore more ready to run risks.

Most of this research has suggested correlations between attractiveness and positive traits. We are at a loss, therefore, to connect any reality with some of our negative stereotypes: that beautiful people are more narcissistic and less independent of the opinions of others. There is some evidence, however, for the truth of this proposition, 'Attractive children appear less able than their peers to entertain themselves when alone,' perhaps because they are less apt to be left to their own devices. Or, suggest the investigators, attractive children are given 'noncontingent' approval and attention – that is, attractive children get these rewards regardless of their behavior, unlike unattractive children, who are rewarded according to their deserts, and therefore the former do not learn to entertain themselves.

Finally, there is some research about attractiveness throughout the lifespan. This is something that women in particular view with deep concern, for it is assumed that growing old means growing unattractive, or at best less attractive. Interestingly, there is evidence that attractiveness in general stays with a person: someone judged attractive from pictures as a small child will continue to be so judged through adolescence, maturity, and old age.(This is true, however, in terms of facial configuration more than bodily shape.) This research, hopeful as it may sound, however, does not really address the pressing question: can we be as attractive in older years as we were when younger? Unfortunately the study did not ask subjects to rate the pictures on overall absolute attractiveness, but rather in relative terms. Thus the fact that the picture of a sixty-year old woman would be rated as 'attractive' as her picture at twenty does not mean that the judge found the two pictures equally compelling and desirable, but rather, probably, that she was rated as being as attractive for a sixty-year-old as she had been for a twenty-year-old, with no comparison being made between the two age-groups as a whole. No research seems to have been done on the latter question, probably because the answer is obvious to us.

We find, then, that empirical research replicates our subjective assumptions more often than not: the attractive enjoy advantages in treatment and in turn become, in some ways, 'better,' or at least happier, individuals. What starts as mere folk opinion becomes scientifically observable reality, thanks to the effect of the self-fulfilling prophecy.

One of the leading researchers in attractiveness attitudes, Ellen Berscheid, was interviewed in 1982 by *U.S. News and World Report*.[1] She reiterated some of the results of her work: attractive people receive preferential treatment, because we expect them to be good and do well. She suggested further that in America at present we are 'obsessed' with beauty to a hitherto-unencountered extent: we make judgments of great importance based on little but superficial appearance, because we are such a mobile society: we change jobs and residences with increasing frequency. As a result, we cannot count on taking time to get to know one another in depth – we must rely on superficial observation, buttressed by stereotypical clues as to how to respond to those surface appearances. Further, she points out that the media have had an influence on our attitudes. Where in the past people did not encounter personal beauty very often – most people probably never even saw a portrait as long as they lived – now, with photography, television and movies, we are so deluged with images of beauty that it is never long absent from our thoughts. The media encourage us to make snap judgments on the basis of superficial physical characteristics, since that is what they offer us. The nubile blond in the twenty-second diet drink commercial may perfectly well be a brilliant nuclear physicist, gifted harpsichordist, and witty conversationalist in real life – but in those twenty seconds we will never find this out, and must judge her only by the blond mane, sparkling blue eyes and 110-pound body. Perhaps we are learning to extend this form of personal judgment to everyone else we encounter as well, in real life, where we may be learning to ignore opportunities for deeper insights.

Berscheid goes on to suggest that unattractive children should be told that there is prejudice against them on the basis of looks alone. (Of course, the child knows this already anyway.) And although almost everyone questioned will say that they like people because of their personality or their actions, Berscheid says, this is less so than we think. We process in our minds dizzying amounts of information incredibly fast, and our first impressions necessarily involve looks more than anything else. At the same time, of course, we are receiving impressions of character and behavior – but these are subordinated to looks. Of course, we would rather not think so. It makes us seem unfair. Berscheid suggests that, in this country, with our 'all men are created equal' public philosophy, the idea that certain physical advantages are given to some, not others, early on is anathema, and we resist recognizing the facts. But we damage ourselves, each other, and our relationships more by our denial than we would with the truth.

Thus empirical psychology speaks, but leaves many questions unanswered – indeed, unable to be articulated in a non-speculative format. Although we remarked earlier that psychoanalytic theory had little to say on beauty, or our feelings about it, there has been some exploration in the literature of our deeper thoughts on the subject, attempts to connect the experience of being beautiful with various kinds of behavior that is stereotypically associated with the beautiful woman. In particular, the special emphasis of psychoanalysis being on psychopathology, there is concern for the unhappiness, narcissism, and sense of emptiness that the beauty may feel: why do they arise? Freud talked about a type of person he called the 'exception': those who, because they were born with some serious defect or handicap, felt that the world owed them something, and therefore they had the right to behave immorally. (He identified Shakespeare's Richard III as one such example, and women, born castrated, as another.) Edith Jacobson, a psychoanalyst, discusses the concept further in an article about the psychoanalytic treatment of such people (1959). After talking about exceptions of the type discussed by Freud, people who are or feel themselves defective, she turns to another type:

At a certain point in my analytic work, I happened to have a few women simultaneously in treatment who were more than attractive or pretty; they were beautiful. It struck me that their beauty seemed, if anything, to have had a devastating effect on the lives of those close to them, on their own lives, or both. Their fates made me wonder why I had hardly ever met beautiful women whose lives had been happy or at least harmonious and peaceful. The answer might be that not only those cursed with physical affliction, but also those blessed with extraordinary gifts, with genius or with outstanding beauty, seem to be a special variety of 'exceptions.' (p. 147)

Jacobson suggests that the very beautiful, like the afflicted, are commonly concerned with the effect their physical bodies have on others; because of the response they get from others, from their earliest childhoods, they are likely to become deeply narcissistic. As with deformed individuals, though for somewhat different reasons, the unusually attractive become convinced that they can get, and have the right to get, whatever they want from whomever they demand it – first, usually, their fathers, who can deny them nothing; later, other men. The lives of beautiful women become an attempt to test themselves and their worth by seeing how much they can get, and their fear is that some day the giving will stop. They know that at bottom they are empty, since they have nothing but their looks to fall back on. Because the human mind reveres beauty, and in its presence cannot see other kinds of imperfections – moral failures, for instance – the beautiful are encouraged to do as they like, without concern for the effect upon others; all will be forgiven, if it is even noticed. But ultimately it is not gratifying to be an 'exception' to the rules of human conduct in this way. The beauty's life becomes empty; she is 'vain' in both senses of the word. Depression and a sense of her own worthlessness plague her – in this theory, as a necessary concomitant of the advantages beauty brings.

Another analyst, Alexander Grinstein (1963), looks at a second kind of 'beauty,' the 'doll': a woman valued for her passive beauty alone, for her function as a symbol of her husband's wealth and power – since he can support such a woman in the requisite elaborate style. This woman's dependency and expensive tastes, while they are ridiculed by others and perhaps eventually by her husband as well, are none the less a part of his display to the world of his success, and he has married her because she plays her part so well. But it is only a part: underneath there is nothing. Grinstein, with perhaps less compassion than might be expected from one in his profession, describes her:

This 'doll' is between the ages of 30 and 35, very well-dressed in the height of fashion. Her grooming is impeccable and her hair is styled in the latest vogue. Her jewelry, of which there is a good deal, is likely to be heavy and noisy. She tends to be overdressed for the 'ordinary' occasion. During the day she uses a good deal of makeup, include eye shadow, mascara, etc., which also seems striking and inappropriate. Perhaps one would not be quite so struck by her appearance at a cocktail party as one is in seeing her attired in her customary fashion in the neighborhood shops. In an effort to maintain the highest level of fashion, current styles are copied so slavishly that she strongly resembles her counterparts with the result that the man in the restaurant could not distinguish one woman from another. (pp. 161f)

Grinstein goes on to describe these women's general uselessness and passivity, as well as their competitiveness with one another, especially over material possessions. Although such women do not generally 'seek professional help as their characterological makeup keeps them symptom-free,' occasionally one does, and the symptoms, while often hard to ferret out from the superficial appearance of contentment and well-being, involve 'a general feeling of an underlying unrest.' More specifically, they are afraid of 'a loss or a threatened loss of a love object' – most often, husband or children. As a result, some of these women are contemplating, or even engaged in, extramarital affairs, a situation which causes them considerable distress, but they can think of nothing other than love from someone else to take up the empty spaces in their lives. Underneath the assurance in dress, the surface charm, is 'a bewildered, frightened child.' Like infants, they have no identity: they do not know who they are, and therefore feel security only when they can be sure they belong to someone. Grinstein attributes much of the narcissism and infantilism of these

women's personalities to the infantile and primitive aggressiveness of their mothers – overlooking, it would seem, the
fact that such behavior patently works to charm men who
will be successful (and presumably was first practiced, with
approval, upon the fathers). He suggests finally that they have
learned to be what they are because it was the only way they,
as girls, could get any positive response from their parents,
who were more interested in their brothers.

Though attractiveness is central for both Jacobson's and
Grinstein's subjects, the two groups approach it differently.
Jacobson's subjects were from early childhood unusually and
naturally beautiful. Their concern is not making themselves
pretty, but in coming to terms with what they have been given.
Their narcissism arises in part out of a sense that they have
been specially selected, that something has been given them
with no expectation of effort on their part, or of return by
them. This sets them apart, and makes it clear that they need
not play by others' rules. The 'dolls' Grinstein discusses are
quite different. There is no indication in the article that they
have any natural or intrinsic beauty. Rather, they are women
who have learned to do the most – perhaps, Grinstein suggests,
too much – with what they already have. They are women
who have learned to equate beauty with passivity, rather than
with specialness or lawlessness: if they take care of themselves, others will take care of them. But it is a bargain. They
must act and look like 'dolls' – artificial, passive, not-quite-
living – if they are to be rewarded in return with appreciation,
love, and material gifts. Their mothers have set the example
and groomed them for their role, and men, starting with their
fathers, have shown appreciation and given them many clues
that if they want continued love and comfort, they must
continue to be doll-like. Different as they are, eventually both
'exceptions' and 'dolls' feel empty, defeated, and depressed.

We must remember that psychoanalysts are generally clinic-
ians, who derive theory and observation from their patients,
who are in distress when they appear, while academic psychologists have subjects who are in general functioning well, or at
least have not encountered the researchers because of any
deep psychic distress. None the less we have to be struck
by the sharp disparity in the two kinds of results. Academic

psychologists link beauty with happiness, competence, and goodness. Psychoanalysts link it to misery, passivity, and immorality. Both claim 'empirical' evidence – one group from interviews with randomly-selected subjects, the other from patients' case histories. The two together form a whole – the whole of our myths, literature, and popular stereotypes about beauty. In real life, we are confounded by contradictions and confusions surrounding beauty. But in psychological theory they are resolved, with one group generally claiming that beauty is positive, another that it is negative. We must assume, tiring as the cliché may be, that it is both, or in between. We may also assume from the evidence we are presented with that some women deal much more successfully with the matter of looks than others. Those who – attractive or unattractive – cannot come to terms with the way they look turn up on the analyst's couch as the case-history. Those who resolve the matter more comfortably do not. But it would seem just as possible to be unattractive and content as it demonstrably is to be beautiful and wretched.

So we get only partial satisfaction from experts. Maybe it is time to go to another authority – non-experts, people who have had to deal with looks, their own and others', in leading their daily lives and forming their characters, usually without the benefit of theory and expertise. People evolve practical ways of coping and general theories that mostly stand them in good stead. They make use of stereotype and cliché, but often derive something living and vital from it, a pattern of response and judgment that gives flexibility and the power to grow.

We asked many women to tell us how they felt: about their own looks, about what beauty is and how it arises, about men's and women's judgments, about what they are willing to go through to be beautiful, how important beauty is to them, about ageing and their hopes and fears for the future, about what they like and dislike in themselves. Some of these women were quite young, in their twenties. Others were older, in their mid-thirties to their fifties. Predictably, we got somewhat different responses from the two groups, but also a great deal of similarity. One thing women said almost without exception, even those who identified themselves as feminists or sympathetic to the women's movement: beauty is important to them.

Some care desperately about their looks and take great pains over them; others profess to be less concerned, perhaps having come to that consciousness only recently – but their eyes still light up when the topic is discussed, and they have strong and articulate opinions about it. Many remarked that concern about beauty seemed antithetical to feminism: all the other things that separate woman from woman, that make individual women frightened and insecure, have been discussed and debunked by writers and theorists of the movement over the last ten years or so. But beauty remains the final great divider, the ultimate thing we worry about as individuals – not as a cohesive group. We deal with our looks in secret, and we feel competitive about them. Perhaps the subject has been driven even further underground by the women's movement, since we are not supposed to be overtly interested in being attractive. Yet we are, and a glance in any magazine read by women will show a healthy percentage of cosmetic and clothing advertising, probably not significantly less than in pre-movement times. But we accept our interest less.

Yet women were eager to discuss their feelings once the subject was broached – indeed, we had a sense of a river overrunning its banks, as if what had been kept in so long needed an escape valve. And everyone had a great deal to say, and had evidently given the topic a lot of concerned, even passionate, thought.

Perhaps most striking in the younger women was the extent of their (reported) good feelings about their looks. On a written questionnaire, the undergraduate women (about fifty answered the questionnaire) were asked to check the word that best described their perception of their own looks: beautiful/attractive/cute/OK/not OK. An overwhelming percentage checked one of the first three. Except for minority women, almost no one checked the last. Moreover, the young women claimed to have no fear of what all women are supposed to fear, ageing. Asked whether they were terrified of growing older, neutral, or looking forward to it, although a few checked the first column, most selected the second or third. When questioned further, they said that they were unafraid because the fresh beauty of youth would fade, but they were confident it would be replaced by more valuable things, character, for instance. If only they kept themselves healthy and fit, age held no terrors for them.

In fact, fitness was a crucial point. We asked our respondents what beauty in a woman consisted of: was it face, figure, or something else? Almost to a woman, their immediate response was: beauty is not in superficial aspects of a person, is not in the hair, the face, or a voluptuous figure. They were somewhat divided on what it was, with many saying it was some radiance of the soul, concern for others, vibrancy, or intelligence. But almost as many placed emphasis on looking healthy, the sound mind in a sound body, fitness, being physically and mentally at one with oneself. The feeling was that one could will oneself to be beautiful merely by taking good care of oneself, mind and body.

In a way, these prevalent statements seemed to reflect an attempt, in the 1980s, to unite the values of the 1960s (everyone is equally valuable, beauty is in spiritual and political action rather than in the static and conventional configurations of face and figure) with the 1970s (be good to yourself, look out for number one, be healthy and fit). But underneath the glowing rhetoric lurked contradictions.

We noted these intellectual and abstract evaluations of 'beauty,' and then turned the interviews to a more personal note. How did they feel about their own looks? We might have expected – at first we did expect – a continuation of the theme: they were fit, they were content, they were beautiful. This is not what we got. Even from those who, on the written questionnaire, had evaluated themselves as 'attractive,' we now got moans of distress. Well, it was OK, but. . . . And 'but. . .' went on for some time, and often covered just about every inch of the body.

In fact, it was inches that mattered the most. We had thought we'd get a fair amount of variation in our answers. A wanted to be blond, B to have curly eyelashes, C larger breasts, D longer legs, and so forth. But what we got was near-unanimity: 'I have to lose some weight.' How much? Anywhere from 5 to 25 pounds, generally from women who looked not at all overweight. (Some of these women, in fact, had a history of anorexia or bulimia.) What was striking in this set of responses was not only the near-unanimity of the women's identification of their self-discontent with body weight, but also the gap the answers revealed between the intellectual and abstract accolades to health and tranquility, and the concrete disgust upon looking into the mirror, the feeling that beauty is being 10 pounds lighter. We came to feel that it was not so much the perception of excess weight by itself that distresses so many women, but its being coupled with the pervasive fairy-tale that beauty can be achieved through a peaceful spirit in a well-cared-for body – something accessible to many more people than the elusive minus-X pounds. If you feel that you simply are out of the running in the beauty sweepstakes, that you don't have the basic equipment at all, you may be able to deal with your discomfort in time and with the growth of wisdom. But if you really believe that anyone who is willing to make the effort not to be a slob can be in the same league as Brooke Shields and Farrah Fawcett, and you do your home-work, and look in the mirror and see the discrepancy – then you may be letting yourself in for some really serious anguish. We have inoculated ourselves with false optimism and at the same time have trained our eyes to detect every possible real blemish, and are suffering from the gap between these two idealisms. It is not the existence of the contradiction that causes trouble, as much as the fact that it is not recognized.

Another odd discrepancy concerned the use of cosmetics and other enhancement devices. Many of the women we spoke to considered themselves feminists; additionally, most had argued that beauty is in health, intelligence, and fitness. But when asked to indicate whether they used cosmetics, and which they used, the overwhelming majority indicated a famil-iarity with many of them. We offered a list of possibilities: hair dye, eye shadow, mascara, eyeliner, rouge/blusher, foundation, lipstick, perfume and nail polish. Virtually no one claimed never to use any. A few frequently used just about every one. There seemed (as we also gathered from oral interviews later) a distinction in these women's minds between two types of cosmetics: those that merely enhanced what was already there, and those that actually changed appearance. In the first category, for example, were perfume, eyeliner, colorless nail polish; in the second, hair dye, lipstick, mascara. Interestingly, virtually none of the young women used foundation: it seemed, in their minds, to be a part of the technique of an older generation, a 'mask,' an artificiality, rather than something that brings out what is merely hidden – as cosmetics, it was felt, ought to do. The 'natural enhancers' were used by a majority of our respondents at least occasionally; the others, seldom or never. We gave our respondents a choice of five frequencies to check: 'never,' 'seldom,' 'sometimes,' 'often', and 'always.' Seldom did anyone check 'always': perhaps it seemed too much an admission of addiction.

We also asked whether they enjoyed a number of activities that, to many people, seem emblematic of women's traditional 'vanity,' narcissism, or concern for surface appearance: wearing cosmetics, getting hair cut and styled, going shopping, dressing up. A rather significantly large majority indicated pleasure in at least one of these; some enjoyed them all. We have to remember that these are young women whose formative years were during the 1960s and early 1970s, when these traditional feminine behaviors were questioned, perhaps for the first time, strongly and publicly. If there is concern that the women's movement is teaching women to abandon their femininity, the answers to these questions by young women enrolled in a Women's Studies course with a strong feminist orientation should put those fears to rest. What is interesting here – and this showed up still more strikingly in the oral interviews – is that beauty enhancement devices like these are not perceived by many women of this generation as opposed in any necessary way to feminism – as was true of many of the older generation of feminists, who have argued that cosmetics reinforce women's passivity and dependence on male approval and on superficial appearance for self-esteem. These young women – as was also evident in a heated class discussion on the topic – feel that looking good is a birthright, something that we owe ourselves and others to take advantage of. To 'put one's best face forward,' in dress and make-up is not only a boost for one's own ego, a means of enhancing self-confidence and productivity in work as well as social settings, but also a subtle compliment to those around one, a way of making *them* feel better – and, as such, a gesture of politeness, where carelessness in appearance or an apparent unwillingness to take pains is felt to be rude. Some women divided the question in

half: it was unquestionably consonant with a feminist orientation to look good as a result of feeling good, to look strong,
capable, and caring about oneself; to 'let oneself go,' say,
through obesity or careless dress or unstyled hair was to
demonstrate low self-esteem and an inability to take oneself
seriously as a human being – the antithesis of feminism. But
other kinds of things were 'primping,' and to be despised:
dyeing one's hair, spending long hours in front of a mirror,
being obsessed with fashion. . . . It is a matter of degree, the
consensus seemed to be. If outward appearance occupied too
much of your inner life, you were narcissistic; if you did enough
to show you felt good about yourself, this was exemplary of
strength and health.

But the issue – the definition of 'obsession' or 'vanity' –
provoked heated debate and some anger and distress among
the hundred or so women in the class. The issue seemed to be
one that had not been examined deliberately and consciously
heretofore, one that very few of these women had previously
developed articulated positions upon.

One woman, for example, told us both on the written and
the oral interviews that she seldom or never wore any cosmetics, and specifically never dyed her hair (she was blond).
During the oral interview she repeatedly insisted that – as a
feminist – she scorned women who were overly concerned with
the enhancement of their looks, that fitness was what
mattered, that she had no interest in how she looked. She was
not at all interested – could not be tempted or bullied – into
talking more than monosyllabically about life as a blond (most
of the blond respondents were more than eager to discuss the
topic). We were puzzled: we had a sense that something was
being left out of the communication, uncharacteristic for this
articulate and forthright woman, but had no idea what, much
less how to bring it to the surface. Then, a few days later, we
received a letter from her. 'There is something very important
that I left out of the interview,' she began. 'I felt compelled to
write this letter because I was aware of an intentional omis-
sion of information from the interview on my part.'

This was shocking enough – from a woman who cared deeply
about being open and direct, and had been eager to participate
in the interview. But what followed was stranger still. She

described a summer she had spent at the age of eighteen in a resort community, with a group of young people her own age. Besides working, what she did was go to parties. The people in this group impressed her as superficial and hedonistic ('it seemed that all these kids cared about was getting drunk or stoned and having sexual experiences that they could later brag about'), but wealthy and 'in.' (As a Jew, our respondent had spent much of her life feeling 'out,' especially in the presence of gilded young people like these.) Hence, physical appearance was very important to the members of this group, and having a certain kind of mainstream 'looks' was instrumental in becoming accepted. As she put it: 'In this environment, *the people (and more specifically, the girls) who got attention were all blonde.*' (Italics hers.)

Her tale continues: one day she noticed that her best friend's hair seemed to be getting lighter. Her friend said something vague about being out in the sun a lot. But later, in the bathroom they shared, our respondent found a bottle of 'Summer Blonde' under the sink, and made the connection. So our respondent tried it herself. The results were satisfactory – she gained acceptance in the group – but what was odd about the experience was that it remained secret. 'We never admitted to each other that we used it. (Suzi and I were confidants – we confessed everything to one another – except this, "the last secret.")' Our respondent returned to her old community, and then found that – horror of horrors! – she could not stop living under false colors. People there now knew her as a blond. To let her hair return to its natural darker color would be admitting that it had been dyed. She could not stop. Although she keeps in touch with Suzi, neither of them has ever let on to the other about this. Further she says:

I can guarantee you, all my shame about 'assuming a false identity' aside, the experience of being a blonde is very different than one of a woman who has darker hair. I know this because I have passed as both and have a vast repertoire of stories, especially involving encounters with men, which to me indisputably suggest that being a blonde is a highly charged symbol in this culture – especially for a woman. I have had experiences where men have gone to great lengths, making themselves terrific fools, simply to meet me because I appear to be blonde – it's the damndest thing.

So here we have a sort of Tiresias – a woman who has lived both as brunette and blond, and has returned to tell the tale, who confirms yet another popular stereotype: blonds do have more fun. And we may notice, finally, that the fear of exposure in this woman – who earlier had claimed nothing but scorn for women who worry about appearances – was so strong that she could not tell her secret orally, in our presence, to the tape recorder – but could only entrust it to the safer medium of writing, guaranteeing that she would not be present when the truth was revealed.

Other women have confirmed our suspicions about blondness. Natural blonds argue that the fact of their blondness makes others – both men and women, but especially men – perceive them as symbols or objects not as human beings. One is 'a blond,' a member of a special, set-apart category, expected to behave in certain ways and to have a particular kind of mind and heart. A blond who does not may be treated with especial anger, like anyone who goes blatantly counter to stereotype. One such young woman, perhaps the quintessential 'California blond' in appearance, rather startlingly announced herself as an engineering major. The men who dominated her field, she complained – from fellow undergraduates to professors – had a preconception of her as a 'blond': she was to be decorative, demure, and none too bright. When she proved them wrong, they were staggered: how could she be blond and an 'A' student in engineering? She said she felt as much a victim of prejudice in her way as a member of a racial minority group: like such a person, she had to exert inordinate effort proving that she wasn't what 'they' were supposed to be, and that she had a character and personality all her own, and a right to be treated as an individual. She said that people generally came around sooner or later, but often with some degree of resentment.

It is interesting here that within the women's movement, we have learned to empathize with all kinds of sufferings imposed by the female condition, even some we as individuals have never personally experienced. We feel that this sympathy and solidarity with one another is part of our being women. But sympathy stops here. We can understand and feel for someone who suffers unfair treatment because she is gay, old, obese, black, working-class and so forth. But we balk when asked to extend our sympathies to someone who claims to be stereotyped and to suffer from being blond and beautiful. At a stroke, we are returned to the uncertainties of adolescence, when acceptance by both boys and girls our age was of critical importance, and that acceptance too often hinged on a very narrowly defined definition of good looks. A girl who was 'cute' reaped the rewards, and the envy of her less-than-cute sisters, who could be expected to feel something less than total sisterhood. A boy, in normal American adolescent society, certainly profits from attractiveness, but can make up for looks or augment them by power – preferably athletic, but permissibly student government, occasionally even academic. A girl who is not pretty according to strictly circumscribed standards can do these things and excel in them, but her effort will not be perceived by her peers as being 'as good as' looks, or an acceptable substitute for them in winning acceptance; rather they are a consolation prize: she's only doing that because she isn't the only thing that really matters – beautiful. Later on, we mature and we learn better; ugly ducklings become swans, the boundaries of 'attractive' are widened so that many more fall into them and we learn other ways of accepting others and being valued ourselves. But the early harsh memories remain – the wallflower sadly comparing herself to the prom queen – and the wallflower always feels a twinge of anger at what she missed out on, and the prom queen's protestations that she suffered too fall on unsympathetic – sometimes downright disgusted – ears.

This is what makes beauty the 'last taboo,' the final issue that separates woman from woman, the topic we do not discuss openly, where the most open of us cannot bring ourselves to speak freely, for fear of ridicule and rejection – whether out of fear that our ugliness will be known and acknowledged, or our beauty. Women cannot join with women in thinking about – much less talking about – looks, without great anguish.

I heard an old religious man
But yesternight declare
That he had found a text to prove
That only God, my dear,
Could love you for yourself alone

And not your yellow hair.
(W. B. Yeats, 'For Anne Gregory')

While age is something we can approach with less contenti-
ousness than beauty, it is none the less clear to virtually all
observers of our society that ageing is a source of fear and
despair. We have no respectable roles for our older people, and
younger people consider the older a threat, an embarrassment,
and a drag on our resources. This is true for men as well as
women, and men certainly feel pressure to remain youthful in
appearance and behavior if they want to retain their status in
the business and professional world. Face-lifts and hair dyes,
once exclusively the province of women, are becoming increasingly acceptable for men, as it becomes axiomatic that any
man who looks a day over forty will be put out to pasture by
his company. But it is all the more true for women, and ageing
affects more areas of a woman's life than a man's. First of all,
a woman grows 'old' – that is, undesirable and therefore judged
unable to fulfill her feminine role – at an earlier age, and with
a more basically 'youthful' appearance, than a man. A woman
is frequently considered, by herself if no one else, to be 'over
the hill' at the first sign of facial lines or the first gray hair.
A man can have a reasonably lined face, and pepper-and-salt
– or even white – hair, and still seem youthful, if he looks
active and vital. A man need consider a face-lift only if the
signs of age and wear in his face become too apparent: pouches
and jowls, not mere lines.

More, even if a man's appearance of ageing diminishes his
value in the world of work, his social desirability is not necessarily compromised: a man remains attractive to women until
a much greater age than a woman to men. Certainly it is not
unacceptable for a sexagenarian to be seen publicly with – or
even to marry – a woman in her thirties or even younger; for
a woman to do the analogous thing would be to raise the
eyebrows off people's heads: it would be seen as perverse and
neurotic. We would impute dark reasons for the behavior to
both partners, and the woman in particular. In recent years,
it is true, we seem to have been developing increasing tolerance for older woman-younger man pairings; but the kind we
mean (those we are tolerant of) are those in which there is, at

most, a ten (at very most fifteen)-year discrepancy, and these have always been regarded as normal and typical in the reverse case. For a woman of seventy to marry a man in his thirties would be unheard of, while the reverse happens not infrequently. There is often some mildly titillating gossip about such a match, equal in intensity to that produced by a ten-year gap with the woman older. If the couple produce issue, it is considered a triumph for the man, a proof of virility. In any event, we view ageing in men and women according to a double standard, which does not appear to be changing as radically as is sometimes claimed.

Then ageing is rightly threatening to a woman. If she has achieved the good things of life chiefly by her looks, she has all the more to fear. She will not have developed other necessary skills, to be used when she no longer has looks to trade upon. And often the very attractive woman has not only failed to develop work skills – since she thought she could count on always being taken care of – but even social skills – since her beauty provided enough excuse for unmannerliness, or served as a shield behind which to hide her shyness. Now, say, at forty, or fifty, she finds herself bereft. Even if she remains married, she becomes insecure, and her husband's admiring glances at the nubile youth cavorting across the TV screen do little to comfort her. With beauty goes power, and often, hope, since women have too often been taught that they cannot achieve or hold power respectably by any means other than looks.

On the other end of the age continuum, this culture in many ways links childhood to age: many of the ways we expect the old and young to behave, and the ways in which we behave toward them, are similar: the ways of the powerless. What has recently become disquieting is a growing tendency to over-value youth – or certain manifestations of it – as much as we undervalue maturity (and how we reach for euphemisms for one side, and not the other). It is curious for instance, in the fast-paced throwaway world of television journalism, that men as they age and acquire wrinkles become (à la Walter Cronkite) more 'credible,' and more valuable to their employers; women, on the other hand, become less so. Virtually all network anchormen are at least discreetly greying and at least fortyish; their female compatriots, on the other hand, while they may in fact be approaching, or even a bit beyond forty, take care to keep the fact secret; their hair is blond, or brunette, their faces unlined, their figures girlish. On local news programs, the disparity is even more marked, with anchormen as often as not grey or balding (only the weatherman is boyish); the women, however, look and act as if they had just emerged from finishing school. It is not clear what happens to anchorwomen who dare to go grey, but the absence of any such women in any visible position should certainly tell us something.

An article in the *San Francisco Chronicle* (October 20 1981, p. 38) looks at co-anchored local programs, contrasting the ages of the male and female anchors: Wendy Tokuda, 32, and David McElhatton, 52; Jan Carson, 32, and Van Amburg, 50;. . . . Terry Lowry, 34 and Jerry Jensen, 47. Further, Dan Rather, the CBS Evening News anchor, is quoted in the same article as saying:

It is said, and it is a fact, that it's very difficult for a woman past 40 to make it on the air. If a woman establishes herself young enough, the odds are still strongly against her staying on the air.

What an anchorperson needs to be is authoritative and believable. To have authority and believability, one must have, or appear to have, power. As we have noted already, power for women is vested in physical desirability, involving youth and beauty; while for men, it is enhanced by experience. Thus, a male anchor ages gracefully, and his increasing age enhances his effectiveness in transmitting the news; a female anchor, on the other hand, is believable only by virtue of 'sex appeal,' which is fleeting. We admire fatherly, or grandfatherly, types behind the desk; but grandma is not, and in all likelihood never will be, seated next to him.

An article, again in the *Chronicle* (February 7 1982), discusses the fact that the currently most glamorous movie stars, male and female, are getting 'older': in their forties or beyond. The article suggests that our tolerance for age extends to both sexes, citing, for example, Jane Fonda, Ali MacGraw, and Barbra Streisand, alongside of Paul Newman, Clint Eastwood, Burt Reynolds; but we have to note that 'old' for a woman is still around forty, while a man reaches that state perhaps ten years later. It remains true that a woman has a much shorter span of time to establish herself in any of the visual media than her male counterpart.

If one end of the age spectrum is still essentially closed to women, the other decidedly is not, as we have seen in Chapter 4. Adolescent beauties have, of course, always been with us: think of Judy Garland or Sandra Dee, or the many teenage models who have been employed as cover girls for magazines aimed at the adolescent market. In the past, teen models and actresses tended to appear as they were: virginal young girls, appealing because they were youthful and not yet womanly. But the current crop represents a different fantasy altogether. They appear heavily made-up, in sophisticated hairdos, wearing clothing that is sexually suggestive and clearly too elaborate and expensive to be appropriate for the school gym sock hop, or indeed any typical adolescent activity. These young women, while undeniably attractive by any standard, seem to have reached the pinnacle by an unusual, and disturbing, combination, which now spells 'beauty' for us: their faces are unlined, unblemished by the ravages of time; but their eyes are knowing, their mouths experienced. Like their cosmetics, coiffures, and clothing, their faces tell us that they are women of the world – and at the same time, virginal teenagers, their hair typically cascading in improbable ringlets down their shoulders. What are we to make of the contradiction?

As a fantasy, these women represent the ultimate in male having-the-cake-and-eating-it. What could be more desirable than a woman at once sexually knowing and yet untouched? It is the dream given words by Vladimir Nabokov in *Lolita*, which struck a resonant chord when it was published precisely because it put a finger on the popular pulse, and diagnosed the disease with such accuracy. There is nothing intrinsically wrong with finding youth and innocence attractive, nor with finding knowledge and experience alluring. It is the expression of the desire – impossible in reality – of finding the two opposites united in one face, one body, that is troubling. If this is beauty for us today, our symbolism represents some disturbing needs. And more – the juxtaposition on magazine covers of the unbridgeable gap in some way represents the objectification of women, and bases beauty on that objectification, more than ordinarily. It is as if we are saying we can create the impossible if only we wish it. We can make and remake the objects in our world, to fit our needs, our tastes, our desires. It is Pygmalion reborn: an explicit male longing to achieve the fulfilment of his fantasies by the manipulation – even the creation – of the female face and body to meet his precise needs.

Since the attribution of beauty is so important to us, and since we live in an age in which everything important is quantifiable and reducible to ranked lists, it is hardly extraordinary that we have seen arise, in this century, the attempt to make scientific sense of the Evil Queen's mirror – to determine, once and for all, who really is the 'fairest of them all.' The Miss America Contest, begun in 1922, is the oldest of these attempts, and still, in many ways, the most meaningful and prestigious. It has brought in its train a dizzying array of beauty queens, from Miss Universe to the County Fair Pickle Queen. All rest on a basic premise: if you can combine the opinions of a panel of somehow-reliable judges, that aggregate will represent 'the fairest of them all.' You can, thus, quantify beauty and determine a rank order, with fifty contestants, ten semifinalists, five finalists, and the one true 'most'. This in itself is an extraordinary assumption, the more so for so seldom having its basic premise examined. How can we quantify and rank beauty, if so many variables – some, by popular testimony, not even visible upon surface inspection, even in a bathing suit – are involved? Not to mention nagging doubts about the authority of the judges, who are selected, typically, from the worlds of cosmetology, modeling, show business, and prior Miss America contests. Who is an expert in determining beauty? More, why do we attempt to select the 'most' in this category – we don't attempt to select the 'best' or the 'most truthful' or the 'happiest' – all virtues as abstract and open to controversy as beauty. Yet every year we go through the same rituals, and some of us take them very seriously indeed.

For instance, it was reported in the newspapers that Miss America 1983, Debra Sue Maffett, Miss California, did not come to the crown by any direct inheritance. It was reported[2] that she tried several times (one story says three times, another twelve) to be crowned Miss Texas, each time unsuccessfully. Then, nearing the age of twenty-five, at which superannuation is a likelihood in this career, she determined, 'for health reasons,' her mother said, to repair a deviated septum, to undergo plastic surgery on her nose (and chin as well, although it is not clear the effect this would have on a deviated septum). She was thus transformed, on the evidence of 'before' and 'after' photographs, from a quite nice-looking young blond to a veritable 'California girl' with pert, sharply-defined features and a straight, short aquiline nose. The revelation brought in its train more than a whisper of controversy, raising the old unsolved problem: how 'natural' does beauty have to be to be real? For example, padding of bras is considered grounds for disqualification in most prominent contests; but there has been no ruling on silicone implants. Are we equating 'natural' with 'irrevocable'? We certainly allow cosmetics; and beyond question, hair dye; but if it were known that a contestant was wearing a wig, there would certainly be an outcry. Clearly there are inconsistencies of position, based ultimately on the culture's own irresolution on the issue of truth-in-beauty. It should not be surprising to us, though, that a young woman would enter a contest three – or even twelve – times in the hope of winning, nor that she would eventually undergo a good deal of plastic surgery – its cost probably in excess of the monetary worth of the 'Miss America' victory – to achieve the goal.

As if the implicit ranking and quantification necessary in all contests of this sort were not enough to satisfy the scientific spirit of modern America, there have recently been attempts to introduce into this realm of age-old fantasy a favorite up-to-the-minute fantasy: the superior judgment of the computer. Before the annual contest in each of the last several years, it has been widely reported that George Miller, a professor of statistics at Northern Illinois University, had fed data about each of the contestants into a computer and has predicted the winner. He is said to have picked winners in 1979 and 1980 by this method, but failed in 1981 and 1982.[3] So it is not really clear that computerization and statistical probabilities give us an answer. The organizers of the contest themselves, in the last several years, have devised a quantification scheme of their own; the judges' preferences for each contestant, in each subcategory (interview, swimsuit, talent) are fed into a computer, which adds up the results and presents them to the television audience on a scale of one to ten, to two decimal places. But all the results of each individual contest are swept aside in the final overall judging, so that it's not clear what all the quantification is meant to achieve.

In general, we can derive from these failures and confusions the slight comfort that, at least given the current state of the art, beauty is not yet subject to quantification, and statistics do not make a winner. There is still, it would seem, the indefinable something which does not appear on the computer printout. But the various attempts to bring beauty (kicking and screaming, perhaps) into the twentieth century show how very seriously we take it – so seriously that we are uncomfortable when we cannot reduce poetry and art to science, which alone, in a couple of senses, 'counts.'

We have surveyed briefly all the many kinds of evidence that show how seriously we take beauty. But at the same time, we are confused by it. We want to define it precisely, but cannot. We wouldn't mind quantifying it, but cannot. We are willing to go to all kinds of pains to achieve it, but deny any evidence that pains have been taken. Beauty is the only means by which women reach power and influence, but we do not take seriously those women who possess it – and they cannot take themselves seriously either, especially with the knowledge that their power is surely disappearing even as it is contemplated in the mirror. Beautification is a tireless and exhausting effort for which women receive little credit if they are successful, and much contempt if they are not. We have examined the voluminous evidence of the academic psychologists that beauty is believed to make its possessors better and happier – and have considered clinical evidence to the contrary.

Further, we are very uncomfortable with the effects of ageing on appearance, especially women's. We do not like the marks of experience to be evident to the observer. On the other hand, we notice a disquieting tendency to commingle fantasies: the chance at ravishing a virgin who, because of her sophistic-ation and experience, will turn out afterward to have loved every minute – and taught her partner a thing or two – but it won't show on her face for all to see.

And lastly we have observed our desire to make beauty a science, to reduce it to numbers, those impersonal marks that rule the universe. We have seen at least partial failure in this attempt, but are still mesmerized by 'contests' that attempt to rank women in order of beauty. We may wonder in passing why we do not see, displayed repeatedly on nationwide television from May to Labor Day, 'Mr America' contests in which males are ranked according to their real-world power – say, their wealth. We do, of course, rank men according to wealth – but not on the television screen. Indeed, we may wonder why men are so seldom publicly ranked at all in this way. Or we may not wonder any more.

# Chapter 6
# The Pathology of Beauty

Most of us have grown up with Walt Disney's version of the fairy tale of Cinderella that had its moments of suspense, but was generally safe and comforting. But there is another, more authentic version of the story that, although its outlines are the same, is disquietingly different.

In this version of Cinderella (or Aschenputtel, as it is called in the collection of the Brothers Grimm), Cinderella flees from the ball and the prince finds the slipper (a golden slipper, in some versions; a fur slipper in the original) and undertakes a search of every house in the kingdom until the woman whose foot fits the slipper can be found. As in the version familiar to us, the prince comes to the modest home of Cinderella's family. The stepmother sends her elder daughter to the prince. She tries the slipper, but it does not fit her foot. The mother takes her daughter aside and hands her a knife. 'Cut off your toe,' she says. 'When you're queen, you won't have to walk.' The daughter does so, and manages to squeeze the mutilated foot into the slipper. The prince doesn't notice what has happened, and goes off on horseback with the daughter behind him. As they ride through the courtyard of the house, they pass a small tree on which there sits a white bird. The tree has grown out of the grave of Cinderella's real mother, and the white bird, who lives in the tree, is Cinderella's guardian spirit, her mother's representative. As the pair pass, the bird sings out,

Look, look!
There's blood in the shoe!
The shoe's too small.
The right bride's still at home.

The prince looks and sees that it is true. He returns. The mother, not at all perturbed apparently, offers her younger daughter; the shoe again won't fit, and the mother has the daughter cut off her heel. Again the bird spots the subterfuge. The second daughter is brought back, the prince asks if there is anyone else. After hesitation Cinderella, covered with ashes, is disparagingly brought forth, the shoe is tried and of course fits, and Cinderella and the prince ride off to be married, become king and queen, and live happily ever after.

The story in this form seems savage to us, but not unintelligible: the mother's counsel to her daughters is not altogether unlike advice we ourselves have heard. What is strange about the Cinderella story is that to the prince, a small foot seems to be the principal criterion of beauty. That does not become fully intelligible unless we know that the Cinderella tale originated in the Orient, where the female foot was long ago eroticized, and its smallness and daintiness considered of paramount importance. Indeed, the punishment the sisters undergo in the story is mild compared to the ritual of foot-binding to which all well-born Chinese women until quite recently had to submit from early childhood.

But although this focus on the small foot as the determinant of beauty, and the concomitant assumption that any process that produces small, delicate feet in a woman is worth the pain, strike us as barbarous and bizarre, the underlying presupposition does not: that whatever is considered the supreme characterization of beauty in a given time and place is worth expending time, money, pain, and perhaps life itself in pursuing. The legend expresses this truism in terms of feet: but translate 'small feet' to 'thin figure,' 'large bosom,' 'curly hair,' 'straight nose' or any of innumerable other possible focal points, and women still take endless pains to achieve those ends.

These thoughts suggest a delicate relation between beautification and distortion. While we prefer to think that what is beautiful is natural, there appear to be clear contradictions to this point of view, within our culture and outside of it. As we look, with admittedly ethnocentric gaze, on what passes for beauty and beautification elsewhere in the world, at times we can scarcely repress our horror at what is done in beauty's name: scarification, full-body tattooing, distortion of the natural shape of various parts of the body. It is difficult for the Westerner to classify such alterations of nature under the heading of beautification.

Robert Brain, in *The Decorated Body* (1979), proposes an at least partial explanation of these apparent contradictions. Beauty, he suggests, is born of polarizations. In particular human beings admire whatever sets them apart most sharply from non-humans. Anything that serves to emphasize that distinction is, *ipso facto*, beautiful. We value patterns of scarification or tattooing, since animals are not given to such stylized adornments. Hence, too, we undergo the piercing of ears, nose, lips; the distortion of the head; the filing of teeth to points; and perhaps this analysis extends even to the use of cosmetics by Western women.

Perhaps we stop in surprise at this point seeing the juxtaposition of these 'primitive' and 'bizarre' rites of adornment with our 'normal' enhancements of what is already there. (We do not purposely *create* scars, or place permanently garish patterns of color all over the skin. We merely embellish and accentuate the *natural* forms the body takes. Make-up is sold on that basis: do the most with what you already have.) But, in fact, animals are not noted for redness of lip, curl and length of eyelash, opalescent blush of fingernail, or luxuriance of hair on the head. In fact, when we find ourselves possessing attributes that are perceived as animal-like – say, unusual amounts of body hair – we tend to find this embarrassing and do what we can to remove or disguise it. And an obvious analog to primitive skin decorations in our own society is our preoccupation with clothing, indeed, with changes in style – what could be less 'natural,' less 'animal,' than presenting a radically different appearance to the world every day, every season? So our views of what creates beauty are not so remote from those of the African tribesman who decorates his skin with scars, or the Japanese use of full-body tattoos.

And yet we wince even seeing pictures of spectacular examples of these cosmetological triumphs. We do not know if the African tribesman has the same response to the clothing and jewels, or lipstick and nail polish, of the Western woman, or whether he writhes in sympathetic discomfort imagining himself in her girdle, or – worse yet – her husband's jacket and tie. In fact, our wincing at these exotic rites of decoration seems in part to underlie our sense that these are 'mutilations.' When we speak of 'mutilation,' as opposed to 'decoration,' or 'beautification,' we are contrasting our techniques to theirs, implicitly but pointedly.

A mutilation is permanent. It becomes a part of its possessor, and the possessor cannot remove it at will. On this basis, we view tattoos as quite different from body make-up, even if the latter were used (as it occasionally is) in garish and 'unnatural' patterns over all our visible skin. We still find such make-up, worn offstage, disconcerting and bizarre, but it is not a mutilation, where tattooing is. There is some evidence that tattoos are becoming increasingly permissible for us, even for women, although even those women who get tattooed (leaving aside a few exceptions) get a small tattoo of a 'feminine' object – a rose or a butterfly – placed discreetly where it is usually covered by clothing (for instance, the hip). We can see this trend, to the extent that it is a trend, as the cutting edge of a new perception of tattooing.

Once tattoos become common, it is probable that even full-body tattoos will no longer be regarded as mutilations. They will be seen as extreme, maybe still a bit bizarre, but the aura of sadism or masochism that still faintly surrounds tattooing will be absent. For there is one more crucial element in our folk definition of 'mutilation': a mutilation is something not typical of one's own culture. However permanent a 'cosmetic' alteration may be, if it is accepted as normal by a group, it will not be a mutilation for them. For example, in some African tribes lips are pierced and rings worn through them. Seeing these pictures, we certainly find lip-piercing bizarre and probably a mutilation. But pierced ears, involving a very similar operation and likewise having rings through them, often dangling, heavy-beaded jewelry as well, do not strike us as either. Again, there are exceptions, since ear-piercing is not totally accepted by everyone in the West. For example, one of the authors had her ears pierced in adolescence, an operation she underwent to cut down on the loss of earrings. But a friend of hers, seeing her inserting earrings once, shuddered visibly and referred with some horror to the 'disfigurement.' The author found this surprising, until she reflected that not long before she had made the same comment to another friend upon viewing someone wearing a ring through a pierced nose. And the wearing of more than one pierced earring per ear – implying more than one hole – occasions shock, even in those quite comfortable with *one* hole per ear. It is all a matter of expectation. We might attempt a paradigm: my beautification, your decoration, her mutilation.

We mentioned earlier the sense, in looking at pictures of 'exotic' cosmetic customs, of sympathetic pain in the viewer. Certainly we are aware, seeing a picture of someone with a complex pattern of scars or intricate tattoos, that these were purchased at the cost of suffering. And with this realization is associated the sense that we are perceiving a mutilation: mutilation, then, is linked to painfulness. In fact, a great many non-European cosmetic rites strike us as undoubtedly extremely painful, done as they generally are without anaesthesia, and often with primitive instruments. But it is equally true that many of our own unquestioned rites and rituals of beautification involve pain as well, and the proverb, *'Il faut souffrir pour être beau,'* is perfectly understandable to us without anthropological footnotes. None the less, one difference seems to exist between the pain one trades for beauty in non-European cultures and in our own: in the latter, the pain tends to be of long, even lifelong duration: rather than the quick prick of the needle, we have the squeezing of the tight-laced corset, the stab of the pointy toe, the asphyxiation of the collar and tie, or the scrape of the razor blade, day in and day out. The pain is perhaps less agonizing at any one moment in our beauty rituals than in theirs, but over time it evens out.

On reflection, then, there appears to be no culture for which beautification is totally divorced from unnaturalness, from permanent change of the body one was born with, from pain. And our judgment that the decorative rites of other groups involve mutilation, while ours do not, is both subjective and ethnocentric. As Brain argues, the very unnaturalness, permanency, and pain involved are intrinsic in all cultures to the effectiveness of the rites. Beauty is worth just what it costs. Here we are talking about the cost in comfort and health; but it is possibly true that one reason we nowadays insist less than other cultures do, or we have in the past, on genuinely painful forms of beautification is that we can pay money instead for our beauty – and we do. It is common knowledge that the highest-priced cosmetics sell the best and are considered the most efficacious, although their ingredients are also well known to have cost no more than those in the cheapest products, and that any difference in cost to the manufacturer lies in advertising. But we consider it fair to trade the stab of the knife for the stab of the charge-account statement once a month.

We talked about why 'mutilating' forms of beautification are universally popular, but we have not really discussed what those mutilations are designed to achieve. We have adopted Brain's suggestion that polarization is a key. Brain speaks of human/animal as the major polarity, but it is not the only one. Another polarity that is important is that of masculine/feminine. Indeed, one could argue that one of these polarities is selected, in a society, to be the important one, the one around which traditions and judgments cluster, the one of which members of a particular group tend to be consciously, if dimly, aware. Brain suggests that for many primitive societies, it is the human/animal distinction that assumes this great importance. But for us, there seems to be much evidence that it is the other. One reason might be that sophisticated cultures such as our own have very little daily experience with wild animals, and so do not experience the possibility of becoming like them, or being mistaken for them, as a threat, conscious or otherwise. But we do encounter members of the opposite sex; and we have all, from childhood, been socialized to fear being too much like members of the other sex – sissies or tomboys. Therefore, it makes sense that many adornments are considered beautifying because they accentuate the differences between the sexes. And it is also not surprising that truly mutilating or distorting forms of beautification tend to be the domain of women. For being constrained and hurt emphasizes one form of the traditional female stereotype: the woman is one who is helpless, weak, ill, dependent – she who suffers in silence. Men are not supposed to be weak or helpless, so that disfiguring techniques that enhance that aspect of oneself would not emphasize one's masculinity. Hence they are not common in our culture. (If we do find men adopting obviously painful or uncomfortable modes of decoration, we may either assume that there is another motive for them, beyond mere helplessness, or that the stereotypical image of men is changing.) But in those cultures where mortification of male flesh is customary – e.g., by scarification or tattooing – it is probably the case that these rites serve to enforce the human/animal, rather than the male/female, polarity. We do, still, atavistically retain some remnants of the human/animal polarity. The shaving of facial hair in men, and their wearing of ties and other constricting clothing, may be examples.

It is important to underscore what we have argued already: that there is nothing inherently beautiful, or inherently repugnant, in any form of alteration of the external self that some group considers cosmetic. In fact, as often as not we find one group accentuating in its cosmetological techniques what another group seeks to minimize. We have seen this historically: small breasts and large replace each other as desiderata over time. In some cultures, fatness is prized in women, and young girls are deliberately fattened before they are considered marriageable; in others, slenderness is the ideal, and brides-to-be go on crash diets to be as 'glamorous' as possible for the big event. We, attuned as we currently are to slenderness being supremely desirable – indeed the epitome of both allure and health – might view the former culture as deliberately disfiguring its women and ruining their health as well as mobility by fattening them; they, in turn, noting if they were to investigate the issue the damage done to women's appearance and health by amphetamines and dangerous diets, tight girdles, and other means of achieving slenderness, might make the same criticism of our ideal. It is not, then, the superficial appearance itself that is inherently disfiguring, in cases like this, but rather its underlying symbolic significance. Either fat or leanness can create helplessness and illness if carried to extremes, and the problem is the frequency with which they are carried to extremes.

With all these distinctions and provisos to warn us to be cautious, we can still attempt a discussion of pathological beautification: those forms of cosmetic adornment that seem to be intimately involved with pain or debility to their users. Granted that all beautification is a departure from the 'natural' in some sense; none the less we can distinguish, at least in principle, between those devices that merely emphasize that difference, and those that actually distort, that use the human body or some part of it in a way it was not intended to be used, and in so doing, do harm. This harm may be physical or psychological (or both); may be temporary or permanent; may be an essential part of the decoration, or an incidental (but unavoidable) side effect; and may be a direct reflection of a group's stereotypical image, or a means of using that stereotype for another, indirect purpose. All of these variations are encompassed in speaking of 'the pathology of beauty.'

Perhaps the most innocuous category is that of incidental pathology: the beauty ritual itself is not intended to be hurtful, but the way in which it is expedited incidentally causes injury. More surprisingly, even when this accidental injury is openly acknowledged and consumers are quite aware of the dangers, the rite continues in its familiar form, the product continues to be bought, used, extolled. To some extent this can be explained by the familiar feeling that disaster may strike others, 'but not me.' But beyond this is the sense that beauty is worth any price: if the product gives the desired results, mutilation – as long as it does not adversely affect what is physically visible – is a small disadvantage.

The situation is probably far better now than it was in earlier times. Particularly in the early part of this century, women found themselves in an exceptionally risky position. At that time, chemistry had made spectacular advances, so that cosmetics could now be manufactured using benzene and petroleum derivatives, coal tars, and other products that previously were unknown or unable to be artificially produced in the laboratory. Hence, previously, cosmetics were only occasionally truly noxious: science was not able to produce much that was severely damaging. That had changed, but – since people had not yet become accustomed to the new potency of science – laws had not yet been enacted to protect consumers from the enthusiasm of the new scientific cosmetic revolution. Horror stories are legion: caustic chemicals causing burns on the skin, even death; arsenic or thallium (rat-poison)-based depilatories poisoning women slowly and irreversibly, hair dyes causing blindness. By the 1930s, activists had started to press for product safety laws, but they were slow in coming. Dr Haven Emerson, a leading health authority of the period, testified in favor of one such proposed bill in 1933, in these words:

As president of the Public Health Association and a member of the Public Health Committee of the Academy [of Medicine, New York], I advise you that we are constantly observing at the medical centers in New York, through the Department of Dermatology and Medicine, the victims of the injudicious use of self-beautification efforts who come to us with many pathological conditions: Patients with deformed faces, patients with poisoned bodies, patients suffering at long time-distance from the time when they used their medications from chronic poisoning, which they could not themselves suspect from their own symptoms at the time of using the cosmetic . . . . (Lamb (1936), pp. 27–8)

As a result of such pressure by influential people, food and drug safety laws have been enacted over the last several decades. But – thanks in part to lobbying by cosmetics interests, and in part to consumers' unconcern (helped no doubt by laws that explicitly exempt cosmetics from the requirement of stating their ingredients) – dangerous products still are found on the market. As late as 1963, *Consumer Reports* warned its readers that, 'despite the prominence of the word in the Federal Food, Drug and Cosmetics Act, the protection afforded consumers of cosmetics under present Federal law is minimal.' The article continues:

The cosmetics sections of the law as it now stands do little more than require sanitary production, honest weights and measures, and disclosure of the manufacturer, packet, or distributor of the product. The buyer of an unfamiliar cosmetic has no assurance of its safety in normal use . . . .
   When injuries do occur, especially allergic reactions, the problem is compounded for the victim and his doctor by the lack of a requirement that ingredients be revealed . . . . That a tragedy of Thalidomide proportions has not brought a precipitous correction of deficiencies in the law, CU's medical consultants believe, can be credited only to good fortune plus the instinct for self-preservation, if not social responsibility, on the part of the large cosmetics manufacturers. (*Consumer Reports*, February 1963: pp. 90f.)

Getting down to specifics, in recent decades the same magazine has contained alarming reports about such common products as fingernail-hardeners (1958); hair sprays (1958); and 'rainbow' diet pills (1968). In all of these, the damage that is plentifully attested is but an incidental side-effect of the product, but one that chemically sophisticated manufacturers might be expected to have foreseen – at least if they attempted to do any extensive testing of their products, from the point of view of safety, before they put them on the market. But the question still remains unanswered: why are women so willing to subject themselves to untried and potent products, and why do they go on using them despite warning signs – allergic reaction, pain, illness? Thus, according to *CR*'s report, hair sprays were implicated in abnormalities of the lungs, the nail-hardener caused damage to the nails themselves. But these kinds of damages were reversible. More serious are the stories about diet pills and silicone implants and injections, where the damage seems more serious and permanent.

Here we find a situation that is truly horror-inspiring. Products or processes that are untested, or inadequately tested, by Federal agencies are advertised by their producers and used by healthy women, in an attempt to reach some ideal of beauty. Here as elsewhere, we must question the desperation of these women: why is thinness, or voluptuousness, important enough to induce a woman to subject herself to drugs and surgical procedures with dangerous side effects? What does it mean that our government sanctions the production, advertising, sale, and use of these products and processes for women who are perfectly healthy? Certainly, we are all aware that many medicinal drugs have potentially dangerous side-effects, that surgical procedures carry risks in all cases. Yet doctors continue to prescribe these drugs and perform these procedures, and in general no one would oppose this. But there is a difference between taking a drug (say an antihypertensive) with potentially severe side-effects, or undergoing an operation, for instance open-heart surgery that carries grave risks, and taking amphetamine pills to lose weight, or undergoing silicone implantation to increase breast size. No responsible doctor would advise a drug, or a procedure, whose clearly demonstrated benefits did not considerably outweigh its risks, so that a health-threatening drug is not prescribed responsibly except to remedy a life-threatening condition. But equally noxious drugs and procedures are medically sanctioned merely to 'cure' moderate overweight or flat-chestedness – hardly life-threatening ailments. The only way to understand the situation is to agree that those conditions *are*, in fact, perceived by women as life-threatening, so dangerous that seriously damaging interventions are justified, any risk worth taking, to alleviate them. It is not that women are masochistic and enjoy subjecting themselves to discomfort, pain, and death – rather, these dangers are viewed as comparatively slight, compared to being undesirable. But just how dangerous are the 'cures' of these prevalent 'diseases'?

Overweight, from the attention given it in the media, could be regarded as America's Public Enemy Number One. Why? We have seen that fashions in beauty do not always correspond to any logical reality, and our preference for extreme slenderness is not justifiable on grounds of health or pure aesthetics – although we like to think it is. Health, the most frequent rationalization for the preference for thinness, is dubious grounds. While it is true that extreme overweight can lead to certain health problems, extreme thinness can as well, and yet it is valued far more highly. Additionally, there is much evidence that the greatest hazards to health do not arise from being either overweight or underweight (except at truly exceptional levels), but rather from frequent fluctuation from one to the other, a state that perpetual dieters commonly achieve. For despite the claims made by sellers of diets and diet aids, virtually no dieter remains slender for very long. Weight loss is maintained for more than two years by only 5–10 percent of dieters. So most people go from one diet to another via periods of corpulence, up and down, down and up; in the process putting extra strain on their hearts and kidneys. So the very existence of diets and diet aids (pills, candy, and so on) is potentially dangerous to the health of the dieter. But beyond that, some diet pills and diets themselves are intrinsically dangerous, producing immediate unpleasant symptoms as well as long-term physical damage, often irreversible.

Dangerous in this way are the 'rainbow' diet pills – so called because they are prescribed in color-coded combinations so that dieters can remember which order to take them in – discussed in *Consumer Reports* in 1968. Each color is a different drug or combination of drugs, and the spectrum taken in the course of a day may include a diuretic, a laxative, an amphetamine, a sedative (to offset the effects of the amphetamine), a thyroid compound, and digitalis, a heart stimulant. Investigating a series of illnesses, with eight fatalities, among women taking this combination, a doctor theorized that the combination of laxative and diuretic depleted the body's potassium level, and that this depletion in turn sensitized the heart muscle to digitalis, causing irregular heart action leading to death. Even though the number of fatalities in this case was small, it is surprising that any initially healthy person would be willing to subject her body to the stresses of combining so many powerful substances, when the side-effects of such a combination would certainly be highly unpleasant, leaving aside the possibility of illness and even death.

Although this report appeared a number of years ago, stories still are found in the newspaper about doctors operating – that is, supervising very loosely – large franchised chains of weight-loss clinics, where the actual examination and prescription – in fact, if not in theory – is done by unlicensed personnel. One such doctor's license to practice medicine in California was revoked by the California Board of Medical Quality Assurance in 1980. Certainly one would think twice before entrusting one's health to an internist, or a gynecologist, who practiced in this haphazard manner, yet in the desperate quest for weight loss, apparently, a great many people are willing to try anything.

Outside of ordinary medical practice *per se*, we encounter the phenomenon of the published 'miracle' diet, which has been with us since time immemorial, as it seems – or at least since plumpness went out of vogue. Anyone over thirty can remember a grapefruit diet, a banana diet, a high-protein, low-cholesterol diet, a honey-vinegar diet, a water diet, and, the current fad at this writing, the Beverly Hills diet. As each of these fads hits the media, armies of doctors and nutritionists rise up to point out that the diet of the moment is dangerous and not effective in the long run, based on misunderstandings of the mechanisms of weight loss and gain, and probably apt to make matters worse rather than better. But no one listens: everyone is in the supermarket buying papayas. The quest for slimness begins to resemble, in curious ways, the medieval quest for the Holy Grail, or the Philosopher's Stone, whose ends must often have seemed hardly worth the risks involved, but the magic of the chase itself spurred the seekers on, making them impervious to reason and the demands of their bodies. Slimness is today's woman's Holy Grail, her Philosopher's Stone – seldom fully gained, in her own eyes, and when gained, painfully evanescent, but she only feels alive, or worthwhile, when actively pursuing it.

Lest we think that these horror stories are things of the past, a report in the *San Francisco Chronicle* (February 24, 1982) suggests that the dangers are still very real. The drug phenylpropanolamine, an ingredient in many over-the-counter appetite suppressants, is indicted by many authorities for causing serious damage to users: according to this report, 'dietary aids containing phenylpropanolamine poison 10,000 people and cause at least 1,000 others to seek emergency care.' (The article also notes that 'last year alone nearly 4 million Americans consumed about 10 billion doses of products containing phenylpropanolamine.') Further, 'many researchers said the drug is virtually useless as a diet aid and may cause hypertension, strokes, and psychoses.' These are rather serious potential side-effects; we would hope that the malady they are taken to alleviate is more life-threatening than the conditions they may cause – otherwise, there is no medical justification for taking the drug. Yet we see that, not only is it used principally for the control of overweight – seldom directly life-threatening – but even in that function, it is considered ineffective by many experts. This is very strange indeed, and leads us to think that things have not progressed as far as we might wish from the days of thallium-containing hair dyes.

All we can make of this – and other reports of people subjecting themselves to extreme discomfort to the point of risk to life for the sake of weight loss – is to assume that overweight has become a spectre to most of us of truly terrifying configurations. This is in part due to the continual revision downward, over the last century, of our mental notion of the ideal feminine figure. It is not so much that women have gotten fatter; rather, we have continually changed our assumptions about what 'overweight' is, so that fewer and fewer of us escape the twinge at the mirror. Like so many other frightening conditions, overweight is in part in our heads – not only because, as weight-loss experts (who are replacing psychiatrists as the modern priesthood hearing women's darkest confessions) like to say, we eat for psychological gratification, but at least as much because we are making more and more impossible demands upon ourselves. We must be slim and fit, or we fail. Although it is always argued that slenderness is 'healthier' than fatness, that it frees women to lead more active and fulfilling lives, spending many of one's waking hours gazing into the mirror in despair, dreaming about inaccessible hot-fudge sundaes, and castigating oneself for giving in to temptation, are neither healthy nor fulfilling ways to spend time. It looks oddly as if slenderness, rather than really being about health and activity, is but another way to encourage women to feel depressed, inadequate, and unable to get their own lives under control.

However much of our time, energy, and money obesity control takes in our lives, it does not normally (short of the disastrous side-effects occasionally encountered) take its toll in direct physical pain and danger to life. But more drastic ways of achieving society's prescription for beauty can be more threatening. Plastic surgery, for example, is becoming more popular all the time to correct real (or, more often, imagined) 'flaws' of face and figure. We are not speaking here of reconstructive surgery: the correction of true facial deformities, congenital or accident-caused; or post-mastectomy breast reconstruction. Such operations are often psychologically life-giving, and overcome real pain and suffering. Rather, we are thinking of cosmetic surgery done to make the patient look better, according to the dictates of his or her society, to make him/her conform more closely to a cultural ideal which is in no sense more 'perfect' than the way the patient looks before surgery, except that popular opinion makes it so. A cleft palate, for example, is a deviation from our basic notion of how a human being (anywhere, at any time) normally looks, and so is distressing to see or have; moreover, it creates problems in speaking and perhaps other true medical difficulties. No one questions that such a problem should receive all the help reconstructive surgery can provide – and the miracles often accomplished are without question worthwhile. But changing a hooked nose to an Irish snub, or rounding Asian almond-shaped eyes, are in a rather different category. There is nothing intrinsically unnatural or universally strange in a hooked nose; if we think it aesthetically undesirable, we do so for rather curious reasons. First, it deviates from the white Anglo-Saxon Protestant ideal, and marks its wearer as not of the most prestigious ethnicity in America. And second (since we notice that women are much more stigmatized than men for having one) it gives a face an impression of strength, of going its own way, while the snub nose, being 'cute' and girlish, suggests a childlike dependency and is thus (though equally a departure from aquiline perfection) much more desirable for a woman. In many middle-class Jewish-American, upwardly mobile groups, a very common rite of passage is the (so-called) 'sweet-sixteen nose job.' With this, the young woman is rendered less 'Jewish-looking,' and, hence, potentially more desirable to her eventual husband.

We will speak later of the psychological dangers of ethnicity-concealing plastic surgery of this kind; what is in some ways more crucial is the recognition that, under less than optimal conditions, such surgery can be physically dangerous, even life-threatening. And since there is no physical justification for subjecting oneself to the hazard, the pain, and the expense, the psychological reasons for doing so had better be very strong indeed.

Like weight-loss schemes (diets, exercise, machinery), cosmetic surgery does not typically involve physical risk as a direct result of the process, but can entail such risks more or less as side-effects. (It has been pointed out, of course, with regard to medications, that 'there are no side-effects, only effects that are undesirable.')

Cosmetic surgery has two major reasons for being. The first is to bring the face, or body, of the subject into conformity with some societal ideal of beauty: rounder eyes, a thinner nose, fuller or small breasts, less tummy and thighs; or it can be used to disguise (some would say, overcome) the ravages of ageing. The latter phrase is one we can reflect upon with profit. Certainly we can agree that growing older – from infancy into old age – creates many physical changes, but why does it seem so natural to us to refer to them as 'ravages'? We should realize, first of all, that the ordinary changes induced by growing older become in our view disfiguring only after the reaching of a certain age is indicated by tell-tale signs. Children, we note, are delighted to tell their age, and often stretch the truth as far as their morals will let them in order to look older. A child will say he is 'ten and seven-eighths' proudly: it's much better than 'ten.' Similarly, adults note with pleasure the signs that a child is growing older: increased height and weight, the changing appearance of the face, bigger hands and feet, signs of puberty, and so on. But once we reach that 'certain age' – earlier for a woman than a man, to be sure – we stop discussing it; it becomes indecent to ask the age, and often a veritable blunder to tell it; and we view every sign of that increasing age in the mirror as a tragedy of major or minor proportions. It is sometimes suggested in the popular media that a woman has a virtual moral duty – to herself and those who must behold her – to remove those wrinkles and bags, tuck that tummy, raise those breasts. We don't want to look at or confront maturity – our own or others'. There is – we need hardly point out – nothing intrinsically revolting about bags and wrinkles. In a man, they are often felt to increase his attractiveness. They show he has had experience in the world, he is knowing. In a woman, though, they are unattractive. They show she has had experience in the world, she is knowing. So the 'ugliness' of ageing for women is very much an outgrowth of our fears of lack of polarization between the sexes: a woman should be untouched and innocent, distinguishing her clearly from a man, who should not. Anything that obscures that line is ugly – inhuman, frightening, no different in terms of our gut response than an actual deformity like a harelip. It has often been noted in literature (as well, of course, as in art) that old men and old women tend to become more and more alike: the sexes are depolarized as they age. This in itself makes growing older frightening, for oneself and in others. We notice old men's weakness, their higher voices; old women's facial hairs and thickening figures. Even if we understand the biological reasons for these changes, they still seem mysterious and frightening. We must remember that the women burned as witches between the fifteenth and eighteenth centuries were usually old women – and therefore objects of fear for men and younger women alike.

Because of this atavistic fear of growing old – or rather, of looking old – experienced by both men and women, but especially the latter, face-lifts, once an indulgence for the wealthy, are rapidly becoming for women one of the normal rites of passage into middle age.

Perhaps the worst thing about a face-lift, though, is the certainty, as one undergoes it, that it will have to be done again – perhaps every five years. While it used to be recommended that the first face-lift be done around age fifty, more recent advice is that women start thinking along those lines as early as forty-five or even forty. Then, supposing a woman lives into her seventies, as she may confidently hope, she might expect to have the procedure (costing at present $5,000–$10,000 and requiring a week or two of discomfort and seclusion) repeated seven or eight times. We must indeed suffer to be beautiful!

On the other hand, there are cosmetic operations done to make one more 'beautiful' irrespective of age. When we look at these too, we see that sexual polarization is at the root of many, if not most attempts at 'beautification.' It has been said repeatedly by plastic surgeons that the most popular form of cosmetic surgery in America is breast augmentation. It is still frequently performed today, despite our increasing emphasis on boyish slenderness: we don't want our women to be *too* indistinguishable from the boys. Breast reduction is also common, though not nearly as common, and reduction is often justified in terms of health and comfort. But augmentation has no discernible health or (physical) comfort benefits, and may in fact keep the patient from nursing children later. Moreover, it has an extremely high (60 percent) rate of complications even when responsibly and competently performed. In non-cosmetic surgery, an operation with that high a rate of complications – many serious, occasionally even fatal – would only be performed in case the risk to life or health from not undergoing the operation was very great indeed. Then it is somewhat curious that such an operation is in fact, so very common for purely cosmetic reasons. Breast augmentation surgery is discussed in two articles in *Ms.* magazine of August 1977.

The problems this procedure has caused are horrendous to contemplate – horrendous because the operation is first of all unnecessary, and second because the problems are often caused by the physicians' ignorance, carelessness, or simple greed. There are two types of breast augmentation, by silicone injections, and by implants containing a liquid or gel. Silicone is a chemical (dimethylpolysiloxane), injected in liquid form. It can be described in terms of its properties and behavior as a cross between glass and rubber and is chemically stable. Because of its physical properties, it seemed an ideal substance to inject into breast tissue to increase breast size.[1]

While silicone was first produced commercially in the 1940s, its use in breast augmentation began in the early 1960s. Not long after, 'side effects' of the procedure began turning up. A summary of the kinds of complications that have been documented since then reads like a medical horror story, from relatively small disasters like hardening of the breasts (so that they feel like 'baseballs') through infections resulting from the procedure, sometimes causing gangrene (in both these cases, often one or both breasts must eventually be removed) to truly catastrophic results: the silicone can 'migrate' throughout the body, to the eyes, for instance, causing blindness; or the lungs, causing death by pulmonary edema. The most serious complications fortunately are rare, but they are attested – for an operation, we reiterate, of no benefit whatever to physical health.

While legislation resulting from stories such as these has curbed the practice of silicone injection (though it is still done by unscrupulous practitioners), implantation, though safe, has its problems, discussed by Marjorie Nashner and Mimi White, in 'Beauty and the Breast' (1977). Over the years, many different materials have been tried for implantation, from plastic sponges in the 1950s through silicone gel to the currently popular inflatable implant filled with fluid (silicone or saline solution) after it is in place. All of these are prone to complications. As with the injections, hardening of the breasts may occur, sometimes necessitating mastectomy. Inflatable implants may leak or deflate; scar tissue may become infected or harden. Pain, reduction in breast size, distortion of shape, and loss of sensation are some of the results, often not correctable.

One story told in the Nashner and White article expresses perhaps one's worst nightmare:

> In 1975 [a woman] was at a party, when a large professional football player suddenly hugged and squeezed her very tightly. 'We heard a loud pop and he said, "what was that?" "I think my beads broke," I answered and fled to the bathroom. My breast had become soft again.'

Other forms of plastic surgery probably have fewer risks to life, health and comfort associated with them. But there is always risk if only from the anaesthetic, not to mention the expense and the pain necessarily involved.

What is curious, in descriptions of plastic surgery and its practitioners, is the frequency with which they are likened to artists, and their patients to the artists' canvases. While the objectification of the subject of medical procedures is hardly novel, this convention seems to carry it farther than usual. One is reminded, as so often, of the myth of Pygmalion, which tells us that a woman is never more desirable than when she can be seen as the pure creation of a man. A story in the *San Francisco Chronicle* (August 12, 1980) about the Brazilian miracle-working cosmetic surgeon, Pitanguy, exemplifies this point of view very clearly:

> Although some of his detractors charge that Pitanguy would not be able to perform in the United States the operations he routinely does in Brazil where malpractice suits are virtually unheard of, this is seen as a plus by the professor of surgery:
> In Rio, because he is who he is, Pitanguy can experiment, and other plastic surgeons can benefit from his results. Malpractice laws are necessary to protect the patient, but sometimes they tend to stifle creativity.

Novel words these, with their reminder of what one suffers for the sake of science, but we must remember that the 'experimental' animals are not laboratory rats in this case, but women.

All the foregoing are examples of risks to health brought about more or less incidentally in the pursuit of beauty: it happens that the procedure that creates what is currently construed as beautiful has attendant effects that are damaging. But there are still more puzzling cases (that is, puzzling as long as we wish to equate beauty with health, grace, or normality) in which the damage is a necessary condition of the procedure. In fact, what may in one definition be construed as damage is in another the form of beauty itself. When we encounter such customs in an exotic culture, we shudder and consider it primitive, or savage – unintelligible. But analogous practices are hardly unheard of in our own. Yet we consider them merely what a woman ought to do if she wishes to be desirable. They are strange and revolting only to the outsider.

Some examples are so well known that we need only mention them briefly in passing. For example, Chinese foot-binding, happily no longer practiced, though women are still alive who demonstrate the results. Here is a case where beauty is directly related to crippling and helplessness: the broken foot, incapable of supporting weight, testified to the woman's having a husband wealthy enough to support a totally helpless wife. Except, of course, that foot-binding had to be done in early childhood, long before it was known whether the foot's possessor would spend her life in that idyllic situation.

Because its common Western name, foot-binding, conceals its actual form we should summarize briefly what the 'lotus hook' involved. The small child had the arches of her feet broken so that the feet could be turned under at the instep. The feet were tightly bound in this position, insuring that healing would not take place. It is notable that, as with so many women's beauty rituals, women were in charge of doing this to – or 'for' – other females, thus apparently relieving men of the responsibility for the damage inflicted.

Or we could consider clitoridectomy – unlike foot-binding, practiced in the past by a great many societies, and still practiced more or less clandestinely by several. The United Nations has spoken strongly against such practices, but they continue; where individual governments have taken stands against them, they continue more or less in secret. Clitoridectomy – the excision of the clitoris, with more or less additional mutilation of the genital organs – is common in many nations of Africa, and is encountered to this day both in relatively isolated tribes and in the most sophisticated urban areas, even in highly educated families. At first it seems irrelevant, in a discussion of beauty, to mention this custom, since the excuse for it is generally that it keeps women chaste (by destroying or greatly diminishing their sexual pleasure). But it is closely identified with femininity and thereby with 'beauty.' Where the practice is usual, a woman who has not been 'circumcised' is considered unfeminine, probably unmarriageable, and her genitalia are considered 'ugly' – as is she, by extension. (Of course, feminine genitals are typically considered ugly by both men and women in many cultures, including our own. What is interesting here is that a practice that distorts these organs and destroys one of their principal functions can *thereby* render these otherwise 'ugly' organs beautiful, just as for the Chinese crippling women's feet automatically made them beautiful.) But clitoridectomy does not merely cripple, symbolically and otherwise. When (as so often) it is performed under unsanitary conditions, it can cause serious infection and illness. Additionally, some of its variants create difficulties in menstruation, intercourse, and childbirth, with pain and risk to life and health.

But of course, these are the practices of exotic cultures, which we need not pretend to understand. We like to think that our society is at present, and perhaps even always has been, exempt from these bizarre customs. Yet if we look around we can see, both in the past and in the present, similar practices – perhaps not quite so dangerous or disfiguring, perhaps not so common – but certainly done in the name of beauty, a beauty based on disfigurement and debility.

Let us consider the wasp waist, beloved of the Victorians and in fashion up to the early years of this century. A moment's thought will convince us that the ordinary anatomy we were born with is not, and cannot be, wasp-waisted in any way approaching the ideal. Somehow those willowy Victorian maidens had to accommodate reality to the dictates of fashion. And there was a way – a couple, in fact. One, extremely common, involved heavy corsets with whalebone stays, laced as tightly as the wearer could tolerate. Perhaps the reader remembers a scene in Margaret Mitchell's *Gone With the Wind*. The southern belle Scarlett O'Hara, who has 'the smallest waist in five counties' is being laced into her corset by a big black mammy. Scarlett has to hold on to the bedpost while Mammy pulls. At last – triumph: 16 inches! but it has not been without a struggle. Later in the book, after Scarlett has borne a child, she tries the corset again. This time, things are grimmer. She can't, try what she may, get it smaller than 20 inches. This is too horrible to be imagined. Twenty inches! That, Scarlett reflects dolefully, is no better than Mammy – impossible to appear in public looking like that!

We are well acquainted with the Victorian female custom of fainting at the slightest provocation. We think of it as a charming psychological trick. But since in fact these women were laced in so tightly that their circulation was impeded, and they could not breathe normally, it was not so hard to faint when additional demands were placed upon the respiratory and circulatory systems, as they would be in moments of emotional stress. Fainting then was not purely a hysterical syndrome, but had real physiological roots. It seems undeniable that the physical debility induced by corseting was part of its appeal. It created the delicate Victorian lady whose helplessness was an intrinsic part of her charm.

In case the wasp waist were not sufficiently created by mechanical means, with the development of anaesthesia, and modern surgical techniques, another method became feasible. It was never really popular, but was available to a woman who was serious about her fashionableness. Since the lowest rib stands between a woman and a true wasp waist (wasps, after all, don't have ribs), someone had the happy inspiration: why not remove the rib? Really determined women did so, despite the risks (due to ignorance of antisepsis, imperfect anaesthesia, and undeveloped surgical technique) involved.

But all this, we say, heaving a sigh of relief, is in the past. What with our greater understanding of psychology and physiology, such dangerous forms of beautification no longer appeal. We have separated debility from beauty. In fact (it has been argued rather often of late) our standard of beauty has changed in recent years. Yes, in the wicked past we did tend to equate beauty with weakness, deformity, and helplessness – but no more. Now, beauty for us is strength, activity – autonomy!

There is some evidence that, in a limited way, this is true. Yet fashion has hardly recognized the fact, if fact it is. Style still defines femininity as embodying immobility or the appearance of uselessness. As we have seen, our models and cover girls still wear hairstyles that take immense amounts of time and effort to keep them looking the way they must (although there is a fiction that they are wild, free, and wind-blown); skirts, currently back in fashion after a decade-long reign of pants, still require care on the part of the wearers in walking and sitting, if modesty is to be maintained (and indeed it is); and long, perfectly manicured, lacquered fingernails are as essential as ever. Silk and wool are the popular fabrics – and everyone knows how careful one must be in wearing them, and the care that must be taken in keeping them clean.

In fact, what is judged beautiful changes as signs of indol-ence and comfort change. A century ago, white, untanned skin was a necessary part of beauty, and a wise young woman who had to be outdoors in the sun protected her fair complexion with a parasol. A tan was the mark of someone who had to labor under the sun – someone not accustomed to leisure.

Today, most women's menial work is indoors, and a white (now called 'pasty') complexion is the giveaway that one spends long hours at work. Persons (male and female both) of leisure and affluence demonstrate their privilege by vacationing where they can spend the winter under the sun and return with a badge of rank – a tan. The tan now indicates higher social position, and therefore health (despite its link to skin cancer) and beauty (despite its link to premature wrinkles). Beauty is not tied directly to health – nor to independence, mobility, or autonomy.

But constraint is not the same thing as debility. Is there anything in the way we currently live that links beauty with immobility or passivity? An answer is as near as your neigh-borhood shoe store. In style again, after an absence of a few years, is the high, narrow heel – some as much as four inches high. Often these are combined with ankle straps – a truly lethal combination for walking, let alone running, as anyone who has tried will attest. At first glance, it may seem strange that high heels are almost universally considered beautiful and 'sexy,' since they make women taller – more on a par with their male companions. But in fact, what makes high heels sexy is not the height of the heels *per se* but rather what they do to a woman's leg. They compress the calf muscle, causing it to bulge. It is this constriction, which makes movement difficult and creates a mincing short-stepped walk, that is attractive. Moreover, the distortion caused by high heels is no more temporary, though of course far less debilitating, than that caused by foot-binding. A long period of wearing high heels every day, generally for hours on end, will cause the tendon in the leg to shrink permanently, making it painful to wear flat heels. Additionally, the regular wearing of high heels is blamed by orthopedists for a good deal of chronic back pain and postural difficulties, and by some authorities even for problems with the internal organs in the abdomen, since the distortion of posture caused by the wearing of heels pushes the pelvic region out of its normal alignment. If even a fraction of the distress these conditions cause can be traced to the wearing of heels, it is strange indeed that women persist in wearing them. Curious too is the way they keep returning to fashion, even after being declared dead in more 'unisex' or 'casual' periods of fashion. During the late 1960s and early 1970s, in part because of the popularity of the miniskirt, as well as the generally informal and practical emphasis of fashion throughout much of this rather unusual period, high heels went into eclipse succeeded by the equally dangerous but less 'sexy' platform shoes, running shoes, boots, and other non-high-heel styles. But at the beginning of the 1980s (widely considered a return to traditional values everywhere) high heels, this time with even more dangerous and constricting ankle-straps, made a return appearance, and women snapped them up with relish – like meat after years of rationing.

There is an odd sidelight to the whole matter of shoes, a flashback to the Cinderella story. During the 1950s and early 1960s, not only were heels high, but toes were extremely narrow and tapered. It was difficult for many women to get their toes into the shoes and wear them comfortably. According to a story in *Time* magazine (November 10, 1961, p. 57), an enterprising surgeon in Texas found a way to help the suffering: he performed literally thousands of little-toe-ecto-mies. While it is true that the little toe is of relatively small use in our daily lives, it is still shocking that thousands of women preferred to run the risk and undergo the expense of surgery, rather than settle for a less fashionable shoe – or put pressure on shoe stylists to bring their designs into conformity with the natural contours of the female foot, rather than vice versa. In general, women's fashions try to fit the female body into clothes designed for an unrealistic ideal, rather than shaping the clothing to fit the woman, while current men's fashion tends to follow the shape of its intended wearers. We don't find men's shoes creating an image of the male foot bearing little resemblance to its actual form, or preventing it from fulfilling the purpose for which it evolved – moving.

But physical damage is perhaps the least of a woman's problems if she seeks to tailor her image to what fashion proclaims attractive. More serious for us today is the possibility of psychological damage. It arises in two ways: first, there is the damage that arises out of the stereotype of femininity in general that beauty represents: beauty as helplessness and passivity. If everything a woman does to make herself more desirable inevitably restricts her movement and flaunts her helplessness and dependency, how is a properly-socialized young woman to break out of the traditional role? It becomes very difficult for such a woman, trying to reach a definition of herself in the first years of her adulthood, to find an identity that is at once active and competent, and attractive and desirable. Sigmund Freud, asked what abilities were part of a normal healthy personality, replied, 'To love and to work.' For a woman in this society, it seems, it is impossible to have both. To seek love – to become feminine and desirable – is to renounce work – competence and autonomy, and vice versa. This message is probably presented today in a more muted form than twenty or thirty years ago, when scores of Hollywood movies were based on the heroine's need to make this choice, and a happy ending entailed a choice for love. Now, of course, there are many movies in which the heroine is able to have and enjoy both. But the heroine is now a superwoman, a person the female movie-goer can only view with a vain longing – not someone to model oneself after, unless a nervous breakdown is the hoped-for result. For most of us, the choice between beauty and autonomy must still be made, but with the nagging sense that if we were *really* marvelous people we wouldn't have to choose. In the 1950s and 1960s, even the most marvelous had to give something up, which perhaps made us feel, leaving the movie theatre, a little more contented with our lot. As with advertising, where the sell is more blatant but not much different, the media as a whole seem to conspire to create self-dissatisfaction in a woman's mind: one is never beautiful enough, never young enough, never accomplished enough. Better buy a new deodorant, that may help. The psychological gap between Everywoman's graspable reality and the fantasy – of fulfilments of various sorts – projected at her from every source feeds upon, and helps at the same time to create, the desperate need for reassurance: 'Drink Tab, and you will be the fairest of them all.' So despite the very real successes of the women's movement, our vision of beauty still partakes, to a very great extent, of the old female stereotypes, and we are still caught in the same old choice.

We see then that women, through their conscious efforts to achieve an appearance approximating an internalized and abstract ideal current in their society, subject themselves to procedures which, physically or psychologically or both, can be hazardous to the health. But they undergo these procedures in some sense by conscious choice. There are other ways in which women subject their looks and lives to the dictates of their societies which are still more dangerous: in which the determination is largely unconscious and outside the will of the woman, although she does not perceive it that way; and the effect of the compulsion is to render her, not so much a reflection of a currently desirable ideal, but a virtual parody of it. What is frightening about one currently prevalent condition is not only its high rate of occurrence, its high fatality rate, and the lack of a reliable cure, but also the fact it is brought into being by unconscious mechanisms – the sufferers themselves have no control over the situation, at least in any normal sense of the word.

We refer to anorexia nervosa, about which a great deal has been written from a great many points of view over the last ten years. And well it might be: not only is it virtually epidemic in the population most at risk (young women in their teens and early twenties; one in ten or so is male), but it has a fatality rate of 10–20 percent and leaves the health of others permanently damaged. Moreover, the population at risk is the middle to upper-middle class, which makes it especially visible.

Anorexia nervosa, appetite loss and consequent drastic weight loss without physical cause, has been attested in the medical literature for several thousand years, but until very recently was considered extremely rare. About ten years ago, the number of cases started to increase suddenly and rapidly: it is currently estimated that one of every 250 young women is affected. The major symptom is that the young victims refuse to eat, or eat very little; if pressed to eat, they may induce vomiting later. (A closely related condition, bulimia or bulimarexia, involves episodes of gorging, with as many as 15,000 calories consumed in the course of a day, with purging via induced vomiting or laxatives.) Menstruation usually ceases if the condition continues; the body's electrolyte balance is upset (the most frequent cause of death); if prolonged, other signs of malnutrition may manifest themselves. The victims claim not to be hungry, not to to be interested in food; rather, they become more than usually energetic, exercising compulsively and getting very little sleep. Anorexia may persist for years, with remissions and relapses.

Many treatments for anorexia have been attempted, depending on the assumption about its cause. Psychoanalytic theorists have related it to fear of assuming a woman's body, fear of pregnancy and sexuality. (In favor of this position they adduce the cessation of the menses, although this normally occurs whenever the percentage of fat in a woman's body becomes extremely low – as it does with non-anorexic gymnasts and ballet dancers, for example.) Other psychologists have argued that it is less a problem of individual psychology than a family problem – hence its onset at an age at which one must face separation from one's parents both psychically and physically, and when one's efforts at independence are apt to be rebuffed by parents. It is argued that those women who fall victim to anorexia are those for whom the achievement of autonomy has been impossible. The parents of anorexics frequently present a picture of an 'ideal family' whose members love one another, do everything together, are interested in one another's doings, and are extraordinarily close-knit. Yes, say the researchers, too close-knit. The only autonomous act possible for the young woman, the only one her parents cannot interfere with, is eating – or rather, not eating. And at first the decision to diet is often approved of by the rest of the family. After all, 'you can't be too thin or too rich.' (Anorexia is a disease of the upwardly mobile.) By the time the parents observe the danger, the child has tasted the pleasures of autonomy – her body, at least, is her own, and nothing can get into it without her consent. (In this way, food works as a symbolization of sex.) It is a dangerous way to achieve adulthood, but seems, to these young women caught in their family situation, the only way.

From this picture of it, anorexia nervosa seems to have little to do with beauty. It is a disease of coming-of-age, of achieving autonomy, whether sexual or social. But there is more to it than that. A pressing question is why the fear of, coupled with the desire for independence and adulthood, is manifested in this peculiar way, at this time. For young people have been dealing with these questions since the dawn of time. It is argued that only very recently have young women been explicitly faced with having to achieve their identity – in earlier generations, women were not expected to find themselves, but only to find a man. Yet even that choice posed problems and it is certainly true that this is not the first time in history that young women have faced conflicts, internal and external, in coming to full maturity.

About a hundred years ago, in America and in Europe, a condition was widespread in precisely the same population in which anorexia is epidemic today: young women, well-educated, from middle- to upper-middle-class families, the women often unusually intelligent and articulate, the families often unusually loving and close-knit. Here, too, 10 percent of the victims were male – generally young men who in other ways were atypical of their gender. The condition so prevalent in Victorian times was, of course, hysteria. There is one major difference between hysteria and anorexia, though: the former involved many fewer fatalities, though it did frequently render its victims helpless invalids for life. Hysteria, too, was often thought of as a disease involving sexual conflict, an unconscious unwillingness to acknowledge one's own sexual needs and desires. But the symptomatic picture was quite different.

Loss of appetite did sometimes occur among hysterics, but never with the compulsive and life-threatening quality it has in anorexia. The symptoms of hysteria could mimic an inexhaustible number of physical maladies, from blindness, deafness, or aphasia, to paralysis, intestinal pains, dysmenorrhea, coughing, and fainting – and many others. The result in any case was to reduce the victim to dependence and passivity, a state of chronic invalidism. While the anorexic becomes unusually active, the hysteric retreats to passivity.

Although early psychological theories about hysteria singled out an inability to communicate about sexual matters as its cause, this was later recognized as but a partial understanding. Rather, hysteria could be understood as indirect communication, the symptoms substituting for words, but too often unintelligible – about whatever one could not be direct about. Although Freud preferred to trace his patients' symptoms to repressed sexuality, reading those case histories we can as often find inexpressible anger at their base. And while Freud did make it permissible for women to acknowledge their sexuality, he made it even harder for them to express anger (which he had defined as penis envy, among other unpleasant things). In any case, we may say that both hysteria and anorexia are diseases of miscommunication: they are indirect ways of expressing wants and needs, when direct acknowledgment and expression of them would put a woman at risk, before herself and her family, as a bad or unworthy person. The Victorian hysteric needed to separate from her family, needed autonomy, whether to understand her own sexuality or to develop other aspects of her personality. The young anorexic also needs to separate, to discover who she is and what she really needs. But although the two conditions are manifestations of the same underlying need, they show themselves in remarkably different superficial symptoms. How are we to account for that?

Let us look once again at the Victorian hysteric's symptoms. What is interesting about them is that they created – in a woman who otherwise might have been an unusually independent and active person – the very model of the sickly, passive female the Victorians had as their ideal. Hysteria tended to occur in women who were supported by their families – their parents or sometimes their husbands. Only they could become hysterics, since only they could be supported, and since only women in the bosom of a family had the benefit of an audience to the sufferings they underwent. There is ample evidence that, very often, a hysteric's more florid symptoms (convulsions, for instance) tended to appear only when there were onlookers, and would subside, rather like a child's temper tantrum, when there was no one around. Of course, if hysteria is indirect communication, what is the point of communicating to no one? At the same time, the hysteric typically feigned unconcern about her symptoms, professed not to be distressed by them ('la belle indifférence'), where a person organically ill and showing the same symptoms would naturally complain and talk about them. But this makes sense, if the symptoms are but the means to an end. We don't ordinarily metacommunicate – that is, talk about the form our communication takes – so why should the hysteric? From this perspective we can see that the surface behaviors of hysteria communicate something deeper as well: they are a sort of parody of the Victorian culture's ideal of femininity – sickly, helpless and dependent. A young woman caught between her own desire for autonomy – which she hardly dared to make conscious to herself, let alone express to others – and her culture's view of appropriate female behaviour could not discuss the matter or negotiate it. All she could do was express, indirectly and ironically, an exaggeration of the stereotype that functioned as a protest – but one for which the protester, having disclaimed responsibility, could not be chastized. But since she had chosen to remove the behavior from her conscious control, she could not call it off when it became inconvenient. Unless something intervened – a way to get autonomy, or a decision that passivity was, after all, the better choice – the symptoms would remain and probably, to retain their effect as communication, get worse.

From this standpoint, anorexia is really not very different from hysteria in function (as opposed to surface form). We have, in the last ten or fifteen years, given up the old stereotype that women should be weak and helpless. But we still have others. Perhaps the most potent – judging from the evidence that we have already examined – is the belief that the ideal woman is always active and busy (generally in someone else's interest or for the enhancement of her own attractiveness, of course) and is also as thin as she can possibly be. While most of us won't get a chance to see if we can be too rich, we can all try to discover whether we can be too thin (but we believe we can't). So just as hysteria's surface manifestations reflect a parodic view of the Victorian female ideal, so anorexia's parody our own, as indirect communication for which the communicator (for all her desire for autonomy) does not recognize responsibility, and cannot be criticized.

If we view anorexia and hysteria in this way, several former mysteries begin to make sense. We see first of all why the epidemiological pictures of the two are so similar. We see why the symptoms in each case take the particular shape they do. And finally, in both cases, we see why the condition, once it starts, is so hard to arrest – we see what makes it attractive, or at least why its victims view it as the only tolerable alternative among a set of bad choices. We see the relationship between a culture's dictates about normal and ideal female behaviour, and preferred female pathology. And just as hysteria is not a disease about sexuality, anorexia is not a disease about dependency *per se*, though both sexuality and dependency are involved. Both are diseases of communication, which arise when a young woman is presented with an ideal to identify with and strive toward which is, for her, untenable. Anorexia nervosa is not then directly related to beauty, but the surface form the condition manifests arises from our perverse notions about beauty, which in turn arise from idealizations not so different from those of the Victorians – that a woman should be manipulable, by the others in her life or by the media. Hysteria and anorexia are last-ditch desperate attempts to subvert these manipulations (though they are themselves manipulations), to preserve some sort of identity of one's own, even at the cost of life itself. And therefore both hysteria and anorexia resist cures by methods that merely concern themselves with superficial symptoms. It is society that is sick, and the woman's relationship to that sick society and its ideas about feminine perfection that must be changed.

In fact, we can see anorexia nervosa as the direct lineal descendant of hysteria. After Freud's work became disseminated widely, during the 1920s and 1930s, a sudden and dramatic drop in the number of cases of hysteria was noticed, so that it has by now become as much a rarity as anorexia used to be, particularly in those segments of the population in which it was most common. The psychoanalytic explanation for the decline was that, since Freudian thought had made female sexuality acknowledgeable, women's sexual needs no longer had to be expressed indirectly. But no sooner did hysteria subside, than therapists noted an alarming increase, in much the same population, in phobias, particularly agoraphobia; and when this in turn appeared to subside, anorexia took its place. So we might argue that the same disease remains, only the symptoms change from time to time, responding to our fantasies. Just as slang changes rapidly – lest those who are 'out of it' become aware of what it means and start using it themselves – so the disease caused by our ideal of femininity and the intolerable constraints it places on real women is protean, changing its surface form to mirror changing needs as well as to hide from outsiders what they must not hear.

# Chapter 7
# Talking About Beauty

The linguist looks at language in a special way. To the ordinary speaker, language is 'just talk,' 'just words,' 'just semantics' – not actions or the reality for which words are mere substitutes. To the linguist, though, language is a map – the most accurate one we have – of the workings of the mind. Syntax – the way we organize words into sentences – reveals a great deal about human cognitive structure and capacity; by the same token, the words themselves, their denotations overlaid and underlaid by nuances and presuppositions and other chiaroscuro touches, tell us about our feelings and attitudes. Especially in a language like English, unusually richly endowed with vocabulary choices, the words we choose tell us more than almost anything else about how we feel toward what we are talking about.

We have already discussed some of our relevant linguistic habits, of course: proverb, cliché, and myth. But these are conscious and intentional structures, employed knowingly and purposefully by speakers. Now we want to turn to another aspect of language use: the words we employ without knowing their histories, or being consciously aware of their connotations and relationships with other words. And although we as speakers do not typically have this kind of information at our conscious disposal when we speak – or perhaps because we do not – to the observer it can provide evidence of our deepest and most pervasive attitudes toward a subject we have thus far found tantalizingly difficult to define and comprehend fully.

In the same way, language has a history that is both parallel to, and deeper than, the history of the deeds of its speakers. The forms we use today are a different language from what was spoken as 'English' one hundred, five hundred, or a thousand years ago, and more different still from progenitors of a thousand (Germanic) years ago, or three thousand (proto-Indo-European) years before that; yet we can trace a direct line of descent and notice similarities, aspects of communication scarcely changed over that epochal length of time. Most intriguing is the comparison between those aspects that have changed and those that have not, and the tracing of the history of the changes. We assume that if a form changes, there is a reason for it, and that, if one does not over a long period of time, there is a reason for that. And these histories, with their reasons, are again a window into our minds, telling us what ideas have particular importance for us, what we avoid, and what we will not or cannot speak of. So for the linguist, the study of language over time and at one time is as exciting as it is informative.

Words, like ideas, have histories. They are born, they mature and change, they die. Like people, they do all this in accordance with systematic rules. Some words, like some people, are orderly: they leave records of where they came from, and what they're doing – and when they go, they do so in a predictable way. We can trace their unbroken history, in other words, from proto-Indo-European to present-day English, observing some changes in form and function along the four-thousand-year way, but nothing surprising or inexplicable. Then there are others. They come into the world apparently without parentage, or at least with no clues to origin and no near relations (in their own or related languages) to give us clues about their origin. Their meanings, once they are established in a language, may change radically throughout their history, in ways that semantic principles do not allow us to account for. And they vanish abruptly, with no clues as to the reason for their passing, their functions taken over by other words, altogether different in form, and previously quite different in meaning.

The first are the solid citizens of the word world, the ones we can count on. They tend to be 'solid' in meaning as well: they represent concrete, everyday notions, ideas we are comfortable with, not esoteric or embarrassing, intellectual rather than emotional in connotation. The second are the flighty members of the family, words that are unstable and more than a little mysterious. Their meanings may be vague because they are principally emotional, and they may refer to ideas that are difficult to define clearly. They may be the black sheep of the linguistic family, referring to thoughts that are, quite literally, 'unspeakable,' unmentionable, and embarrassing – in which case we feel the continuing need to replace euphemism with euphemism, so that the meaning is expressed, over time, by constantly shifting forms. Or the word may be so strong in emotive content that its cognitive component may be lost, or easily shifted from one idea to another. All these work against stability in the linguistic world.[1]

Using lexical semantics – the way words are structured in terms of meanings, compared with others in the same general meaning-class – and historical principles, we can approach the problem of the human understanding of beauty in a new way. Let us try to trace some of the words that have been used for 'beauty' in the Indo-European language family, and more specifically, the histories of the words now current in English, to see what they tell us about how speakers think of beauty.

Our word *beauty* comes into English from French, where it has had (in the form *beauté*) the same meaning as the English form. In French, the noun *beauté* is clearly derived from a more basic adjective, *beau*, 'beautiful.' It is interesting that in English, the adjective must be derived from the noun with the addition of an adjective-forming ending, *-ful*. This is not true, in English, for most of the other words of this semantic class, in which the adjectival form is basic to the noun (cf. *pretty*: *prettiness*; *handsome*: *handsomeness*; *lovely*: *loveliness*). The French adjective, whose historically more basic form is seen in the feminine *belle*, is ultimately derived from the Latin *bellus*, with a meaning approximately that of English *pretty* (or French *joli*). The usual word for 'beautiful' in classical Latin, however, is *pulcher*.

There are a couple of interesting things about the historical situation. One is that there has been a replacement, between classical Latin and French, of one form meaning 'beauty' by another, etymologically unrelated. This sort of lexical discontinuity is far from uncommon in the history of languages, but when it occurs, we often discover that the switch was not merely random: something about the original word, whether its form or its meaning, encouraged the change. So, for instance, if in a language one word sounds too much like another, unrelated to it in meaning, a substitute is likely to be found for one or the other, sooner or later. Or, a meaning might be represented by a series of quickly changing forms because it referred to something we typically avoid confronting directly, and resort to euphemism. Then the original word vanishes, with the euphemism taking its place. After that the original euphemism, now the basic word, requires substitution by a new euphemism, and so on. Words for 'bathroom' in English have undergone this process many times. But *pulcher* does not resemble other Latin words, nor is 'beauty' an idea we seek to avoid talking about openly.

The mystery is deepened when we discover that *pulcher* itself is a word without history or family. There are no words in Latin, or any other Indo-European language, etymologically related to it, nor can we give it an etymology. The standard Latin etymological dictionary, under its entry, comments: 'Adjectives meaning "beautiful, pretty" differ from one language to another'[2] – in other words, display semantic inconsistency. That is, generally in the Indo-European language family, a more or less basic meaning (and we might argue that 'beautiful' is a basic and essential concept) tends to be assigned the same form from language to language. But if we look over the languages in this group, there is no etymological sharing of forms meaning 'beauty.' Aside from the types of situations we have already mentioned as favoring etymological instability, another is meaning that is emotive, rather than objective or intellectual, in character. Words whose main, or major, sense lies in the emotional realm, because that sphere seems to us indefinable and shifting, relative to concepts that are concrete or objectified, tend to have a patchwork sort of history, and the words for beauty certainly seem to behave this way. Here is a clue, helping us understand some of our earlier difficulty in defining beauty: we were looking in the concrete and objective spheres, because consciously and intellectually we want to believe that beauty is an objectively observable phenomenon. But if beauty is indeed subjective, located in the emotive faculties of the observer, definition would be harder to agree upon, and the etymological history of the concept would be in accordance with our expectations.

Not only does Latin *pulcher* lack family connections, it is short-lived as words go. Even in the Classical period its semantic domain is being competed for by another word, *bellus*. *Bellus*, as we said, means 'pretty' in Classical Latin, and is used mostly of women, and ironically of men. Etymologically this word, too, is interesting. The form is historically opaque (that is, native speakers of Latin would not have recognized its origin from its contemporaneous form), but it is in fact a diminutive of the word for 'good,' *bonus*, itself derived from a form like *\*dwen-us*, with *bellus* coming from its diminutive, *\*dwen-olus*, which would ordinarily mean something like 'dear and good,' or perhaps 'rather good.' It is odd that a word meaning 'pretty' should be derived in this way from the moral-utilitarian, rather than the visible-aesthetic, sphere. The etymological dictionary comments on the semantic history of the word, 'because of its emotive character, *bellus* tends, in the popular language (which, rather than Classical Latin, is the immediate progenitor of the Romance languages), to replace *pulcher*, which it has supplanted, in the Romance languages, along with *formosus*.'[3] *Formosus*, which becomes the Spanish *hermoso*, the ordinary word for 'beautiful,' originally had a purely visual-physical meaning, derived from *forma*, 'shape, form.' *Formosus* in Classical Latin means 'stately, shapely, elegant.' Thus, Romance seemingly divides the semantic area occupied by *pulcher* in two: the emotive part of it is taken by *bellus*, in Classical Latin a word having largely to do with emotional response; and *formosus*, which covers the physical and objective territory. It is as if *pulcher* were trying to do too many things at once, and had to have its sphere of influence divided. By modern French and Spanish, of course, *beau* and *hermoso* have come to occupy the territory formerly held by *pulcher*, and those languages have in turn developed words that take over the space previously occupied by *bellus* and *formosus*. Interestingly, Spanish has, alongside of *hermoso*, from *formosus*, both *bello* and *bonito*. *Bello* is defined as essentially equivalent to *hermoso*, but tending to occur in exclamatory utterances: *Qué bella mujer*, 'What a beautiful woman,' but this is hardly an inflexible rule. It is worth noticing in this context that *bello* tends to precede the noun it modifies, *hermoso* to follow. As a general principle in Spanish, adjectives that precede tend to have emotive significance, those that follow, more objective. (For instance, some adjectives may either precede or follow, with somewhat different meanings in each case. When it precedes, the adjective has more of a metaphorical, subjective force. *El pobre hombre*, 'the unfortunate man,' and *el hombre pobre*, 'the poor [economically destitute] man.') Thus Spanish has retained some of the original emotive force of *bellus*, in contrast with the more purely objective *hermoso*: *formosus*. There seems to be some evidence, moreover, that *bello* is encroaching more and more on the territory of *hermoso*, working its way up from the less to the more frequent word for 'beautiful' in contemporary Spanish. At the same time, coming into Spanish to occupy the territory vacated by the original *bellus*, 'pretty,' was a new word, *bonito*. And, very interestingly – since the etymology of *bello* is surely as opaque to today's speaker of Spanish as *bellus* was to a Roman of the Classical period – the word is derived etymologically in precisely the same way: *bonito* is a diminutive of *bueno*, 'good,' itself of course originally the Latin *bonus* which gave rise to *bellus* long ago. The connection between goodness and beauty seems still to exist for us at some level, recalling the Greek καλοκἀγαθός, another way of achieving the same combination of ideas. In this context, we might note in passing that the Greek καλός, 'beautiful'[4] is as innocent of etymology and familial relationships as is *pulcher*; and further, that commonly in the Indo-European languages roots with an *a* vowel signify heavily emotional concepts. As much as we may think the Greeks intellectualized beauty in their philosophical discourse, the etymological evidence suggests that for them, at least originally, the word was as laden with affective content as its semantic equivalents are in other languages.

The repetition – in Greek, Latin, Spanish – of the subliminal link between beauty and goodness may puzzle us, as speakers of English whose lexicon contains no such hint at any accessible level. Can it be that speakers of languages that do draw this connection as a result, or as a cause, experience beauty in a slightly different way? A famous postulate of psycholinguistics, the Sapir-Whorf hypothesis, difficult to prove in any empirical way, yet powerful at an intuitive level, has something to tell us here. Benjamin Lee Whorf, in the 1920s, articulated the proposition that the form, and forms, of a language influence the speaker's mind. Thus, since a language like Hopi (for example) is different in many significant aspects from English, a Hopi speaker will organize the universe otherwise than a speaker of English. But one could also argue, of course, that a pre-existing mental framework influences the shape language takes: that speakers, based on their own psychological structures, create their language accordingly. Moreover, neither proposition is absolute, nor is it entirely clear what kinds of relationships between mind and language might actually exist, which must exist, and which are never encountered. Whorf's hypothesis, as given later shape by another anthropological linguist, Edward Sapir, is more an intriguing suggestion than an empirically validable theory. But it can direct our thoughts along profitable paths.

Thus, several languages, as we have seen, equate beauty and goodness at some psychologically relevant level, though probably not in a way immediately accessible to the ordinary speaker. Some languages (in fact, all those that we have been talking about) equate male and female beauty by using the same word for both, while English normally forces us to select one (*beautiful*) for women, and another for men (*handsome*).

What are we to learn from these choices? It is tempting to speculate (and speculation is all, obviously, that we can do) that speakers of languages which express the concept of 'beauty' differently see it differently, and that a language which – however opaquely to its speakers – equates physical and moral attractiveness has a different slant on the issue of beauty than one that doesn't. Perhaps, too, if Whorf and Sapir were right, the speakers of such a language have more or less differently constituted conceptual systems in their minds than others have. And these languages are to be contrasted with English, where none of the words in common use for good looks is related to moral virtue. (As we shall see, words with physical attractiveness as their denotation can be allusively pressed into service to describe moral values, but this is a different kind of linguistic development.)

We might also dwell, in the same speculative mode, on differences in the subliminal perception of the role of the sexes in cultures where male and female attractiveness are normally covered by the same word, and in those like ours where they are not. Does a language like ours, forcing us as it does from early childhood to differentiate verbally between men and women in this semantic area, also force our thoughts into unnecessary dichotomization elsewhere? Do speakers of a language in which one word applies to both sexes perceive men and women more readily as a unified group, less polarized, even to this small extent? By forcing speakers to learn early that one word describes attractiveness in women, another in men, does our language inculcate sexual stereotyping, insisting explicitly in this way that good looks in a man are altogether unlike, totally unrelated to, good looks in a woman? Perhaps it is too strong an argument to make, resting cultural behavior as deep as this on the choice of a single word, where other adjectives in our language (say, *tall, intelligent, rich*) cross the gender barrier with no difficulty. And yet ... it must make a difference that we assign one set of semantic characteristics to 'beautiful,' and very different ones to 'handsome.' For we typically think that the existence of a word for a thing legitimizes that thing, or makes it an actuality. Advertisers and propagandists are well aware of this tendency on our part – quite illogical, we need hardly point out, since the human mind can easily both conceptualize and lexicalize unicorns and other non-existent creations – and know that if they can only set in our minds a catchword or phrase ('Lebensraum,' 'blood, toil, tears, and sweat,' 'white supremacy'), they have a good chance of convincing us that the idea behind it is valid, in fact, unquestionable because there is a word for it. Then in the same way, the fact that in our language we have two words with clearly differentiated connotations puts in our mind, subliminally or otherwise, the notion that polarization of sex roles is valid, makes sense, has always been, and is right and normal. Perhaps a language that does not make such distinctions does not legitimize these habits in the same way. Or perhaps it is the other way around: people who don't make so sharp a distinction between the attributes signifying attractiveness in males and those in females are less likely to enshrine formally in their language that particular distinction. We cannot say which way the logic works, and probably it works both ways, the mind feeding on the language, the language depending on the direction given it by the mind. But as long as the difference is there, and the choice is ours to make, we will feel both authorized and enjoined to make it.

But 'beautiful' and 'handsome' are not our only choices for describing personal beauty. The English language, for historical reasons, is unusually rich in synonyms (perhaps the reason why we, almost uniquely, have separate words for male and female attractiveness). We have, in fact, virtually a continuum of choices, covering a large and subtle semantic sphere. And while meanings may overlap, each is unique in some way. *Roget's Thesaurus* gives us some idea of the riches we have to work with, organizing the relevant ideas into three broad categories:

beautiful, beauteous, endowed with beauty; pretty, handsome, attractive, pulchritudinous, lovely, graceful, elegant, fine, exquisite, flowerlike; aesthetic, eye-filling, easy on the eyes, good for sore eyes, not hard to look at, long on looks, looking fit to kill, pretty as a speckled pup (all slang); pretty as a picture, 'lovely as the day' (Longfellow), 'fair as is the rose in May' (Chaucer); tall, dark, and handsome.

comely, fair, good-looking, well-favored, personable, presentable, agreeable, becoming, pleasing, goodly, bonny, likely (chiefly dial.), sightly, braw (Scot.); pleasing to the eye, lovely to behold; shapely.

gorgeous, ravishing, raving, devastating, stunning, killing (all slang); glorious, heavenly, divine, sublime; resplendent, splendorous, splendrous, splendid, resplendently beautiful; brilliant, bright, radiant, shining, beaming, glowing, blooming, sparkling, dazzling.[5]

This is almost too rich for the blood. Where do we begin? We notice, first of all, some interesting things about the items listed. A great many of them come from odd places in the vocabulary – slang, borrowings from poets, dialectal words, frozen expressions, whether poetic or merely stilted (e.g., *beauteous* vs *pulchritudinous*, neither of which most of us have occasion to use more than once or twice a lifetime.) Only a few items on these long lists belong to our daily linguistic life. This too is typical of a semantic area the force of which is largely emotional: it will constantly seek to augment its lexicon with 'fresh' words, still emotionally charged, to replace those whose expressive connotations are dwindling away, and it will borrow from slang and dialect – which are like an ocean breeze to the stagnant air of the standard language – and poetry, where we find our emotion ready-made.

The division into three categories seems intuitive, though it is harder to define precisely what each of these categories covers. The first is the most general and, in a sense, the semantically central category, involving both emotional and physical judgment, the subjective and objective together. On the other hand, it also contains some highly specialized words for very particular impressions: *exquisite*, *flowerlike*. It covers both personal and other forms of beauty, or at least some of its members do.

The second set covers the more intellectual, objective senses of beauty, the reasoned judgment, not swayed by over-whelming passion. Interestingly, very few of these words are in current standard use. They are mostly either poetic (*fair*), obsolescent (*comely*), or dialectal (*bonny* – which, we might notice in passing, probably has the same etymological history as *bellus* and *bonito*, but has not survived in standard English). Those words in this category which are in the vocabulary of standard English seem not to make principal reference to looks, but rather to demeanor or general impression, based in part on looks, but looks of an unprepossessing, non-threatening, and not exciting sort: *agreeable*, *personable*, *presentable*. If asked to describe someone in terms of looks, it is extremely unlikely that we would spontaneously select one of the words in this list as our primary choice.

The third set is the complement of the second, containing as it does those words that are principally emotional and subjective, and none really evaluative-objective at all. If, asked our impression of someone's looks, we respond with one of these, what we have expressed is our emotional response, and aside from that given very little other information – not some-thing one could use for purposes of identification. The words, all generally metaphorical, cut across two categories: the homicidal and the religious, perhaps because religion and death are two truly transcendent experiences, death and reli-gious ecstasy being, at opposite poles, favorite poetic meta-phors for the act of sexual consummation and, generally, uncontrollable emotion. The rest of the group suggests a visual experience so extraordinary as to be physically painful: brilliant, dazzling, radiant.

What is interesting about the three sets is the rapidity with which lexical items in all flit among various levels of usage – from slang to ordinary language to formal to poetic, and back. The situation in English is like that of the older Indo-European languages: this class is not semantically stable. We have to keep reaching into the cache of dialectal, slang, learned and poetic words as we deplete our supply of items with this meaning in ordinary language: they become 'obsolete,' and others must be found to take their place. They fall out of use as their emotional impact is exhausted – a more serious hazard for words whose primary content is emotional than for others. To have a strong emotional impact, a word must strike its users as fresh, startling and new – more or less spontaneously created. So emotional-meaning words lose their effectiveness as soon as they lose their freshness, and thus lose their place in the vocabulary, in favor of new words brought in from places that strike users as lively, exciting, emotionally stimulating. These are, principally, the areas of slang (which, like poetry, has a heavy metaphorical component and generally stresses the emotive aspect of communication); dialect (which seems to users of the standard language to be uncluttered by white-collar intellectualization and formal coolness); and poetry, whose language is specially created to be emotionally evocative and richly allusive. Metaphor, of course, jogs our emotions – in poetry, slang, and other special linguistic types – by equating more or less ordinary experience with the transcendent and highly charged. Our repeated borrowing from this level to create, again and again, 'ordinary' words to cover the extraordinary concept of beauty none the less is doomed to fail in the long run as the metaphors, as re-used metaphors will, become frozen and no longer evocative. On the lexical level, then, we continually recreate our mythology: beauty is too hot to handle, the line between supreme pleasure and ultimate pain very thin. Perhaps (as some of the items on the list – raving, ravishing, killing – suggest) we blame the possessor of beauty for the pain her (or its) very image could conceivably cause. It is worth noting that our few words for male good looks do not carry this connotation. *Handsome* is down-to-

earth: its etymological roots go back to words meaning 'useful.'
And of course, the stunning emotional impact of someone or
something extraordinarily beautiful *is* shocking, *does* cause
the beholder spiritual unrest. Is it merely that second of
emotional unbalance that these metaphorical terms describe?
That momentary shock of impact seems, finally, to be the
important part of the meaning of 'beauty' to us, necessarily
encoded in our word. Once the powerful impact of the word is
lost, once its use does not suggest, any longer, the involuntary
wincing, the sudden intake of breath, it has exhausted its
usefulness to us. We cast it out and look for a replacement.

We find, then, that the history of words for beauty in English
is a repetition of the situation that pertained from proto-Indo-
European to the Classical languages to modern Romance: the
words are unstable because they cover primarily emotional
territory, and therefore, the language or its users, to retain
the meaning of these words, must continually reinvent ways
to create an emotional jolt in speakers and hearers.

If we look at a few of the words we use whose meaning is
closely related to 'beautiful,' we find their histories and
patterns of current use illuminating. We have mentioned
'handsome' and 'pretty' as members of this set. Both of these
words have semantic histories quite startlingly different from
*beautiful*.

*Handsome* is etymologically transparent: the *hand* that is
its first part is our English word 'hand'; *-some* is the suffix
found in many words: *toothsome, winsome, troublesome, tire-
some*. That suffix started out with a meaning something like,
'fit for, appropriate to.' Thus, what is handsome was originally
something fit for the hand, that is, easy to handle, or convenient, or useful. (Hence the proverb, 'Handsome is as handsome
does.') *Handsome*, then, is first introduced into the language
as a word applicable to behavior or action, and only secondarily
does it make reference to appearance appropriate to 'useful'
behavior.[6]

*Pretty* has a different history. Its origin, through an Old
English word, *praettig*, is ultimately in the noun, *praett*: 'trick,
wile, craft.' As this source suggests, the original meaning of
*pretty* is 'cunning,' 'clever,' which then becomes 'nice,' and
finally turns into our current sense, given by the *Oxford*

*English Dictionary* as 'having beauty without majesty or state-liness; beautiful in a slight, dainty or diminutive way, as opposed to *handsome*. Of persons (usually women or children): of attractive and pleasing countenance or appearance; comely, bonny.'[7] Here, as with *beautiful*, the principal focus seems to be the effect on the viewer, but the effect seems one derived through calculation, through the observer's physical perception or the observed one's knowing how to present him/herself to best advantage, rather than being naturally and passively endowed. Since prettiness is thus by implication artificial rather than mysteriously given by nature, it is without the emotional force of *beautiful*. And since its effect is primarily through physical means, *pretty* is largely descriptive of manageable physical impression, probably impermanent. Prettiness, as the definition suggests, is a property of the small and delicate – the very antithesis of handsomeness.

In our interviews, when we asked respondents to differentiate among these words, we got general agreement that prettiness involved purely physical (as opposed to spiritual or active) attributes, and physical charm that correlated with smallness or youth. *Handsome*, of a woman, was much less a part of people's active vocabulary, but it could be used of someone with dignity and strength as evinced by her physical appearance. Thus, *handsome*, of women, suggested something worked for, the result of activity and good experience; *pretty*, the antithesis, the absence of any sign of wear, passive physical attractiveness. *Beautiful*, predictably, was the most troublesome. People were not sure just where to apply it, as might be predicted from its emotional, rather than intellectual basis – we were, of course, providing intellectual-evaluative determinants. People generally felt that younger women would most appropriately be described as 'pretty,' much less as 'handsome,' and that for younger women, the latter would be no compliment. But for older women, 'handsome' could be complimentary, 'pretty' much less, suggesting an unpleasant passivity and failure to grow. But it remains true that to say to a woman, of any age, 'Gosh, you're pretty,' is apt to be interpreted with pleasure as a compliment; but telling a woman of any age that she is 'handsome' is a much riskier proposition.

Generally, too, people felt comfortable referring to men as 'handsome,' and associated this with strength, whether exemplified by muscles or firmness of facial features. To refer to a male beyond childhood as 'pretty' was never complimentary, and always carried a connotation of effeminacy. 'Beautiful' was, as usual, more problematic. Many of our respondents said they would call men 'beautiful,' but it did not appear that their doing so referred to a different sort of physical configuration than would be implied by 'handsome'; rather, of a male, 'beautiful' seemed to be used to mean 'handsome,' with added emotional emphasis on the part of the speaker (not unlike *gorgeous*, when used of men).

Moreover, when we speak of 'handsome' women and 'beautiful' men, we are making an additional statement that goes beyond and behind assessment of physical attractiveness. We are saying that the person so described is crossing over gender lines, and as such, the use of these words carries an aura of daring, of not-quite-appropriateness. A macho man, a he-man, is not 'beautiful,' and even less would we describe a Marilyn Monroe type as 'handsome.'

Other words in this semantic area take other portions of the field for their own. *Gorgeous* and *lovely* (the latter usable only of women, even more, perhaps, than *pretty*) stress the emotional impact and assert it, presupposing the physical configuration. (*Beautiful*, on the other hand, seems to do the reverse. That is, if we say, 'She's gorgeous,' we mean something like, 'It's given, or assumed, that she is physically attractive, and what I want to communicate now is the strong emotional effect seeing her has on me.' With *beautiful*, we are suggesting rather, 'I'm communicating to you that she's physically attractive – oh, and it certainly affects me powerfully, by the way!' These are abysmally rough paraphrases, but perhaps they give the idea.) *Pretty* and *handsome*, on the other hand, circumvent the 'emotional' aspect almost totally. *Attractive* goes even beyond *handsome* and *pretty* in this respect: it is purely intellectual-evaluative. It usually refers to pure physical appearance, sometimes to features of personality, without reference to looks – or refers obliquely to looks on the grounds that they reflect the character.

Finally, we have words like 'sexy' and 'charming,' at the

periphery of this category. Our respondents generally agreed that one could be sexy, or charming, without being physically beautiful, or even pretty/handsome. (But any of these attributes would make someone 'attractive.') We generally know, even if we do not always agree, from time to time or person to person, what 'sexiness' entails, a combination of appearance and actions. But 'charm' is more elusive. The very word hints at the mystery of the concept: charm, as in 'magic charm,' something that affects us against our will, without our conscious volition. *Charm* in this sense is related to two other words, *glamour* and *fascination*. *Glamour* is derived from *grammar*, in the sense of special knowledge, hocus-pocus, charm, or incantation. *Fascination* is derived from the Latin *fascinum*, a charm or amulet (incidentally or not, often in the shape of a phallus). All these words, then, hint at the mysterious transformation in the mind of the observer that occurs when an object with these qualities presents itself. We do not understand, we are not in control, but we don't really mind.

We find then, three major components to the definition of items within this semantic area: (1) the objective physical reality itself; (2) the subjective emotional impact on the observer; (3) the actions or behavior displayed by the object. And the various members of this class arrange themselves at various points around a triangle, which we might visualize thus:

**behavior**

| glamorous | sexy |
|---|---|
| charming | handsome |

**effect**                                      **appearance**

| beautiful | pretty |
|---|---|

But we have been speaking as if all these words were solely applicable to visual sensations, or the emotions aroused by them. Yet we know that most of the words in this category can, under more or less well-defined conditions, be used for other pleasant sensations as well. What is less clear is which can be used where; and whether these additional uses are, in some sense, direct, as legitimate, as it were, as the visual uses, or whether they are used metaphorically and thus indirectly, with the user likening these other sensations and evaluations to those that are based on eyesight, but only by allusion. What exactly is the relation among pleasurable effects upon the senses and the judgment? We can set up a chart, indicating how the words we have looked at can be used in any of a range of transferred meanings.

|           | sound | taste | smell | touch | intelligence | morality |
|-----------|-------|-------|-------|-------|--------------|----------|
| beautiful | x     | x     | x     | x     | x            | x        |
| pretty    | x     | –     | (x)   | ?     | x            | –        |
| handsome  | –     | –     | –     | –     | –            | x        |
| gorgeous  | x     | (x)   | (x)   | (x)   | ?            | –        |
| charming  | (x)   | –     | –     | –     | –            | –        |
| lovely    | x     | x     | x     | x     | (x)          | x        |

On the chart, an entry of x means that we can use the word in this way; (x) means that it is conceivable that the word might be used this way, or that it is occasionally encountered, but not idiomatic or normal; ? indicates that it isn't clear whether it can be used this way; and –, in the writers' opinion, that it cannot be used in this way.

Thus, for instance, with *beautiful*, which can be used for all of these, we might find, under the appropriate circumstances, people saying any of the following and the utterance being understood as normal – not, for instance, technical or ironic or poetic – English:

She played the Chopin piece beautifully.
That is a beautiful soufflé.
You smell beautiful tonight.
Silk feels more beautiful than cotton.
Dr Snurch made a beautiful argument in favor of his thesis.
When Mary gave her last dime to the beggar, it was a beautiful act.

By contrast, the other words in the set are more restricted. Thus, while we might say, for instance, 'The Chopin prelude is a pretty piece,' we would be less likely to use *pretty* for moral concepts. (An asterisk here signifies the impossibility of saying the sentence it precedes.) For example: *'Giving up your seat to the old man was pretty.' And *handsome* is even more restricted. So while we might say, 'You smell pretty tonight,' we would be unlikely to say, even to a man wearing a fashionable cologne, *'You smell handsome tonight,' but would use *beautiful*, instead. On the other hand, *handsome* can be used of moral judgment: 'Allowing his graduate student to take credit for the work she had done was a handsome gesture on Professor Nurff's part.' But not intellectually: *'Among the handsomest proofs of relativity theory was the Michelson-Morley experiment.'

*Beautiful* covers more semantic territory than any of the other words in this group. The reason seems to be that since the sense of this word is primarily emotional, that emotion is most readily transferred to other meanings. But at the same time, since it has an intellectual-evaluative component, it can be applied to concepts normally judged on this basis. With the other words in this set, either because they are principally evaluative and primarily definitive of the visual experience, they cannot readily be transferred to other kinds of experience (like *handsome*); or, because they are so strongly subjective, cannot be used for situations involving intellectual judgment without seeming frivolous (like *lovely*).

It is not clear how to evaluate these uses of the words. Are they just extra definitions – meanings automatically and directly transferred from one sense to the other – or are we dealing with evocative, allusive language, that is, metaphors? If they are metaphors, they are frozen: as contemporary speakers, we do not have the sense, in using these words outside the visual sphere, of actively likening the other senses to seeing. If we were to say, for example, 'I was blinded by the radiance of the music,' we might argue for active metaphorical extension, but when we merely say that it was lovely, we seem to be doing something rather less powerful with language, merely suggesting that sensory experiences have something in common.

In any event, we see that words are, in themselves, historical records and psychological clues. They reflect changes in attitude over time, as well as our own current assumptions. While words are in one way 'just words,' they can tell us things that other analytic tools leave unexamined. And by looking at the history of words having to do with beauty, we can understand why the concept is so baffling, and rich, and evocative.

Part 3
# The Politics of Beauty

# Chapter 8
# **Men and Beauty**

Narcissus was a youth whose beauty seemed, to him, more trouble than it was worth. What he really liked was pursuing the pleasures of the hunt with his male friends, throwing the javelin, engaging in all the other activities that a young man in ancient Greece enjoyed. But he was continually bedeviled by unwanted female attention: because of his looks, women flung themselves at him. It was all he could do to keep them at arm's length. Some of them felt he was selfishly trying to keep a good thing to himself.

Echo was a nymph with a past. As a member of Hera's entourage, she was expected to be loyal. One of Hera's most frequent activities was keeping tabs on her husband, Zeus', liaisons with nymphs, other goddesses, mortal women – anything female. Hera couldn't do too much about his predilection – he was, after all, king of the gods – except get in his way as much as she could, and nag him about it afterward. For obvious reasons, then, Zeus preferred not to be caught by Hera in his fun and games.

Though Echo owed her loyalty to Hera, when she came upon Zeus indulging in his favorite pastime, knowing Hera was not far behind, she warned Zeus of his wife's proximity, saving him from the usual tongue-lashing. But Hera knew that she had been thwarted (as dalliance was Zeus' favorite hobby, nagging was Hera's), and by whom. As punishment for taking an unwarranted initiative in speaking, Echo was condemned to the opposite fate: to speak only when spoken to, only in words previously supplied by her addressee. She could echo; she could no longer initiate.

One day Narcissus, hunting in the forest, got separated from his comrades. In a lonely glade he sensed another presence. 'Who's here?' he asked. 'Here,' came the reply. 'Come,' he said. 'Come,' replied the female voice. Curious rather than desirous, the youth called, 'Come join me.' 'Join me,' said the voice, and out of the shadows the nymph Echo darted in response to Narcissus' invitation. How she wanted to offer herself to him! But she could not, unless he supplied the means. All she could do, words being impossible, was to throw herself at him, embrace him passionately. 'Take your hands off me,' he cried in disgust. 'I would rather die than let myself be yours.' 'Let myself be yours,' the nymph sighed, eagerly if ungrammatically. But Narcissus, by now thoroughly repulsed, tore himself free and ran off without a kind word – his usual way with the ladies. Poor Echo, heartbroken at the rejection, pined away and died, leaving only her voice to sound back at us from caves and mountain peaks.

But Narcissus' coldness – to Echo and every other woman he encountered – did not go unremarked by the powers on Olympus, who felt that something, finally, had to be done: the youth was setting a bad example. One day, again separated from his companions in the hunt, Narcissus stopped by a limpid pool. He stooped down to drink and, in so doing, caught a glimpse of his own fair form. Never, he thought, had he seen anything so irresistible. Forgetting his thirst, he reached down into the waters to embrace the object of his desire, but, fickle youth, it retreated from his arms. He leaned down to press his lips upon the smooth face, but the face, too, eluded his touch, dissolving in the roiled waters. Was he – who had hunted down so many a deer, hurled the javelin further than any of his companions – to be unsuccessful here? He determined to wait, to pursue until he found success. He grew haggard with hunger and sleeplessness; finally, in time, he pined away in unrequited love. Taking pity on him in death, the gods changed him into a flower as beautiful as he, nodding gracefully by the pool, casting its reflection ceaselessly into the still waters. The flower, as if to remind us of the tragedy, bears his name – Narcissus.

For all their charm, Greek myths are intended by their creators for a sterner purpose than mere aesthetic delight. They are cautionary tales, instructions to the young about proper behavior and the dangers of transgression. We have seen how Echo was punished for disloyalty and taking undue liberties: in Greek myth, the punishment always, however ironically, fits the crime. And Narcissus' story, too, was intended to tell the reader something about how to lead his life – proper deportment for the Greek youth. And since the story continues to exert its power today, although we no longer consider it a part of religious upbringing, as it was for the Greeks, we may conclude that the message still has meaning for us: what Narcissus needed to learn is something we are even now apt to overlook.

Echo, who sins through her voice, becomes – just a voice. Narcissus becomes a beautiful but quintessentially passive thing – a flower. A flower is the symbolic embodiment of all that is both useless and lovely – all the more lovely for uselessness. A flower does not hunt, nor throw the javelin: it waits to be plucked, its highest purpose is being appreciated. But in fact we cannot speak reasonably of a flower's 'purpose.' As an inanimate object, it cannot have one. Its function is purely in the eye of its beholder.

The stories of Echo and Narcissus are inextricably intertwined. One makes no sense without the other. And in a very real sense they are complementary. Echo suffers because, a woman, she has taken the active, initiatory role, made things happen. This was not the role appropriate to the young Greek woman, the story warns. And Narcissus? He, so the story suggests, despite his aggressive 'macho' or hypermasculine stance, is none the less not behaving appropriately for a man. He is showing only one side of a manly self. As a punishment – or a message – the gods make him show the other side with equal vengeance. In effect, he is turned into that which he, inappropriately, despises beyond everything. Narcissus is turned into a woman. His final transformation into a flower is only the symbolic epitomization of this. If you are not enough of a man, the story says, you might as well be a woman: you are – presto – a woman, or even worse.

This reading of the myth strikes the reader, perhaps, as a bit perverse, or at least hard to understand. To the modern sensibility, Narcissus is indeed all man, the stereotypical he-man; the sheriff in the western who lives to shoot bad guys, says little but 'yup' and 'nope,' and don't have no truck with women. Women, in the American myth, corrupt men, emasculate them. The true male truly enjoys only the company of other men, or his own, solitarily, like Narcissus in the glade.

And it would be misleading to deny that this myth of masculinity was attractive to the Greeks. Certainly many men must have believed in living like Narcissus, or the myth, as cautionary tale, would not have had to be invented. We know, too, from literature, of the position of women throughout most of Greece during most of its history: women were distinctly second-class citizens, denied the chance to become full human beings through education or experience in the world, then despised for their silliness. But, of course, a culture whose males prefer to have nothing to do with women is a culture headed for extinction. So the Greeks, realizing the problem, create the myth as antidote.

And yet, 2500 years later, the stereotype exemplified by Narcissus is instantly recognizable, and the cautionary tales still have force. Our explicit myth is: get too close to women, you become like a woman – useless, inert, waiting only to be plucked. But at the same time we warn ourselves, as the Greeks had to warn themselves: nothing – not even manliness, whatever that might be – in excess. Manliness in excess is death. The culture wastes away, does not produce or act, becomes effeminate – through excess of stereotypical masculinity. The Greeks, noted for their espousal of the Golden Mean – 'nothing in excess' – realized this perhaps more fully and poignantly than we do.

Since the time of Narcissus, our mythology and all our arts derived from it swing back and forth on an uneasy pendulum: either men and women grow dangerously close, or dangerously apart. We have our cult of 'real men,' just as the Greeks did, and yet they tend in our minds to become pathetic caricatures of themselves, one-sided, self-preoccupied. Narcissistic in a way that is permissible for women, but not for men, certainly not for he-men.

Female beauty, like the beauty of the flower, waits to be plucked. A real man plucks, and leaves. A man is out in the real world, having adventures, while a real woman waits at home. A man who gets sucked into female ways will pine and die, will be no true man, in fact, nothing. Again, our myths illuminate the facets of this stereotype. Here – starting with the Greeks again – is Odysseus, dangerously close to losing all he has struggled for by listening to the sirens' song, or by bedding down too long with Circe. That alluring danger is continually to be repulsed. Samson, another real man, a muscleman, is done in by devotion to Delilah. The real man knows how to use women but not be used. Aeneas, the Trojan refugee, uses Dido's hospitality to refresh himself and his crew after seven years of wandering; but, when the time comes for the man to go forth to recapture his destiny, he is ready to go with scarcely a pang, knowing he is leaving the woman who loves him and has sacrificed life and reputation for him to certain death. To do otherwise would be shameful. Aeneas, given the assumptions of his – and our – culture, can do nothing else. A man is most attractive when he is doing something; a woman, when doing nothing. Dido and Aeneas came perilously close to reversing roles. He got out in time; she paid the price.

Since men are attractive by activity, in one sense looks don't count for them as they do for women. Narcissus gets into trouble through being too close to feminine standards of beauty, he is pursued by women because of how he looks. Perhaps (a Freudian interpreter might suggest, if mythic heroes could take time out for psychoanalysis) Narcissus' avoidance of women is ultimately born of terror that, in fact, he is too much like them. He overcompensates, the time-honored device of the anxious. He will do, and do, and do, kill and kill and kill, throw and throw and throw . . . then he will be all man. He must avoid all taint of woman if this is to succeed. But the gods ferret out the insecure root of the overcompensatory behaviour, and make of him what in fact he has always been. Woman, the looked-at, the object, not the subject. The supreme narcissist.

So a man can feel respectably manly only in case he feels that he is desirable because of what he does (or has done) rather than how he looks. It doesn't hurt, of course, to be good-looking, but a man can't be seen working at that. For a man, beauty is suspicious. Good looks have always involved a kind of cragginess, a sense of scars won in battle, rather than prettiness through mere genetic caprice. And yet, at the same time, male good looks – whatever is supposed to create them – are clearly represented in literature and art, and represented as extremely important. While for women the conflict is between nature and artifice, in men, it is between seeming to care, and seeming not to care, but the conflict exists none the less. For men, *beauty* is a problematic word, and there is nothing that really replaces it.

It is a problem for men in several ways, which we want to examine in detail in the rest of this chapter. First, we have alluded to men's ambivalence about their response to their own looks: can they be comfortable with 'handsomeness' – let alone care enough to take pains? If beauty in women resides all over the body from head to toe, where do men locate their 'beauty,' if we can even use that word? In what ways is the symbolization of beauty different for men and women, and what consequences does this have? We acknowledge, then, a different mythology for male and female attractiveness. How do men visualize themselves when they are concerned with their looks?

Then, according to men, what *is* a good-looking man? Is he different in every way from his female counterpart? Are some attributes 'feminine,' others intrinsically 'masculine'? Aside from the symbolic aspects that we have talked about already, what in a man strikes a man as attractive – how does he wish he looked, of what is he consciously proudest? Are the standards for men as severe as those for women? We are speaking here largely of straight men, and assuming that – contrary to the myth – they care, whether they wish to establish that publicly or not.

Next, we have suggested already that men are and stereotypically are supposed to be the consumers of beauty in others, rather than the objects themselves. And that consumption is facilitated by polarization: men find it easier, it would seem, to fantasize about female beauty that is as unlike male looks as possible. This is the myth, but how close is it to reality? What can men tell us about what they want in a woman . . . and is there a difference between what they want, what they say they want, and what they think they want? All these are the facets of male concern about looks. Traditionally, men shy away from confronting these questions. But what can they tell us about themselves, and about human perception of beauty in general?

The Greeks had a clear and unambivalent appreciation of

youthful manhood. Their very statues speak poetically of that ideal. The expressive faces – more sensuous even than in their female counterparts; the heads of curly hair; the muscular torso, poised to throw the javelin; and the legs prepared to run at full speed – all these combine activity and passivity in one: the Greek ideal. A Hermes or an Apollo could match any Aphrodite in sheer beauty. While male and female statuary, for the Greeks, seem parallel in their conventions to an extent somewhat surprising to us with our clearly differentiated masculine and feminine stereotypes, in one respect there was a difference. Female statues were decorously veiled; folds of garments swathed them from breast to thigh, or even to the ankle. But male statues stood naked in all their glory. Not for nothing did the Romans refer to the female genitalia as *pudenda*, 'those things it is right to be ashamed of,' while the analogous male parts were revealed for all to admire. A glimpse at the statues indicates clearly that the Greeks idealized male beauty, as the Renaissance did later. And yet, despite these models, through most of Western history it has been deemed inappropriate for men to dwell on their looks as women could take pains on theirs.

And we speak differently about men's and women's looks. Not surprisingly, language gives us an abundance of ways to speak of feminine beauty, each possible aspect covered in loving detail. But we have a much poorer vocabulary – and, we might note, many fewer opportunities in ordinary non-poetic discourse where we can appropriately utilize it – to talk about men's looks. On the other hand, while for women the language has devised ways of taking them apart, seeing them piece by piece, organ by organ as it were, not really as a composite whole, with men we do not have the words to idealize the parts, at least not in contemporary English. But the situation is reversed with one part. While women have very few words for their genitals, as often as not referring to them by indirection and euphemism – 'down there,' 'that thing,' men lavish an abundance of names redolent of affection and tenderness on theirs. Directly (as in D. H. Lawrence) or symbolically (as in practically everybody else), the male organ is at the center of our descriptions of men: the sword that cuts, the knife that penetrates, the musical instrument that beckons ladies' fingers to pluck and causes them to tremble. It is as if women's general physical beauty is a substitute for the beauty of that one male member – or, *pace* Freud, vice versa. In any case, the lack of words in one is for both sexes made up amply by the plethora for the other. It is almost as if, for men, to name or to detail the different parts or the different ways of seeing masculine beauty would take from them some magic, mystery, or power. Perhaps we perceive the division of women's bodies into separate parts, each to be admired (or reviled) as inanimate and unconnected to a living being, as a kind of symbolic dismemberment of women, and the fact of women's being divisible and rendered inanimate in this way as a means of depriving them of power and control (and indeed it is). Then it follows that men indeed should avoid such dismemberment of themselves, since they are the ones who have devised the vocabulary and grammar of sexual admiration for women. And yet have they not done much the same with themselves, with the objectification of the penis? But, in a sense, this works for men symbolically. For men, the penis is the organ that in fact they can't control: it is a part of them yet not a part – it does what it wishes. To objectify the organ is to remove oneself from blame for 'its' behavior. So the objectification of women's parts, and men's 'part,' serves different functions, but both work for the advantage of those who create the vocabulary, men.

Apart from this arcane sort of symbolism, it is clear why men have, in general, removed themselves from contention in the beauty game. Beauty is a losing contest, as we have seen. If you can achieve power and admiration in other ways, gaining them through aspects of your behavior that are under your control, why leave such important matters up to others? Women have to, since they cannot do anything on their own. But men, having this option, are well-advised to use it.

Directly and symbolically, literature abounds with evidence of men's identification of their self-image with the phallus. Here, for instance, is a high priest of phallus-worship, D. H. Lawrence, describing in *Lady Chatterley's Lover* the gamekeeper Mellors revealing himself in all his splendor to the lady:

The sun through the low window sent a beam that lit up his thighs and slim belly, and the erect phallos rising darkish and hot-looking from the little cloud of vivid gold-red hair. She was startled and afraid.

'How strange!' she said slowly. 'How strange he stands there? So big! and so dark and cocksure! Is he like that?'

The man looked down the front of his slender white body, and laughed. Between the slim breasts the hair was dark, almost black. But at the root of the belly, where the phallos rose thick and arching, it was gold-red, vivid in a little cloud.

'So proud!' she murmured, uneasy. 'And so lordly! Now I know why men are so overbearing. But he's lovely, *really*. Like another being! A bit terrifying! But lovely really! And he came to me!' – She caught her lower lip between her teeth, in fear and excitement.

The man looked down in silence at his tense phallos, that did not change.[1]

There he stands tall, dark, and handsome. D. H. Lawrence has given the penis a life of its own. Indeed, by the end of the passage, Mellors has become a huge, dark phallus. This, Lawrence wants us to know, is all that Lady Chatterley sees. Her eyes are full of it, full of this proud, lordly, and lovely thing. The lady is transfixed and terrorized as she gazes at such beauty and such power. In fact, the phallus strikes terror the way an awesome natural phenomenon would – it is more than beautiful. It is sublime. It is, incredibly, close to achieving godhead on its own. It is glorious, it is almighty, it is mysterious, as it rises 'thick and arching . . . gold-red, vivid in a little cloud' a mountain rising above the mists. Lawrence, neatly turning the stereotypical tables, places phallic masculinity on the pedestal heretofore reserved, in song and story, for feminine pulchritude. Women's subjection to man's raw masculine power is basic to our modern, Laurentian myth of masculinity. But anyone who has read Lawrence knows well that what he offers as the female point of view, in this case Lady Chatterley's, is really his own. He is seeing Mellors; he is seeing brute masculinity; he is looking at an idealized version of himself through Lady Chatterley's eyes. Again a man is interpreting women, and what is essentially narcissistic male self-adoration is translated into a woman's reaction: thus our stereotypes remain intact. Women are self-absorbed, vain, narcissistic. Men don't care for mirrors. Women *are* their mirrors.

Both men and women are narcissistic, but while women's narcissism is spread over all their bodies (creating more opportunity for anxiety but also, perhaps, a kind of fail-safe device – should the hair be less blond, perhaps the breasts will be more buxom and will save the day) men's is pinpointed and concentrated on the penis. And, paradoxically, while the penis is worshiped, it is worshiped in secret. Women normally are allowed to be exhibitionists, at least in that it is permissible for them – nay, preferable – to show what they have to offer to best advantage, and a woman who does not, in this culture, is abnormal. Hence it is stated in the psychological literature that women are seldom 'exhibitionists' in the pathological sense of being under compulsion to reveal their genitalia. This is normally interpreted in the same literature as meaning that since women already know that they are castrated, they do not require reassurance of their wholeness. But some men are exhibitionists – they have to display their genitals – usually to women, the younger and presumably less sophisticated in judgment, the better. But perhaps there is another way to look at this disparity. If women are allowed to reveal – and love to reveal – the source of their beauty, should not men have the same impulses? For complex reasons, men are socialized (as are women) to keep that source hidden; but some men, perhaps, cannot resist the temptation to show it off and be reassured that, indeed, they are 'the fairest of them all,' that, like Mellors, their phallic beauty inspires awe and terror in woman. A young and naive woman is best for the purposes – she is most apt to be properly dazzled. And then, finally, socialization aside, perhaps men and women are not all that profoundly different after all.

But men of leisure by the accident of noble birth have from time to time been willing – or forced – to acknowledge that they enjoy looking into the mirror. The Renaissance courtier, for example, took infinite trouble with his appearance. Ruffles were *de rigueur*, and silks and velvets for men. In England during the Elizabethan age men were peacocks parading around in tights with codpieces that accentuated their noble parts, wearing blouses with lace and ruffles, wigs and hats, and worrying about their 'well-turned legs.'

The relationship between leisure and feminine behavior is

not accidental. Gentlemen have always acted more 'feminine' than the less privileged classes: softer and more elaborate in dress, language, and manners, daintier in tastes. A gentleman was, indeed, a *gentle* man. The roughness and toughness that we associate with masculinity were for a long time considered appropriate demeanor only for the lower classes. In fact, even now, it is hard to think of a gentleman as someone with bulging muscles, a weatherbeaten 'manly' face, or the boisterous behavior that we usually associate with rough 'n' ready good ole boys. When we think of a gentleman we think of an elegance that contradicts the stereotype that men don't care about appearance.

In other periods, non-conformist men have worn clothes that call attention to themselves, in order to question society's assumptions about appropriate male behavior. This subversive choice of dress has often been deliberately linked to the expression of emotions, itself usually regarded as the prerogative of the female sex. We need only think of the poets of the romantic period who glorified the thin, sepulchral, tubercular, weak, and even feminine look. For them, the frailer the look, the more spiritually-minded the man. Muscles in men and flesh in women were considered too worldly.

It is true that those who made the look popular were poets or artists – men who are always outside of power, a leisured, if unmonied, class, and who, because of their position in society, are allowed to express emotions. At the turn of this century the poets and artists took dress to extremes. Men truly wore their hearts upon their sleeves, parodying the more conventional fashions in dress. The dandies in France and the pre-Raphaelites in England, for example, tried to show through dress their overcultivated sensibilities. Dress was more than fashion. Men delighted in its artifice, emphasizing it whenever they could, using devices that would draw attention to both the clothes and the man. Clothes were like a canvas on which the artist's idiosyncrasies were painted. Indeed, in function, clothes were not unlike Narcissus' pool.

More recently, in the late 1960s, men used their looks to wage an emotional protest against the status quo and against its prevailing political institutions. During this time of unprecedented economic abundance, leisure became a prerogative of the middle class. Those young men who didn't go to Vietnam stayed in school or otherwise out of nine-to-five jobs, thereby gaining free time to protest against the war and other forms of economic and social injustice, and often to indulge in drug-induced fantasies. They freed themselves of the concerns and constraints of mainstream America by declaring that they were off to do 'their own thing.'

The ways of the socially and politically marginal were newly revered. The new male heroes were anti-heroes, figures of the past and present who had turned their backs on the conventional and opened themselves to unconventional experiences, sexual or psychological. Eccentricities were 'in.' Ginsberg's howl could be heard loud and clear. It had been picked up by a whole generation of men. Artists and revolutionaries became important cultural figures. Men were no longer to be penalized for the expression of emotions. It was a time of rebellion and men rebelled against the mainstream's responsible mandates for manhood.

Like the dandies or the Byronic 'brothers' before them, the male youth of the 1960s used clothes to express their rebellion. Men let their hair and beards grow long. They wore necklaces of colorful beads, bracelets, rings, and sometimes even earrings in their reach for eccentricities. Everyone seemed to be searching for new, innovative looks which would best express the 'far-out' emotion of 'mindblowing' experiences that they were undergoing. Ponytails, braids, richly embroidered shirts all made their way into men's fashions of the period. Men and women often traded clothes, throwing off old uniforms with their strict sexual designations, sometimes even throwing off clothes altogether in the process. Clothing had always been a badge of identification. The ideology of freedom and fantasy was to be expressed in the unrestricted and fanciful wear. It was a period when androgynous looks were favored – Mick Jagger's for instance.

The 1960s thus changed the way men and women looked at men. In the first place, men, like women, could be and were encouraged to be narcissistic, to be openly concerned with their appearance and how it reflected their inner reality. And that inner reality – emotion, sensitivity, extra-logical psychological experience – was suddenly the mark of someone who was a worthwhile person in the culture: no longer the athlete or the millionaire, the threadbare hippie doing his own thing, letting it all hang out, was the new culture hero. And, with men able to see themselves as passive – perhaps helpless for the first time to control their destinies, under the sway of the stars if not Uncle Sam – fashions in dress and cosmetics perforce became androgynous. Male and female fashion became interchangeable, and 'unisex' boutiques sprang up like hallucinogenic mushrooms.

Any reminder of mainstream masculinity was put down. Anything in uniform was looked at with suspicion, even hatred. Hardly any distinction was made between a cop's uniform, a football outfit, a suit, and army gear. Indeed, for the young men of the 1960s there was hardly any difference between a policeman's club and a baseball bat. Even sports, the basis of the American male's identity, were seen as expressions of fascism – and regimentation. Those who still participated in the sports fantasy were 'jocks' (named significantly after athletic jockey straps) – that word used derogatorily of these young men who failed to oppose the trinity of money, masculinity, and might.

But the period of androgynous display was short-lived, and by the early 1980s men and women were showing strong signs of reverting to the normal polarization. Frilly silk blouses and feminine skirts – not to mention six-inch stiletto heels with ankle straps – were in again for women, and for men, short hair and the three-piece suit. However, while we may think that male narcissism is again in retreat, with only a few last holdouts clinging to a tenuous life, the influence of men *outside* the mainstream is pervasive.

Perhaps the most explicit form male narcissism takes at present is observed in the gay community, which has come out of the closet and into public visibility in the last decade or so. Gays, interestingly, adopt two basic styles of presentation of self: the aggressively hypermasculine, complete with big motorcycles, chains, uniforms, and crew-cuts; and, if not ultra-feminine 'drag,' the well-tailored, cared-for look, reminiscent of feminine styles of dress and deportment. But for both, as disparate as they seem, the underlying perception is similar. Like women, gay men frequently regard their own bodies as passive objects for the enticement and attraction of others. Therefore the costume, whichever it is, is designed to make a statement in a way straight male clothing traditionally has not. Hence, physical attractiveness is of especial importance for gay men – about as important, it would seem, as it has always been for women. And that attractiveness, again much more parallel to women's traditional behavior than men's, is a concomitant of youth and youthful 'beauty,' boyishness rather than manliness.

Male beauty is as central to courtship among gays as female beauty is to the courtship of heterosexual couples. Gays have made a great deal of male beauty. One need only read the personal want ads of gay newspapers to see the emergence of a vocabulary that begins to speak of male beauty.

For most gay men there is no feeling of shame in vanity. On the contrary attention to outward appearance is very important. Good grooming covers everything from body-building to posture, movement, hairstyle, dress, and facial cosmetics. It is not unusual to see gay men pampering themselves with facials, manicures, pedicures and the like. The ideal gay lifestyle is one of leisure and comfortable affectation. Gay men are the gentlemen of today. They feel no sense of shame about looking into the mirror and deciding who is the fairest.

A young man we talked to who had been engaged in homosexual activities since his teens told us that ever since he was very young, he found his body, and all men's bodies, both aesthetically and sexually pleasing.

It was such a turn-on to look at myself . . . at first I would look at other men with curiosity, sometimes just to see how much bigger or smaller they were compared to me [he said]. Then I found myself feeling sexually aroused by the experience.

At the same time, while gay men, admiring the male physique, work toward beautification, many find the increasing emphasis in the gay community on youth and beauty demoralizing and draining. An attractively muscular thirty-five-year-old told us that his perceived physical flaws (he felt that he was too fat, that his hair was thinning) were keeping him from full participation in San Francisco's gay community.

'I'm over the hill,' he lamented. 'In the gay community here, once you are past your 20s, it's over. There are so many beautiful young men out there that I feel I don't have a chance.' He spoke of the many times he had been turned down in favor of younger, more beautiful men; of the drugs he used to forget his pain; his inability to meet the gay standard of beauty; his need to be loved for qualities less tangible than outward appearance; his desire to find a long-lasting relationship that would free him from the fear of ageing and easy disposability. 'In the gay community,' he told us, 'at least among the people I know, men look at other men as sexual objects, nothing more. If you are young and beautiful you have it made.' He spoke about how sometimes he wished he were straight, so that his beauty would be less important.

We have heard all this before, of course, and as much as we sympathize, we see the unavoidability of this man's dilemma: if you (as a man) choose to opt out of the heterosexual male's drive for dominance via wealth and status – or if you are, as a woman, not allowed to opt into it – you are in the same position: only your fleeting physical charms will work for you. As painful as this realization is for a woman, it is all the more so for a man, who has been unable to escape our culture's male socialization: the gay male cannot – as women sometimes can – feel entirely comfortable as a sought-after and cherished object, always on the verge of the discard heap; the male has learned that the male should want to be the seeker and the doer, and not the object of the search. As repugnant to the gay male, and the liberated woman, as are traditional male standards of success, they offer some hope of surcease: to be the chooser, not the choice. Yes, straight males are buying cologne and pumping iron; but they aren't leaving law school or medical school to be kept by older and wealthier men, or women.

Although we said that gay men's influence on mainstream male fashion has been pervasive, another way to look at the situation is that gay and straight ideal modes of presentation of self are becoming more alike, both moving toward a common center. Perhaps as being openly gay becomes more acceptable to the mainstream, gay and straight men will feel less pressure toward polarization, less compelled to accentuate their differences. Interestingly, the concern of gay men for appearance has influenced, and even extended the limits of what is considered acceptable behavior and acceptable appearance among 'straight' men. In fact, we find current styles in straight male looks influenced by gay styles: facial hair, for example (which is also in part a relic of the 1960s); more colorful and form-fitting clothing, designed to catch the eye (male or female as the case may be), excite and seduce as women's clothing always has; the growing permissibility of cosmetics, hair dye, and even face-lifts for straight men similarly exemplify this trend. But straight men, unlike women and gays, cannot compete sexually on the basis of looks alone. The mainstream male is still judged by what he does. The image of man as doer, man as worker, rather than that of a leisured, finely spun gentleman, has its roots in the epic hero of the past who, like Aeneas, was ready to sacrifice everything for destiny, or who, like Odysseus, measured his worth by the power of his brain and of his 'cutting blade.' From then to now, the man with toil-roughened hands, weather-beaten and weary-looking face, the grizzled look of age and experience, an appearance that shows that he has been gainfully employed, is intrinsically attractive. Work is the basis of attractiveness.

Actually the equation of work = male handsomeness is not quite direct. It isn't merely toil that is beautifying. Rather, what attracts are the outward signs of being affected by, and having an effect upon the external world, whether through gainful employment, military or athletic exploits, or political power. Acting leaves its signs upon the actor, and it is these that are coveted as masculine good looks.

In the same way that stereotypes of women ranging from the dumb blond to the sultry seductress have been used as quickly understood symbols by the visual media, the symbolic wrinkle, the appropriate muscles, work for men. Ads directed at men offer a variety of looks which are intimately associated with work or activity. One Winston cigarette ad in *Playboy* portrays a group of male workers in hard hats, wearing work clothes and a look of relief; they have put in a hard day's work and can now enjoy some real male camaraderie – and a Winston. The ad reads, 'This is your world. This is your Winston. Smooth. Rich. Taste it all . . . . Nobody does it better.'

The ad is selling an image of virility as much as cigarettes. A man works hard, he plays hard, he smokes the cigarette that makes him a member of his hard-working, fun-loving male world. Advertisements in women's magazines sell a product by suggesting that if a woman wears or uses the product she will be more beautiful and as a result good things will come to her. Advertising directed at men relies on the immediate identification between the product and men's performance. 'Doing better' means both work and smoking Winstons, but what makes the ad work is the subliminal association of work, smoking, and performance in the sexual area, suggested by words 'Smooth. Rich. Taste it all,' and the climactic line, 'nobody does it better.' The use in magazine ads and television commercials of popular athletes to endorse products carries the same message. Athletes are known for their tough physical performance on the field. For millions of American men these supermen in their form-fitting athletic attire are the epitome of masculine good looks.

Ads directed to a more selective audience, say business executives, doctors, or lawyers, suggest the luxuries that money can buy, including women. The caption of an ad for Mumm Cognac VSOP reads, 'Fortunately, Mumm's the word in cognac, too,' and the accompanying picture is of a man in his late thirties toasting a slightly younger bejeweled and sophisticated woman. There is little need to wonder what else this fortunate couple must be mum about, for the ad speaks clearly of elegance and quiet seduction.

He is thirty-five, has plenty of money, drives an expensive high-powered sports car at full speed, lives in a well-appointed pad which, among other fashionable amenities, includes a bar that is fully stocked with the finest brandy, liqueurs, and wines, and that overlooks the glitter of a city where activity never stops. He can go out to dine at a moment's notice at the best restaurants with his friends, who just happen to be well-known and well worth knowing. He is home infrequently. But when he is home he knows how to relax and enjoy music on his powerful and expensive stereo equipment or he can turn on his video recorder and watch all the sports games that he has missed. His bed is circular and big enough to accommodate as many nubile bodies as he can. But no, he would prefer to have a quiet evening with one woman at a time, even though there are many beautiful and sexy women who would find it a privilege to step into his pad. No fear, the luckier ones will have their turn. After all, he needs variety to prevent boredom (a word that is not very familiar to him since he has rarely used it). And he never need be bored, since he has enough money in his fashionable pockets to go anywhere and to buy anything that may suit his momentary whim. He is a successful man. As he stares into his many mirrors he feels content.

This is the image of the playboy formed by the magazine of that name which millions of men read and which has fed at least a couple of generations of American men with fantasies of wealth, power, glamour, success, and women. Generally, we talk about men's looks in terms of what they do, their activities or work. In fact, a number of men to whom we talked could speak initially only of their ideal of masculinity in those terms.

It's not so much what a man looks like but an attitude that he has [one man in his late thirties told us]. I think it is hard for men to look at only beauty. There are attitudes, there's power, there's something in other men that you could admire . . . . If you think of a businessman you think of one type of ideal. Then you might see someone rich, a woman's man, who goes to parties on the Riviera . . . the playboy. But I don't think you look at a man and say, 'God, I'd like to look like that man.' You say, instead, 'I would like to be in his shoes. I'd like to do what he has done.' Some women see a solution in looking like someone else but a man says, 'if I had done that I'd be in a position to have limitless money, sex, beautiful women, material possessions, partying . . . .' I would never, for example, say, 'I wish I looked like Mick Jagger,' but I might say, 'I'd like to be in his shoes.' It's more the things that they have done. It's not just their looks.

A number of men echoed the notion that they could imagine being in other men's shoes, even though an ideal physical type eluded them.

There is kind of a man's image that is ideal [another man told us after thinking awhile about physical types]. It's sort of the busy executive, the guy in the three piece suit and he can have a lot of different faces but he's on a jet flying someplace important. He has all the trappings of success, the credit card, the nice car, the women . . . . That tends to be more important than what his face is shaped like or how big his nose is. I do notice that as part of the same image that these men always seem to have a nice head of hair.

One might say that the ideal is that of *Playboy*'s mythological playboy. What we know about him, above all, is that he is single (and if he is married he acts single), and successful both in and out of bed, and that, yes, he has a full head of hair.

From month to month, indeed from year to year, the cover of the magazine, its advertisements, its editorial pages, and even the well-publicized bachelor lifestyle of its publisher Hugh Hefner – his mansions, his planes, his bed, his pajamas, his parties, his women – have all helped to create the *Playboy* image. In fact, when we think of a playboy it is hard not to think of Hugh Hefner, the modern Casanova, surrounded by beautiful bunnies hopping in and out of his massive circular bed. *Playboy*, to a large degree, is the fantasy of a single man that has been transformed into a powerful modern myth about masculinity.

'What sort of man reads *Playboy*?' the magazine asks each month. Why, indeed, does a man read *Playboy*? What does he hope to learn? 'The skill to make wise choices . . . is what he gets from *Playboy*,' the January 1981 issue answers. 'It is essential to him, the reliable guide he needs to experience the pleasures of life.' *Playboy* knows its reader well. The average *Playboy* reader looks to *Playboy* to guide him, to enable him to experience vicariously 'the pleasures of life.' He finds gratification in the monthly mate who demands nothing of him, who looks willing and available as he unfolds her on the coffee table.

Like the ideal playboy, he too can be a womanizer. When he is through with his playmate he need only flip the page to find another woman. Even if he tires of this month's Playmate he knows it won't be long before a new one arrives. All the men we talked to had peeked at the pages of *Playboy* at least once. The *Playboy* Playmate, just like the *Vogue* cover girl, has become part of the mythology of female beauty.

Of course, the real playboy – that ideal image – would not need a guide such as *Playboy* to experience the pleasures of life. Instead, he would be out there experiencing them directly. The myth exemplified in the *Playboy* philosophy gets its power by appealing to men who feel powerless. Its continuing success depends not only on the inevitability of male frustration, but also on its ability to convince a large number of its male readers that they need a guide to masculinity. So, while it promises to make 'playboys' out of men, what it is actually doing is reducing men to boys, and relying on the hope that these boys will remain boys, satisfied to play with paper harems. *Playboy*, of course, would not have its mass appeal had it not been able to tap the cultural myth of the American male and build on it, and had Hefner not perceived the less than satisfying reality of American manhood. Then, at a deep psychological level, the myths men have about their own beauty are quite different from those women have, but perhaps not in the way we had originally thought.

For we are concerned not only with how men see and wish to see themselves, but with how they actually wish they looked at a superficial level. We saw earlier, in talking with women, that they tend to have a rather clear idea of ideal femininity, and how far they fall below it. Do men have fantasies of perfect male looks, and do they measure themselves against them?

Currently, the whole notion of masculinity is undergoing drastic changes. It is not just, as many claim, the women's movement that has made many men reassess their roles, although for a large number of men it has been influential in that process. Some men experience the women's movement as making them feel powerless and therefore have more need to show that they can still flex their muscles, still be sexually dominant – even if other masculine prerogatives are ebbing away. But even as their psychic need to show physical strength is increased, men have fewer and fewer opportunities to show physical strength at work. Also threatening is the decreasing distinction between men's and women's work through modern technology. Hence, if doing is becoming less and less unambiguously the arena in which male prowess is to be demonstrated, men feel both comforted and justified in borrowing tried-and-true feminine ways of gaining prestige and self-esteem; no longer is it enough for a man to be powerful. He also has to look powerful – young, sleek, and virile.

Men are beginning to face the mirror with less hesitation. They are beginning to look at themselves the way they customarily look at women. It is still not quite the same for men as it is for women, but a lot of men are beginning to fear not having a healthy and youthful appearance; they are becoming willing to get facials, and face-lifts, to lift weights not for muscular strength, but for muscle definition. The media have been quick to discover this new fascination – no longer just eccentricity or protest – with looking good and beauty products designed for men as well as cosmetic surgery on men are on the upsurge. 'Cosmetic surgery [for men] is no longer strictly a Hollywood phenomenon,' one article notes.

Today, middle-aged men make up 20 percent of a cosmetic surgeon's practice. . . . We live in a youth-oriented society. Men . . . exercise and diet not only to feel better about themselves, but for advancement in their careers. People in high visibility professions need to look good. They need to look healthy. Cosmetic surgery used to be a luxury – sometimes a necessity – for entertainers, politicians, homosexuals, men in unstable marriages, or men just new on the singles' scene. Now, prospective cosmetic surgery patients include men from stable families, bankers, salesmen, businessmen. In recent years, high-level management has discarded or passed over for promotion men who don't look fit *and* young. For most male cosmetic surgery patients, it comes down to economics. . . . Cosmetic surgery can help to produce renewed feelings of confidence toward work and the opposite sex. (*San Francisco Chronicle*, June 2 1982, pp. FF-1)

For men, good looks are very often justified by their link to money and power. An energetic and youthful appearance is becoming a prerequisite for promotion. When we asked men how far they would go to change their looks the majority said that, while they didn't look down upon other men who underwent cosmetic surgery or even used cosmetics in an understated manner, they would only consider cosmetic surgery if they were in an accident *or if not having it would seriously threaten their jobs*. As one man put it,

[Good looks] make a lot of difference in my business. Depending on how well they present themselves physically, or how well men exploit their looks, it will do a lot for getting them places . . . looks are important for everybody these days. . . . If I thought [cosmetic surgery] would seriously affect my income, I would seriously consider it.

While most of the men we spoke to mentioned economic considerations as the major reason they would undergo cosmetic surgery or use cosmetics, many felt that pressure from the media impelled them to want to look better. Mainstream masculinity is beginning to admit that men have always been somewhat concerned about their looks and that they are more so now than ever. The attention they once could only give to woman's beauty they can now legitimately lavish on themselves.

I feel sad for people who need those things [one man in his early forties told us], expecially women. . . . We live in a society where growing old is frowned upon and people are neglected and rejected because their age appears to show and so people feel a great need, almost a franticness to retain that youthful quality.

He remarked further that he saw nothing wrong with cosmetics or cosmetic surgery, but for personal reasons he wouldn't undergo either. 'I've never been particularly taken with decoration . . . having tattoos, ears pierced. But,' he added, 'I wouldn't feel it would detract from my masculinity.' A man in his early twenties assessed the need to look good in a slightly different way:

There is a lot of commercial influence. Most people on TV are good-looking. . . . There is, for the most part, a strong push for men to look their best. A strong influence from all sides of the media but that doesn't mean all men adhere to what's shoved down their throat.

Nevertheless, there was a feeling among the majority of our subjects that too much was being made of looks and that it had an effect on the way they were beginning to see themselves as well as other men. The media's emphasis on male looks was clearly making some men nervous. While maintaining that they would undergo cosmetic alterations primarily for success at work, many admitted to their fear of growing old and not looking good. Others suggested that looks were important to them in and of themselves, to enable them to attract the opposite sex and bolster their feelings about their own sexuality. One twenty-year-old maintained, for example, that he 'wouldn't have a face-lift. I wouldn't want to fool someone. . . . I wouldn't think it's necessary for women either.' But he did add that

The only type of cosmetic surgery I would get is if I were balding, I'd try to get a hair transplant or something like that. . . . I don't know. . . . I just don't feel that I'd look attractive bald. The prospect of losing my hair scares me. . . . My friends feel that way. Ask any twenty-year-old man, they'd fear balding above all.

While men have been reluctant to admit it, there has always been an aesthetic of masculine good looks which is only now beginning to make itself explicit. Men are becoming able to perceive themselves purely visually, as sex objects. To be sexy, a man must have hair, since – as mythology suggests – the loss of hair can be symbolic of impotence (as one man put it, 'I'd sense a certain sense of loss of something'), and to the conscious eye, baldness just doesn't look good. The same type of concern was expressed about height. Men should be tall, at least 6 feet, if not more. And all men talked about being in good physical shape (which means being muscular without looking like a body-builder), and lean. Of course, tallness and muscularity contribute to the image of strength and power that is masculinity.

While most men spoke only in general terms about men's looks, emphasizing tallness, muscularity and the like, and stuck more closely to defining ideal looks on the basis of job-related activities, one man did venture to give a portrait of his ideal-looking man that was vaguely reminiscent of the way men tend to describe women.

I would say he'd be around 6 feet [he said of the ideal look], have broad shoulders, be thin at the waist, strong, with very direct eyes, full head of hair, relaxed, so even though he is physically strong he wouldn't look flexed, strong neck and back muscles, strong calves, good arches on his feet, suntanned and so on. . . . His face would be clean-shaven, I'm not exactly sure why, no rings under his eyes, sparkly eyes, not sallow but thin enough so that cheekbones are well-articulated, square jaw without looking like a cave man.

The portrait was clearly one that looked best in photos or on the movies screen and he emphasized this.

The other men did not have nearly as clear a view of what ideal masculine good looks might be, but it was evident that the media had given them at least a vague notion of what they were looking for. With the exception of a couple of men, the men we spoke to had all looked at or browsed through the pages of *Gentleman's Quarterly GQ*, but they were still reluctant to admit to caring very much about their own looks. It is not unusual to see advertisements portraying older, well-dressed, distinguished-looking men with younger women, but in the past few years there has been a trend towards younger male models. With the exception of men modeling fashions for the business executive, the majority of the men in *GQ* are young and seem to fit what is becoming an emerging aesthetic for masculine good looks. We need only think of the young muscular bodies, and the more or less chiseled faces of the young men in Calvin Klein or Jordache jean ads to get a notion of what the ideal in male models is. But it isn't only Klein. As one young male model said: 'There is a trend towards a sporty look now and younger men will get those jobs. . . . For the business man look, selling suits, cigarettes, liquor and what have you . . . geared toward older people they'll hire older men.' But a look through *GQ* reveals that Gianni Versace, Perry Ellis, Armani, Missoni, Valentino, and other major designers were all using young, handsome (beautiful, even, in the way we would see female models) men to advertise their wares. The magazine itself carries numerous ads for male cosmetics, advises men on cosmetic skin care, on 'conditioning regimens' (exercise and diet); hairstyles and so on.

Beauty and the enhancing influence of specific fashions – previously an issue for the women's magazines – are beginning to make their appearance on *GQ*'s pages. The August 1982 issue, for instance, features a discussion on 'How Uniforms influence the Way You Dress.' Talk of uniforms epitomizes men's sense of masculine good looks by emphasizing occupation through dress.

The most striking aspect of a uniform [writes Anne Hollander in that issue] remains its isolating character: It sets the wearer apart from the humdrum and haphazard, the domestic and the personal, all ordinary commercial and social elements in life. A man in uniform is responding to a call; there's something fearsome about him, a kind of threat. (pp. 94–5)

For men, uniforms, especially military uniforms with their connections to weaponry, have always been potent, a sign and symbol of their masculinity. Uniforms symbolize crisp and unbending masculine decorum, suggest the ideal in male social and sexual behavior. They glorify male strength and conquest. 'Dazzling elaborations and minute distinctions of color and insignia,' continues Hollander, 'proliferate in peacetime, when the uniform's visual power becomes a matter of competition and overt virile display.' Unlike the garb worn by men who have flirted with the counterculture, which, in its extravagance and eccentricity, externalizes and legitimizes emotions, uniforms, however dazzling the insignia, suggest regimentation and hierarchy. Even in men's ordinary dress, suits and neckties reflect a degree of regimentation, of a constricted and contained sexuality.

It is interesting in this context that we currently have very different gut feelings about male and female cross-dressing. Women's wearing of male clothes – pants with front flies, button-down shirts, ties, even tuxedos – goes unremarked or at most, is 'cute' in paradoxically accentuating the femininity of the wearer. A woman wearing such clothes remains a woman. She is not 'passing for a man' or engaging in transvestism. But consider a man in a skirt. For one thing, men who want to be thought of as masculine do not wear female clothing in public, except occasionally to costume parties – where the very fact of cross-dressing is hilarious (rather than adorable). He is seen as imitating, if not becoming, a woman, with very different audience response depending on the verisimilitude of the imitation. A man who is too good at it creates nervousness; a man who leaves traces of his masculinity (beard, chest hair) is seen as only kidding, and that is funny. But men do not ever casually adopt female fashions as women do men's. Similarly, in part as a badge of togetherness, women often appropriate 'their' men's pajama tops, old shirts, sweaters. The reverse never occurs.

As men get more leisure time, and as their raw physical strength becomes less useful, they are acknowledging that it is just as important, if not more, to 'look like a man' as to 'act like a man.' As more emphasis is put on visual appearance, open disdain for looks, for some, is on the verge of becoming a thing of the past. There was a time when paying too much attention to physical appearance, holding jobs which emphasized looks, such as dancing, modeling, and even acting were considered not quite 'manly.' According to Zoltan Rendessy, young men are becoming increasingly interested in modeling. 'Whereas before,' he observes, 'to be a dancer, hairdresser, or model, was always tabu, now many of the athletes right out of college want to be models.'[2] Indeed, Jack Scalia, one of the top male models, was a pitcher and a first draft choice of the

Montreal Expos before an injury prevented him from playing professional ball. He chose modeling only when he was rendered useless on the field. But by and large these days there is less of a feeling among men that it is not a manly occupation. The men we spoke to saw nothing wrong with modeling, although most would not choose it above other equally lucrative careers.

It has long been a popular notion that good looks in men actually work against them. Mothers could be heard talking about little boys as being *too* pretty or *too* beautiful, as if there were some stigma attached to it. Good looks in men were not to be trusted; there was something feminine about looking good. But men are admitting, albeit sometimes reluctantly, that they want to be counted among the fairest. When asked how they would feel if people referred to them as beautiful, the majority indicated that they might at first feel confused because, as one man put it, 'it's very hard for a man to say another man is beautiful unless he's gay,' but all of them felt pleased at the thought of being considered beautiful. 'I'd be flattered,' said another man. 'I'd be embarrassed and try to deny it, because I haven't grown up believing that.' Another young man reflected,

The minute you said that I sensed this fear that you or someone else might think that if I thought men were beautiful I would want to be physically involved with them or that my saying that men were beautiful would connote that or imply that to the public in general . . . it would be hard for me to accept because I've never believed that . . . yes, I would want to be considered beautiful.

Fear of homoeroticism was not enough to keep men from wanting to be considered beautiful. Masculinity was not only admired by these men, but considered beautiful as well. There was a larger fear of being considered pretty. Prettiness to all men we spoke to implied femininity, a devaluation of manhood, a diminution of virility.

Are men vain?

I don't think that there is any question about it that they are [one man said, echoing the opinion of several others]. Sometimes I think even more so than women. I have friends . . . who'll take hours to get ready to go out, shaving, combing their hair and making sure every little hair is in place, making sure they're wearing the right clothes and that everything is right. They spend the same time in the front of the mirror as the stereotype of the women that we grew up seeing in cartoons and magazines.

Men are beginning to define themselves in terms of outward appearance, beginning to feel bad when their appearance does not measure up to some vague standard. But even those men who have most thoroughly adopted the new attitude feel some residual unease in the role of object. One man suggested that male models in magazines are not as appealing as female models because they don't project energy and they don't work with the camera as well. 'The male figure becomes a very interesting formal subject,' he said, 'but the only time that that's appealing is when it's done in relationship to the way the female in the same picture is responding to him.' Men, in other words, have yet to learn to flirt with the camera in order to project themselves comfortably to the world as objects of desire. Hence they cannot be playful as women can. The photographs of men in *GQ* lack the whimsicalness, the fantasy, and the hints of sexual kinkiness often found in *Vogue*. Male models tend to look directly, purposefully into the eye of the camera. They mean business. Still, the young man we spoke to found the type appealing, and felt that male models offer prototypes of masculine good looks. But,

I might be denying being attracted to the figure of the male model [he added], maybe some sort of jealousy, perhaps because they have an advantage that I don't have in the sense that if you're not born with it you don't have it . . . . I respond to the image of a male model with a bit of jealousy.

The reaction is reminiscent of women's reactions to beautiful women – the 'catty' jealousy thought to be exclusively female. One man told us that he was sitting one evening with his girlfriend watching a *TV* program that featured a *Cosmopolitan* (male) centerfold talking about how and why he was chosen. When his companion expressed admiration of the man's looks, of his lean, muscular body, he admitted 'I felt jealous. I could see now what women must go through always having to compare themselves to some airbrushed ideal that they think men admire.'

While the majority of men we spoke to maintained that intelligence, money, and charisma (all the men we talked to indicated that charisma was extremely important to men in terms of attracting the opposite sex) were highly valued because they provide access to power, very few denied the importance of good looks in their lives. One man indicated that good looks had always been important to him and that he suspected that it was so with most men. As a child, he said 'I tended to overemphasize the importance or value of my looks .... I think I saw at an early age that good-looking people – good-looking boys and girls – in school managed to have, or at least seemed to have, an easier time socially.' Some men even felt that attractive males had an advantage over men with money in their ability to make women respond to them, although they did acknowledge the cultural myth that women associated sexiness with power, that women still could be bought and men were still buying, and that money and power gave men a way out of the futile game of beauty. 'I think a lot of women are attracted to physical beauty. I think a lot of women are attracted to power. I think a lot of women are attracted to charisma,' one man said. 'There is no simple formula.'

There is, however, still a stigma attached to being too good-looking, but the reasons given are not the obvious ones. Not so much that good-looking men are seen as less manly but rather that emphasis on external beauty lessens a man's chances of developing inner qualities of moral strength and outer characteristics of power.

I think [one man told us] that handsome men have a more difficult time of it even though there is a tendency to revere beauty in our society, and I think that one of the reasons for that is that men that are good-looking, if they find it out early enough in their lives, have a more difficult time applying themselves to their life's work. They use their looks in attracting women, playing sexual games. Whereas men that are more average-looking, I think, tend to have to apply themselves to something else in order to gain a sense of identity.

The argument is not much different from the one often applied to beautiful women who, because of their outward beauty, are suspected of not having developed a deep emotional or intellectual life. But for women that failure seems to matter less. Echoing this sentiment, another man suggested that the reason unattractive men can be powerful is that 'it may be because they have had to overcome not particularly resplendent physiques in order to get what they wanted. It's almost like a little Caesar complex.' Reasoning on men's physical appearance is at times rather contradictory. Yes, beauty gives men an advantage both in work and in love. No, beauty in men does not give them an advantage. It is too easy. They don't have to work hard and therefore don't feel the urge to 'get ahead' in the world. While for women, beauty alone is heralded as the only source of power, for men power fully compensates for unattractiveness. Men value their 'beauty,' but without it they can still strive for money and power, which will assure them of success with women. In the end, for men, whether beauty or power, it all seems to come to one thing: doing it better. Physical beauty is just another way for men to advertise their virility. The strong jaw, the direct gaze, the full head of hair, the hairy chest, the tall body, the well-developed muscles all speak of male potency. In the stiff, taut, strained, studied pose of Mr Universe, we see the *Playboy* ideal: Mellors the gamekeeper, the respectable outward representation of the phallus and its proud possessor.

And finally to our last question: now that we understand the complexity of the emotions with which men view themselves and the way they look, can we understand men's fantasies about the female image of their dreams? We know that women tend to be rather unspecific about what an 'ideal man' should look like: men's characters and accomplishments, what they 'do,' rather than how they look, are the major concerns. Though more recently the media with their male centerfolds, or male strip-tease joints, hint that men, too, can be looked upon as sex objects and that pear-shaped bodies and flabby stomachs might fall short of the ideal masculine look, by and large these media displays of formidable masculinity provoke laughter, joking and prurient curiosity at most – but only rarely masturbatory fantasies in women. The popularity of female centerfolds and pin-ups, on the other hand, tells us that men respond to female erotica in a very different way. Men grow up on images of paper playmates, and are socialized to use them freely in their erotic fantasy lives. Surely this colors their perception of what an ideal woman looks like, and how she should behave. Women have no counterpart. Do all men share an image – say, 'five foot two, eyes of blue'? And is it in fact true, as is often suggested, that the parameters which define and delimit female attractiveness are much more constrained than those that limit male good looks? We are talking here about male views of female beauty. We have already seen the severity of female views of the same topic. Are these related to men's, and if so, how?

By men's own admission, the *Playboy* ideology has created conflicts both in men's view of themselves and in their attitudes toward women. '*Playboy*,' one man in his late twenties told us, 'represents women as an extension of yourself. Then if you're confronted with real live women, you end up masturbating rather than communicating.' The schism created by the myth has made many men insecure and unhappy in their relationships with women.

I have always felt torn [another man in his twenties said] between trying to acquire what masculine culture tells men they should have – that is, money, cars, and, especially, beautiful women – and wanting to not worry about such things, wanting to be with someone interesting, someone I could communicate with no matter how she looks. I think that is what most men want deep down ... but our culture teaches us differently, teaches us to be alone, actually, since no one can measure up to the touched-up image of the beautiful women that the media tell us important men sport. Too much is made of beauty.

The notion of the solitary bachelor having the freedom to tempt his fantasy with money, beautiful women, or whatever, doesn't work so well when translated into reality. Many men spoke of the loneliness and inadequacy they felt as they searched for their 'ideal' mate, forever unable to find her. Yes, they realized it was a fantasy but it was difficult to shake. After all, other men did it, why not they? What was wrong with them? Another man spoke of the fear of rejection that men experienced, a fear which drives men back to the safety of solitude, or into making do with women or relationships that don't meet their standards.

Men are frightened by good looks in women [he said]. I find men frequently try to rationalize their fear of being rejected by a woman by saying that just because she's a beautiful woman she's empty-headed, probably really stupid. They're afraid of rejection.

It is interesting that many of the men we talked to, who

had faith neither in their attractiveness, nor in their abilities to have power in the world, confessed that at some point in their lives they had dreamed of being seen with beautiful women. Beautiful women are ego-boosters. Women seem to be the best outward sign of men's success or lack of it.

But while men all had encountered the image of the successful man and the beautiful woman in the media, most had totally different ideas not only of female beauty, but also of the kind of relationship they wanted with a woman. Contrary to popular mythology, many of the men we spoke to did not particularly prefer young women to older women, although they could appreciate nubile beauty. The majority of men said that, to them, the ideal age for women was about their own, sometimes even older, as long as they were in good shape. When we asked about wrinkles in women most said that they weren't bothered by them, that they tended to add character. While we have heard people say all of this about men, it was hard to believe that men were now able to think the same way about women. A man in his early forties, who had read *Playboy* with a passion in his teens, said that he always 'considered *Playboy* women to be vacuous and . . . found nothing attractive about their faces . . . there's a certain hardness, it seems like their personality's been wiped out . . . something's missing.' Another young man in his late twenties who told us he was in a serious relationship with a woman ten years older than himself offered a similar opinion of the image of women that *Playboy* sold. When asked what type of look he liked, he admitted that he found the *Vogue* model much more appealing.

Somehow [he said] I don't respond to them as models but rather as people, as women . . . The *Vogue* cover girl has a slightly darker side. She has a certain kind of mysteriousness about her . . . *Playboy* centerfolds are always young and physically always very voluptuous and very sexual and sensual combined with being naive at the same time. But they're not as appealing to me. . . . I guess the *Vogue* cover girl seems more intelligent. . . . I like the look of older women.

We were, of course, speaking of ideal looks. What he found most attractive in women, as he put it,

has more to do with the way she moves than the way she looks. . . . Beauty, for me, is something that you grow into more (like for a man

I guess). . . . It seems like the more in touch you are with yourself the more beautiful you are. . . . What attracts me on a sensual, visceral, intellectual level is something you have to grow into.

Many men spoke of movement, gracefulness, a direct look in the eyes, an aura of mystery, attributes which cannot quite be captured by a camera, as what they felt constituted female beauty.

Similar opinions have been recorded by men who work behind the camera, by men who photograph the women we deem the most beautiful in the world. Photographer Uli Rose, for example, told *Mademoiselle* in July 1980 that

Women look best – and sexiest – when they're in love. In general, the women I find sexy are in their late 20's and up. Women's bodies seem to change at about that age. Maybe they have children; maybe it's just experience, or self-confidence. It must be chemistry. . . . What's sexy isn't long hair and a red mouth. That's a cliche. Fantasy is important, so is surprise.

Photographer Patrick Demarchelier also suggested that physical appearance goes only so far.

There's too much emphasis on finding a '10,' the perfect beauty. What's really beautiful and sexy is always less than perfect. To me, what's sexy is how a woman moves, laughs, smiles – that's how she shows her personality and intelligence. And a little mystery is very important. If I look at a woman and don't see any mystery, I lose interest. (p. 106)

And men who work in front of the camera also spoke of a woman's beauty as involving something more than just another pretty face.

I like long dark hair [said top male model Frank Dzurenko in the same *Mademoiselle* interview]. I like women who are graceful, who move well. Ballet dancers are sexy because they move so beautifully. . . . The physical part has to come first; it's the first thing you see. But what's really sexy is another level – maybe it's vitality of the body chemistry or spirit. It's like an extra dimension and not everyone has it.

Model Jeffrey Aquilon adds 'What's really sexy in the long run is a woman's attitude – liveliness, spark, energy. You have to be able to talk to someone; there has to be a little challenge.' (p. 54) A young man we talked to, who started modeling at a young age and who at the age of twenty is entertaining notions of an acting career, seemed to sum up best the attitude of many men.

I'd say they're pretty important [he said of women's looks], but some women aren't very attractive, yet they have a way of carrying themselves and I'm attracted to that. . . . Beauty is not more important than personality. I'd much rather go for a woman average in looks and great in personality. . . . I'd say intelligence outweighs beauty.

Even when pressed to provide a prototype of their physical ideal, most of the men we interviewed did not describe the *Playboy* centerfold, although they were quite familiar with it, or any of the more common stereotypes of blondness and buxomness. Other men said that at some point in their lives they had been lured to the *Playboy* mate. But, as one man in his early forties maintained, this was primarily because when he was growing up the 'fair-haired and fair-skinned' were considered ideal. He still likes the bodies of *Playboy* women. 'But,' he continued, 'we've been inundated with lots of different people from many different cultures in America in the last twenty, thirty years and it has sort of changed our image of what is attractive.' As one twenty-year-old man put it,

I'd have to say it's all in the eye of the beholder. There are many ways to interpret beauty. . . . I would interpret it as something that you can see and touch and makes you feel good to see and touch. . . . It depends on what your individual concept of beauty is. . . . I think there are different kinds of beauty and you can't restrict yourself to one type of beauty. There is no perfect beauty. Every country has a different people and all are beautiful in their own way. . . . The beauty of blond-haired, blue-eyed, of black, of Asian, or of anything in between. Western features aren't important to me. All features are different and can have their unique beauty.

As for his ideal, 'long, black hair, a slim, trim body with dark brown copper skin, dark brown to black eyes. About my height but not taller. . . . I'd like to look someone straight in the eye . . . be on an equal plane.'

In the same way, many men took exception to the softly rounded, passive, 'bunny' image as an ideal. They found more 'masculine' traits appealing in women. The majority of men said they liked thin women in good physical condition. A few even said they felt muscles were particularly sexy. As one man put it, 'I don't want you to think I'm attracted to men, but I like almost boyish-looking bodies on women – small breasts and thin hips, muscular-looking legs and arms while still being svelte.' Perhaps some men are becoming more able to acknowledge openly their attraction to androgynous looks, or even to the androgyne in themselves. Or perhaps strength and power – autonomy – in and of itself is attractive to some people.

These observations seem to contradict what the media not only tell us men want but also what they propose women should look like. Some of our interviews were particularly surprising, for they seemed to be moving away from the paper dolls that *Playboy* sells. These men no longer were buying either the magazine or the image. As one twenty-year-old put it, 'Each picture is its own reality . . . but that's not you. . . . It's fantasy. All of it is just make-believe.'

These results certainly seem to be grounds for optimism. From the interview data, men would appear to be moving away from the old stereotype: they seem less interested in dewy and inexperienced youth, less concerned with superficial and bland prettiness. Perhaps – dare we hope – men and women are moving into a new age, in which they value each other for the kind of people they are under the skin, for intelligence, vitality, compassion, wit – those qualities which, unlike physical looks, not only last but become better with age.

But before we break open the champagne, we had better reflect a moment. It is still Utopian to hope that men are becoming able to see women as individuals and not types. *Playboy* still sells and turns a handsome profit. How can we explain the discrepancy between what we heard in our interviews and what we see in the media? Certainly, the media are hardly out of touch with popular fantasies, nor were the men we talked to – who were of all ages and all walks of life – immune to the media, but most of them had come to grips with their frustration and realized that the centerfold promise wasn't enough for a life together in reality, that looks counted for less in a relationship than we are told. Perhaps it is simply, as one man put it, that 'we are so bombarded with visual images that men are taking refuge and looking for the real thing . . . someone you can speak to across a coffee table rather than fantasize with in some magazine.'

Perhaps these are cases of wishful thinking – a reflection of the way men may ideally want to, or think they should, see women. After all, men, too, are living in the legacy of the 1960s, which encouraged individualism and self-reflection (the encounter-group generation), and of the women's movement, which made known its preference for more sensitive men, for men who could understand the problems of oppressed groups, including women. Just like the women we interviewed they too may be hoping that they (unlike others) are immune to the lure of superficial appearance and that it is that 'special quality,' something unobservable, that attracts. Yet, all of them talked about the importance of physical attraction on their first encounter with a woman – how if there were two available women, they would probably approach the most attractive.

Interestingly, the women we interviewed seemed to buy the stereotyped notions of looks much more readily than the men, and seemed to be harsher in judging the looks of other women. There were a number of women who, although they felt put off by the emphasis on looks, thought that Cheryl Tiegs and Farrah Fawcett represented what men wanted to see, and thus how they wanted to look. But among the men we interviewed only the older ones (some old enough to be fathers of these young women) were dazzled by the Fawcett-Tiegs look. Other men felt that these women, at worst, looked vacuous, at best, were no more than pretty. Beauty was something more. A beautiful woman was not necessarily 'perfect'-featured; a pretty woman had flawless skin, and regular features. Youth seemed less essential than we might have thought.

But a glance at reality shows that the issue is far from resolved. After all, we can merely look around us; in a typical academic community, how many male professors, ending marriages with wives of their own age, say, thirties, forties, fifties, are soon thereafter seen in the bedazzled company of nubile young ladies barely into their twenties? And how often do we see the reverse – women professors with male students of comparable age? Not very often, for the second question. Regularly, for the first. Look around in any circumstance where men and women are together in couples. Note the frequency of couples in which the man is old enough to be the woman's father. Perhaps men are becoming more open to acknowledging the idea that other kinds of relationships are possible, and perhaps even, in an abstract sense, desirable. But seldom indeed are these philosophical convictions acted upon, and when they are, the women tend to be unusually attractive or successful. When men speak of preferring older women, they are usually not speaking of the average middle-aged woman. But in general, men seem to be more forgiving of the ravages of age than women give them credit for.

Women have always justified their preoccupation with youth on the grounds that men care deeply about it, and women face rejection if they don't meet men's fantasies. The disquieting thought surfaces: can it be that women's attribution of these fantasies to men is in part a projection? Do women suffer to be beautiful less for men's sake – and more for reasons (whatever they might be) of their own?

# Chapter 9
# Beauty and Ethnicity

'Black is beautiful!' Who of us does not remember first hearing those words during the politically explosive 1960s? Who can forget that first gut response – confusion, incredulity, then deep reflection. And these were not just the responses of the dominant white culture, but of those men and women of color to whom, principally, they were addressed. Black . . . beautiful? Too many myths, too many examples suggested the reverse.

That very mind-wrenching perplexity was the root of the tremendous political power of the slogan. More than anything else the leaders of the movement could have created, 'Black is beautiful!' galvanized mind and heart, united people of color in a way more intellectually rarefied words could not have done. Slogans could be – indeed were – created on the basis of economic, social, and political lack of parity, all of which might have been interpreted as more important and pressing issues in the revolution. But this one above all struck a resonant chord; the confusion of its early use gave way to something else.

To say 'Black is beautiful!' reminded hearers that, in fact, in the real world as it currently existed, few people were likely to agree. Black was *not* perceived as beautiful – as the sales of skin-lighteners and hair relaxers could attest. There had never been – and everyone knew there could never be – a black Miss America. Blacks and whites felt that the closer a black's skin approached whiteness, the more beautiful it was and marrying light was, in the black community, a form of marrying up. In no way could a black both be unequivocally black, at that time, and be beautiful. As well be male and female. No political change could last as long as the ingrained sense of unworthiness lingered in the heart. Hence the slogan, and hence its dynamic effects on black and white alike. It forced a 180-degree reversal of some very deep and formative assumptions in the minds of both races. Black could only be beautiful in a world turned upside down. Then, the slogan said, turn it upside down! But could it be done by a slogan?

As the 1960s wore on, evidence began to mount that, in fact it could. Members of non-dominant groups found it easier to feel pride in the very difference between their looks and the white ideal. And the dominant white culture, perhaps for the first time, was forced to question its assumption that beauty and identity with the blond, blue-eyed stereotype were one and the same thing.

Tolstoy wrote: 'Nothing has so marked an influence on the direction of man's mind as his appearance, and not his appearance itself, so much as his conviction that it is attractive or unattractive.' As painful as is the ordeal of women of the dominant culture who spend so much of their money, their time, and their emotions trying to live up to the modern ideal of beauty, how much deeper is the agony of the woman who – whatever she does – inevitably must find in the mirror that her hair is too kinky, or too straight, or too black, that her nose is too broad, that her lips are too full, that her eyes are too narrow, or slanted, or too dark, and if this is not enough, that her skin is irrevocably the wrong color. Where women of the dominant culture struggle to compete, she knows that from the start she is barred from that competition. Barred, not by some universal ideal of beauty to which she doesn't conform, but rather because one culture has given itself the right to dictate and to promote an ideal of beauty that both arises from, and reinforces, its political and social hegemony. At the same time America encourages conformity and – not averse to profit – offers its spas, its beauty shops, its surgical skill, not only to those who are too fat or too old, but also to the woman who, money permitting, feels that with a nose job, or a lip tuck, or breast reduction, or processed hair, or bleached skin, she will be less 'ugly.' In her, all women's concerns with beauty are crystallized and given their cruelest form. Like other women she is sold hope, but privately she knows all too well that her case is hopeless. As much as she may desire to attain that ideal of beauty which announces itself in the cascade of straight blond hair, the bluest and widest eyes, the longest and thinnest limbs, and skin like polished porcelain, she knows that she cannot ever look like this. Her beauty may be acknowledged in private, but in public she is reminded that she is unattractive, and her feelings about herself are affected by that.

Looking different inevitably suggests being different and that in turn, being worse, which gives the majority the rationalization for imputing to the minority every trait feared in themselves, traits which range from immorality to intellectual inferiority.

More to the point, that difference is both feared and welcomed by the dominant culture. Feared, because what is different is frightening, unpredictable and dangerous. But welcomed for more complex reasons, not accessible for the most part to our reasoning minds. We create stereotypes, in part, to enable us to project out, to attribute to others those negative characteristics we all possess and know we possess, but hate to acknowledge. The more clearly someone is identified as different, the more readily we can attribute these flaws to him or her. We need to have people around as scapegoats who look radically different from us; and as long as we are insecure about our own goodness and lovability (and our obsession with beauty guarantees our continuing doubts) we will need these scapegoats. So the dominant group gives the non-dominant a terrible double message: (1) Be like us (because otherwise we will fear and avoid you, and keep you down) and (2) be unlike us, don't try to 'pass' for us or become one of us (because we need you for our own purposes just the way you are). So the woman of color is caught in a terrible bind. She is being asked, on the one hand, to work to hide her differences, and, on the other hand, she is being told that she must and will always be different. In her quest for assimilation, for acceptance, she might try to forget her language, her culture, even her whole behavioral style. But the color of her skin, the shape of her eyes, the texture of her hair, the form of her body, will speak more clearly than her perfectly shaped words. She might be able to silence her own voice and to adopt a more public one, but she will never be able to hide, to 'not be seen,' even though she may feel and be treated as if she were invisible.

Given our ethnocentrism, it may be difficult to believe that other cultures may have a notion of beauty that is totally different from ours. Even though we may know that, in the name of beauty, women in non-Western cultures have broken and flattened their noses, decoratively scarred their faces and bodies, elongated their necks, stretched their lips, put on a shine to enhance the blackness of their skin, lengthened their earlobes, flattened their heads, and so on, we call it disfigurement, never pausing to think that the anorexic slimness or extreme pallor that we have at one time or another admired so much is, to people of other cultures, equally 'ugly' – if, that is, they have not been seduced by Western ideals. Ethnocentric definitions of beauty, as much as anything else, create barriers between peoples and worse, create feelings of confusion, conflict, self-doubt, and inferiority among those who find their way of looking at the world and at themselves not appreciated. Beauty is never more political than when it is used to prop up the power of one race while it renders others powerless, immured in self-hatred.

It is painful to reflect that all non-dominant groups have had, at some time, to carry this baggage and, confronted with the constant bombardment of images conveying the message that white is beautiful, have also had to ask 'Who am I?' or 'Who are we?' Poignant questions such as these are responses to a culture which, in giving more and more value to physical appearance, has to devalue those whose looks stray too far from the norm. (This is true despite the recent token appearance of blacks, Asians, and other 'exotics' in fashion magazines or news programs.)

Not that this is a new phenomenon. The literature of the period provides copious examples of how antebellum southerners used blacks as a foil to protect their own image and create a myth about their own perfection by contrasting their whiteness with the more sinister image of blackness. Margaret Wilkerson explains that white people's fear of blacks arises because blacks both visually assault their sensibilities, and because our language is charged with connotations, positive and negative, about 'white' and 'black.'

There is something about color [she told us], and it has to do with all of the evidence through language, all of the adjectives, all of the definitions that are used, all of the connotations attached to 'black' and 'white' . . . language is often an expression of people's sensibilities

. . . You don't have the same negative connotations attached to red and yellow and brown, which are the supposed colors of all the under-represented groups in this country, as you have to black.

The dualism of white as representing goodness and purity and of black as connoting evil goes back to the Greeks and Romans. White was lucky, black unlucky. White was the color of celebration, black of mourning. For Christians, white was the color of good, black satanic: black cats, black magic, the witches' black hats and capes. Even those white writers who try to argue against the idea of intrinsic white superiority in all qualities seem unable to avoid falling into the usual ethnocentric assumptions. Thus William Blake:

My mother bore me in the southern wild,
And I am black, but O! my soul is white;
White as an angel is the English child,
But I am black, as if deprived of light,

My mother taught me underneath a tree,
And sitting down before the heat of day,
She took me on her lap and kissed me,
And pointing to the east, began to say:

'Look on the rising sun: there God does live,
And gives His light, and gives His heat away;
And flowers and trees and beasts and men receive
Comfort in morning, joy in the noonday.

'And we are put on earth a little space,
That we may learn to bear the beams of love,
And these black bodies and this sunburnt face
Is but a cloud, and like a shady grove. . . .'

Thus did my mother say, and kissed me;
And thus I say to little English boy:
When I from black and he from white cloud free,
And round the tent of God like lambs we joy,

I'll shade him from the heat, till he can bear
To lean in joy upon our Father's knee;
And then I'll stand and stroke his silver hair,
And be like him, and he will then love me.[1]

Except that, as we have seen, he will not either. So slaveholders point to the black skin of their slaves as an outward sign of their moral turpitude. They were black, evil, impure, lewd, devilish, not to be trusted, and thus eminently fit for slavery.

But not only did the whites' church support their notions of black inferiority, so did the intellectuals of the day who invented explanations for their own intellectual superiority. According to Barbara Christian,

Blacks were defined in America as being in some way not quite human because they lacked beauty. . . . When Thomas Jefferson talked about why blacks were inferior to whites he said it was because they were ugly. . . . What was being said was that basically they hadn't evolved to the point that whites had, in other words they were closer to apes. The whole chain of being concept . . . had an impact on the way they were looked at.

Thus beauty, morality, intelligence and the right to political domination are conflated.

For white women, the stereotypes were more than a comfort. They also helped to rationalize a philosophical, economic, and political system that gave rise to and encouraged what Barbara Christian refers to as the stereotype of 'the lady,' a stereotype which is most apparent in southern and black literature of the nineteenth century. According to Christian, the stereotypes of black women, including that of the matronly mammy, the comical darky, the sensuous mulatta, all emerged in direct response to the southern myth of the lady who, to this day, remains the ideal of female beauty for many black women.

But black women are everything the lady is not. Some of us may still remember old advertisements in which the buxom figure of a broad-smiling and bandana-wearing mammy was prominent. Aunt Jemima became a household name, an example of the sugary sweet, servile, nourishing female image at the center of the stereotype. (The stereotype still survives today in the figure of the black matriarch popularized by the Moynihan Report in 1965 which offered America an image of an independent, domineering female figure who not only made black men look weak but also undermined the black family by reversing the roles of male and female.) The lady, of course, in her submissive dependent posture is there to maintain the order of the ideal white southern household. Unlike the mammy who is a surrogate mother to her children, who with her ample body is as strong and loyal as a she-bear and who is black, fat, and ugly, the lady is as slender, fair and beautiful as she is disdainful and remote. As the repository of southern culture the lady must be chaste. But elsewhere life on the plantation was full of sexuality. For these purposes the southern gentleman sought out the 'mulatta,' a cross between lady and animal, the beauty and the beast, the white woman and the black woman. Brown and with muted negroid features, she is white enough not to offend the gentleman's sensibilities, yet black enough to invite lust, rape and defilement. A foil to the virtuous southern belle, she is seen as lusty, impure, accessible, and base.

The mammy and the mulatta represent the opposite poles of the black female stereotype. In black society's hierarchy of beauty, the mulatta is at the top for approximating the look of the lady. Since, in black society, as Barbara Christian observes, 'the beauty issue is always connected to class,' the mulatta helps to create within black society an order of social rank based on beauty. Even though within this context the mulatta may represent an ideal type, from the vantage point of the majority culture, she, like all other black women, cannot escape the stereotype which puts her on the threshold of 'whiteness' but which keeps her a perpetual outsider.

It is true [says Margaret Wilkerson] that white women suffer under the notions of beauty but black women suffer doubly, triply under them because in one sense the standard for white beauty has been defined in opposition to the black norm. . . . Thin lips, aquiline nose, color of eyes, are in direct conflict to what is the norm for blacks.

The myth of beauty as whiteness that whites imposed on blacks, was more than an attempt to force the value system of one culture upon another culture: beyond that, it was a means of utterly denying the validity of black culture. Blacks were, after all, seen by whites as being closer to animals than they were to the white man with all his culture and beauty. Tragically – but unavoidably – blacks began to believe in the myth of their ugliness themselves. Barbara Christian calls this 'cultural mutilation,' and shows how Toni Morrison's poignant and eloquent *The Bluest Eye* demonstrates the devastating consequences that the Western ideal of beauty has had on the black American, in general, and young black women, in particular. The line between myth and reality dissolves as

Morrison sketches a picture of the Breedloves, a black family which embodies all the ugliness of the race:

They lived there because they were poor and black, and they stayed there because they believed they were ugly. Although their poverty was traditional and stultifying, it was not unique. But their ugliness was unique. No one could have convinced them that they were not relentlessly and aggressively ugly. . . . You looked at them and wondered why they were so ugly; you looked closely and could not find the source. Then you realized that it came from conviction, their conviction. It was as though some mysterious all-knowing master had given each one a cloak of ugliness to wear, and they had each accepted it without question. The master had said, 'You are ugly people.' They had looked at themselves and saw nothing to contradict the statement; saw, in fact, support for it leaning at them from every billboard, every movie, every glance. 'Yes,' they had said, 'You are right.' And they took the ugliness in their hands, threw it as a mantle over them, and went about the world with it. Dealing with it each according to his way.[2]

The horror of Morrison's tale is not so much that 'some mysterious all-knowing master' has handed out ugliness, has created creatures not in his own beautiful image, but rather that through centuries of habit, of quiet acquiescence to the whip and the word, of adoring his public image, the initial lie had become credible to its victims. Morrison shows us ugliness seeping through the skin, becoming conviction. Not only have the Breedloves been victimized by others, but, worse, they are the victims of their own self-hatred, believing that love and happiness and virtue are awarded only to the beautiful, to those with bluest eyes. Outward beauty becomes a sign of inward possibilities and, conversely, ugliness, a sign of moral decrepitude, of a purposeless life wasting away.

Morrison shows us how black women suffer because of their vulnerability to the dominant culture's myth of beauty. In the hierarchy that beauty creates, Pecola, the youngest of the Breedloves, and the passive center of the novel, stands on the lowest rung feeling powerless and unloved, wishing for blue eyes, imagining that blue eyes will bring her happiness and love, and save her from scorn and solitude. The obsessive concern with ugliness is passed from woman to woman in the family. Her mother has finally learned to come to terms with her ugliness by submitting herself to the order of a white, middle-class Dick-and-Jane household, by imagining, for moments, that she, in all her blackness and with her crippled leg, is needed in this white paradise of blue eyes and blond hair. But in a brilliant and haunting passage Morrison lets us know that Mrs Breedlove's self-hatred was also deeply rooted, and cemented in a movie theatre, stronghold of cultural images. In the winter of her last pregnancy, 'she learned all there was to love and all there was to hate,' as she watched the image of Jean Harlow.

There in the dark [Morrison tells us], her memory was refreshed, and she succumbed to her earlier dreams. Along with the idea of romantic love she was introduced to another – physical beauty. Probably the most destructive ideas in the history of human thought. . . . In equating physical beauty with virtue she stripped her mind, bound it, and collected self-contempt by the heap. (p. 97)

But while Mrs Breedlove finds an escape, first through the illusory world of movies, and then through her service to a white household, Pecola swallows, like poison, the dominant culture's image of beauty. She cannot separate image from reality. Morrison shows her consuming the image. As she eats a Mary Jane candy she cannot separate the wrapping from the food, the image from the substance. 'To eat the candy is somehow to eat the eyes, to eat Mary Jane. Love Mary Jane. Be Mary Jane.' (p. 43) Pecola's madness grows with her self-hatred. She requests the bluest of eyes, and imagining that she has acquired them, she believes she will live happily ever after. But she does not. She cannot escape who she is.

Pecola's story can be seen as an ironic inversion of a fairy tale. Although in her imagination her desire approaches fulfilment, the harsh reality is that her wish does not come true. She is not transformed from a black duckling to a blue-eyed swan. Nor is she saved by a handsome prince. Her goodness, her chastity, her beauty are not privately rewarded or publicly acknowledged with marriage. Her life is not one of regeneration but of degeneration. Because of her ugliness, her loss of innocence, her 'badness,' she is publicly shunned, left alone to remember the terror of her rape, to remember that her father, however brutal, was the only one to acknowledge her, to make something 'meaningful' out of human contact. There is, finally, no reconciliation of any sort, no celebration of a new order, of a new union. There is only the painful recognition that she has become the repository of all black women's fears, all their feelings of unworthiness and self-hatred, all their 'ugliness,' and that beyond that she stands stupid and alone, walled in by her madness, a symbol of the alienation and 'ugliness' of her race.

All of our waste which we dumped on her [the narrator recalls], she absorbed. And all of our beauty, which was hers first and which she gave to us. All of us – all who knew her – felt wholesome after we cleaned ourselves on her. We were so beautiful when we stood astride her ugliness. (p. 159)

Morrison's fable about blackness and beauty taps something intrinsic to the politics of beauty. She shows us that female beauty cannot be seen from a purely objective, amoral, apolitical perspective. The whole notion of female beauty depends on a hierarchy which exists to distinguish the 'haves' from the 'have nots,' those who merit visibility from those condemned to invisibility. Moving a bit beyond the novel, we can see that Pecola is like the black woman on whom white women dump their waste, on whom they can clean themselves, against whom they can measure their own beauty.

But the problem clearly is more than a black-white issue. While antebellum southerners may have used the black stereotype to bolster their own sense of beauty, American Indians and the subsequent flow of immigrants from Asian and Third World countries added to the set of images with which white Americans defined their own beauty. These women, too, have been bound by crippling stereotypes. The Latin woman is hot-blooded, more animal than lady. The Asian woman is seen as a prostitute, a bar girl, a dragon lady, or as a delicate, passive, desexed doll. The American ideal of beauty is defined by contrast to any non-white ethnic look.

The real damage that the stereotype causes among non-dominant ethnic groups is in forcing women in these groups to judge themselves according to the American ideal. Like blacks they have created a hierarchy of beauty based on the closeness of their approximation to the white ideal, thus establishing a caste system based on beauty, a system which has been extended into other countries, where women scramble to bleach or straighten their hair, undergo operations to round their eyes, narrow their lips, or reshape their noses. Jane Fonda tells of

a huge billboard in Saigon showing a larger-than-life Asian woman in a *Playboy* bunny type of pose. The billboard was advertising the services of an American plastic surgeon whose specialty was changing Vietnamese women's eyes from their natural almond shape to the rounder shape of the Caucasian eye. For a little more money, he also performed operations to enlarge breasts and buttocks.

According to Fonda,

a prostitute could increase her price with her American tricks if she conformed to the Western playboy sexual standard. And these operations weren't confined only to prostitutes. Many were done on women in 'high society'. . . . These women literally had their faces and bodies Americanized.[3]

With few exceptions the minority women to whom we spoke told how deeply ugly they felt, or had once felt. It was not just a matter of wishing they were thinner, or that their eyes were bigger, or their noses smaller, like some of the Caucasian women we talked to, but rather they remembered what it had been like growing up believing they were ugly and knowing that there was nothing to do about it. To many, billboards, movies, and magazines showed images that they would rather not see. For these women the American Dream of beauty was a perpetual reminder of what they were not, and could never be. Many of their stories revealed how tortured and powerless the dominant culture's ideal of beauty made them feel. Others spoke of anger, of conflicts in families and communities, of hatred they felt toward those who 'had it.' Unlike women from the majority culture who try to measure themselves against the ideal, most of these women tried to ignore it, not always successfully.

One topic that kept coming up in conversations with these women was their feeling of being caught between two cultures, of being asked to look and behave two different ways, of being told from very early on that they had to conform to two different standards of beauty. And beyond this, of having to confront what they really looked like, which often approached neither the standards of their own ethnic group nor that of the majority culture. For many the conflict between private image and public image, between reality and the ideal, began at home. A number of women commented extensively on the way their mothers looked. Some spoke of the difficulty they had in reconciling themselves to their mothers' looks, while others mentioned being troubled because they felt that they did not look as good as their mothers. In a few cases daughters blamed the mothers (not the fathers) for their 'ugliness,' their feelings of unworthiness, and their unhappiness. Often their feelings about both themselves and their mothers were divided: in public they saw their mothers in one light, at home in another. As in Morrison's novel, anxiety about beauty was passed from one woman to the next in the family. Most revealing is the power that culturally imposed notions of beauty had in creating or accentuating problems in the home as well as the community.

A young black woman of high school age from a lower middle-class family confides some of her dark, and up until now, secret thoughts.

A couple years ago when all this shit was coming out about Lady Di and how shy and pretty she was and all that, I wished I could look like her. I started straightening my hair and trying to get it to sort of flip up and all that. But it wouldn't go that way. I remember crying ... it seems like I was always crying in those days ... wishing that my hair would fall out and grow back in again straight and smooth like they have on TV. I used to always feel ugly, especially when I was little, when I'd go out and play and some of my friends were little white girls and their hair flied in the wind. With me all the boys called me big ass or black ass. Even black boys. I hated them. Sometimes I'd go home crying and dreamed that I was never born or that if I was my mother would be white. I never told her how much I hated looking at her. ... I love her but I hated looking at her. ...

A Japanese-American woman whose mother did not speak a word of English tells how, in her youth, her mother was virtually locked up at home cooking, caring for children, and mourning her separation from her youngest child. During the difficult economic times that followed World War II, one of her sisters had been temporarily given to an American couple to look after. A couple of years later when the mother and father felt they were able to care for the child they asked for her return. Not only did the couple not want to give up the child, but the child, who by this time was six years old, did not want to return home. 'She's so ugly and can't speak English. She is not my mother,' the woman recalls her sister crying out on her Sunday visits, always afraid she would be made to stay.

I must admit [the woman tells us], I couldn't help but have a little of her attitude rub off on me. There she was dressed in her Sunday best, looking as American as a Japanese could look and there we were barely making it ... our sister but not our sister. My mother toothless with a kind but somewhat stupid looking grin on her face seemed not to understand anything that was going on. But when my little sister left she would sit in the corner and cry softly. I felt sorry for her.... I felt ashamed of her. In those days even American mothers stayed home and it was just as well. Part of me didn't want to be seen with her. The other part was her daughter.... we were a close family but what I knew about my mother no one else knew, she just looked a certain way to them.

A young woman of Central American descent reveals her fears of growing old and looking like her mother. She speaks of her mixed feelings of pride and shame.

When I was growing up [she tells us], I always thought my mother was pretty and I used to imagine growing up and becoming beautiful like her. Her body seemed so soft and womanly. She had a pretty smile. Her eyes seemed to sparkle and speak, to say so many tender things. I used to like to look at her. But when I got older, when I started going to school things seemed to slowly change. She used to walk me to school at first, to stand around a while and look at me playing in the school yard. Sometimes she would go up to the teacher and talk to her. I used to see the two of them standing there, one tall with light brown hair, light complexion and light eyes, the other short and round with jet black hair, eyes to match and skin with an olive brown cast. The difference struck me but it struck me more when I began to feel not pretty, when I began to look at some of the other little girls around me who looked so angelic with their blond, blond hair and blue eyes. They were always called pretty girls ... big round eyes like those Keane paintings. I would go home and seek comfort there but I began not to feel the same. My mother began not to look pretty. She did not look like the mothers of some of the girls at school ... I remember one mother who kind of looked like Lana Turner but not as sexy.... She was always dressed up with hair in a curly bouffant style. She spoke English so clearly. My mother with her accent and her hands, which tried to make up for the words that she didn't know, seemed out of place, not right, there. When I was a teenager I sometimes wished she'd go away. Not really, but I did. I mean I wanted her there with me but I wanted her to speak differently even look differently.... I feel awful saying all this. I feel guilty. People tell me she's attractive. The worst part is that now that I am older I understand a lot of things that I didn't then and still feel afraid that when I grow old I will look like her, look like all her friends who don't seem to care about getting fat and growing old. I wouldn't mind so much if people didn't always put it down.

A woman of Mexican descent unravels a story about how beauty not only drove her away from home but drove her to the brink of despair. She was born in a city in northern Mexico, the second of three children. Her mother, as she tells it, was the third daughter of a family of moderate means. All three sisters were light-complexioned and considered beautiful. With the exception of her mother, the daughters married at a 'suitable' age. When her mother reached the age of twenty-four her parents panicked, thinking that she would never marry, and married her off to an up-and-coming bureaucrat who was largely of Indian stock. Her grandparents never fully approved of his background, but felt he had a promising future. She said:

There was always this thing about color of skin and gradations of color. . . . it was almost as if we were only skin. . . . I was born the darkest of the three. That marked me for life. My grandmother would not let me forget it. It was always my sister she played with and picked up. . . . my sister had green eyes like my mother. . . . I was called 'indita' or 'negrita.' I looked like my father. I was ugly, no doubt about that . . . at least that's the way I felt for years. So ugly and so dark that I wasn't to go out in the sun. . . . my father punished me for this once. . . . and why didn't I do something to my 'indita' hair. This is mostly what I remember when I think about my childhood. How ugly I was and no one would let me forget it. In my late teens I met a Mexican from the US. He had green eyes. He told me I was beautiful. Imagine. Me, beautiful? No one ever said that to me before. I left with him, came to this country, almost like I was leaving my ugliness behind. But you don't just pick up and leave those things. They stay with you. It was no different here. Only worse. I was Mexican and that said it all. Dark and Mexican. In those days people said 'greasers' . . . you know, thinking we were dirty and women sorta sexy dirt. Problems from 'gringos' and problems at home. It would have been easier if I weren't so dark. . . . My husband called me 'negrita' too, at first as a cariño [pet name], but then with the fights it was bad. It was always better here too to be a white Mexican because you could 'pass.' I don't know . . . you know pale is seen as ugly and then they want you pale. All the love songs about dark women and then they look at blond. . . . I remember one fight when my darkness was thrown at me and how güera [blond], fulana de tal [what's her name] next door was, and all this. That was it. The end.

I cried about my ugliness. I cried about my marriage. He was sorry but it was too late. He wanted his 'negrita' back. I couldn't forget about my ugliness. I had a dream about my mother and that I looked like her. I always thought she was pretty. . . . I wanted to get out of my skin. . . . For many years I felt no purpose but my children helped me through. . . . my daughter looks like me and I think she's pretty. I don't know any more. Now in the pictures sometimes you see dark women and I think they are beautiful. Don't you?

A black woman talks about how in her youth her mother offered, with her light skin and refined features, a picture of prettiness, a picture which she felt because of her more negroid looks that she could never hope to match. She felt inadequate. She considered cosmetic surgery once to have her lips reduced, to have herself made into an image closer to white, like her mother.

I've never had very positive feelings about my looks [she reflects]. As a teenager I remember being very upset by the fact that my lips were full and that my hair was far more curly than my mother's was. . . . that was a bit of a problem. My mother is lighter in skin color than I was and her hair is nearly straight and having that comparison of 'here's a woman who is considered very attractive' and having a daughter with hair that has to be straightened if it's going to be anything approaching straight, and with a very full mouth. It was very difficult accepting myself as being an attractive person at that time. . . . I can remember the first time anybody said to me that I was pretty I said to myself 'are you serious?' I didn't see myself that way.

Now, she says, people say that she looks more and more like her mother. The gleam in her eye betrays her satisfaction.

A black woman who grew up in the Caribbean reflects on how beauty was an integral part not only of the way her culture saw itself but also of the way she saw herself. Her family, she tells us, to a large extent measured itself by how it looked. In this hierarchy of beauty, her mother, though from an economically and socially inferior class, was definitely looked up to. Beauty wielded power.

I can't remember a time when it wasn't [she says about the traumas caused by beauty at home and in her personal life]. My mother's very light of skin and my father's very dark and from the time I can remember he always made a point of saying one of the reasons he married my mother was because she was light-skinned, because he was so dark. . . . You see, if you're black in the Caribbean, as opposed to being brown, especially at the time he was growing up, you couldn't get anywhere. Your color . . . your shade stopped you from moving into another profession. He was the son of a sugar-cane cutter who ended up being a lawyer and he was very ambitious. . . . One of the reasons that he married my mother is that he did not want his children to go through what he went through, so he was concerned that they be lighter . . . but also that they not be different colors because all the problems of the caste system, which was based on shade, would begin to erupt. When I was growing up everybody was classified, both the men and women, in an informal way, in terms of the color of their skin, the texture of their hair, the features, whether their features were keen or broad, negroid, or Caucasian, the form of their body, whether it was round or lean . . . and all of the people of the upper middle class were sons and daughters of Danish and black or British and black . . . so there was a clear class system based on the way you looked. . . . the way you looked helped you. It was a criterion for your growth in terms of economics, in terms of status. . . . So for my father if he wanted to improve his life it was important for him to be connected with that . . . so his children would be better off. . . . I resented tremendously being cast in that mold. People would say she's pretty even though she is dark. My sister, on the other hand, was looked at as being ugly. I don't know, maybe because her features were flatter, more negroid.

There are other stories. Many more, which detail the pain and the trauma of being made to feel inferior, of being told that you are an outsider because of language or looks, of knowing that, through no fault of your own, through no flaw in your character, you are an outcast.

It is [as one woman put it] like having a hell inside you. Like being in hell . . . not knowing who you are or even what you want. Not being able to say anything really about it because there is nothing to say, nothing you can do. You're born that way. That's it.

It is tragic if a child can come to accept media images as normal and desirable and find her mother an insult to her eyes because she violates the ruling aesthetic. It is tragic if shame can make a child want to hide her mother away, to make her want to go and hide herself, or to fear that when she grows up, she will have to bear the burden of her mother's looks. It may be difficult for us to understand how feelings of powerlessness, of ugliness can all be blamed on a mother. It is too simple to say that for the child the mother is a reflection of herself, someone she hates to look at, who is, like herself, 'ugly.' These mothers embody ugliness not because they are literally ugly, but because they are considered ugly by a culture that likes to see itself as beautiful. Even when mothers are all that is desirable in an ethnic group, the daughters suffer as much, if not more. As the woman from Mexico told us, 'Sometimes I felt as if I were the only black spot on the family, the ugly one who made all of us ugly. . . . it was like betraying my mother. Anyhow, that's the way my grandmother made me feel.'

Of course, for these women, their mothers were only part of a larger picture. Those who had daughters spoke of their daughters as well, or of conflicts with sisters and brothers. Often in minority families, like the Caribbean woman's, the degree of similarity to the dominant culture creates a hierarchy within the family. The father marries the mother hoping that his children will all be the same shade so that the caste system outside isn't duplicated in the home. For the Mexican woman, the tragedy of that duplication is realized, with herself on the bottom rung and her mother on top.

All these stories point up the tension that exists between a non-dominant ethnic group and the dominant culture. The young girl hating to look at her mother but liking the images presented on TV is an extreme example. But even women who grew up at a time when integration was not usual and when TV was just beginning its intrusion into homes reflect on how peer pressure held up whiteness as the standard by which all were to be judged.

I think about predominantly negative experiences as I grew up [a black woman told us]. Now, I grew up in a predominantly black neighborhood and went to a predominantly black high school and junior high school and elementary school . . . so even within a black context . . . the majority standards were felt in certain ways. . . . The whole attachment was to be a very white, small, and thin, very aquiline featured woman, very 'feminine'. . . . there were often negative comments just in teasing each other about looks, about big lips, big hips or whatever. . . . for example, I was very large for my age. . . . the tendency was not to see large girls as attractive. I never perceived myself as being beautiful or particularly attractive so I developed my mind.

It is normal for children to absorb the values of the majority culture; in fact, it is difficult not to. The adoption of these values is largely responsible for the agony that so many children have endured.

The woman of Japanese descent, for example, kept referring to her divided feelings of loyalty. Her need to cut and curl her hair the way 'all the popular girls did,' to speak English perfectly, to succeed in school and, later in the world, in short, to become a full-fledged member of the American community caused her to pull away from her mother and her home. She felt deeply guilty (as did most of the women we talked to) for dividing her world between public fantasies and private affiliations. At home, she told us, she felt 'at home.' There was no conflict with Japanese culture which to this day she esteems highly but which wasn't part of the 'American way,' within which she had to function daily. She admitted that from the time when she would gaze in wonder at her little Americanized sister, she would spend days and nights fantasizing how to look more 'American,' how to become more American, and all the social advantages she would enjoy once she achieved her goal. There was nothing she could do about her round moon-shaped face, but she could redo her hair, learn how to dress, act, and speak like those she admired. She laments now that the price for all this was breaking away from her family, becoming literally unable to speak to her mother, their communication reduced to a few words which always triggered emotional responses but inevitably ended in silences, eyes that yearned to speak, and hands that touched

But even those who – out of cultural pride or principle or preference – try to keep to the standards of their cultures cannot help feeling the strain of having to live in a society which still tends to punish differences and reward conformity. So the woman from the Caribbean spoke about the innumerable contradictions within her family, the fierce pride in her culture, on the one hand, the private feelings that white was not beautiful but deathlike, that whites lacked real sexuality and the ability to find pleasure in color and dress and song, that they did not know how to laugh. And, on the other hand, the inability to feel comfortable with her own culture, the color of her skin or the texture of her hair, because another way of looking was supposed to be better, and skin color or hair could be passports to success. She spoke of her continual concern with my hair. Whether my hair was going to become more kinky or less kinky was a very important issue as it was for all my brothers and sisters and cousins and everyone who I knew. You couldn't change perhaps the color of your skin but the concern with the hair ... here was a very interesting contradiction for me because my father came from a family whose father was very proud of being pure black. When my father married my mother, my grandfather did not speak to my mother until I was about six or seven because he looked at her as being a mongrel.... my father had some of that too. When I was five or six – and this was one of my first precise memories – my mother pressed my hair for an occasion (which by the way was an awful experience because your ears burned and the smell of the burning hair and so on). My father came in and saw me with my hair all straightened. He was furious. He put me under the shower. He was livid. Yet he admired that quality in other women. So there was this contradiction. When I came home from college with my hair in an Afro and I walked off the plane my mother started bawling. I don't mean crying, I mean bawling like when somebody dies.... But my father's reaction to it was very interesting because it reminded him of his mother and the older women he had known when he was a boy.... He would knock it down in terms of what he felt it meant politically and radically but he still responded to it aesthetically. So there was this contradiction. On one hand you had the whole culture say the best thing to have was lighter skin, white features, straight hair, on the other hand, people themselves didn't always respond that way so I got a lot of double signals when I was a kid.

Yet, she told us that despite her father's pride in the black look, despite the fact that he remembered with admiration the older women he had known when he was a boy, despite having a little of his own father's attitude rub off on him, 'my father to this day thinks blacks are ugly.' He married a light-skinned woman.

One of the most painful experiences for women of minority cultures is the way they think men see them. The attitude of the sexes toward each other in an ethnic group shows that group's confusion about its standards of beauty.

It is not simply a matter of little boys in a school yard unknowingly deriding the look of their ethnic group by making fun of little girls – their big lips, their dark skin, or their Chinese eyes. It lies more in the husband's confused criticism of his wife whose appearance he first praises and later derogates as 'negrita,' a word at once full of endearment and insult; or, in the story of the man who marries a woman of lighter skin thinking that by so doing he is marrying 'up.' These are not uncommon stories. Their familiarity breeds strife in ethnic communities, assures women that what they have feared all along is true: they are ugly. Yet, in truth, the men are just as confused as the women about female beauty, because it is charged with so much cultural, social, and political meaning. The majority culture teaches us that power and money are not only ways out of poverty but give meaning and substance to the life of anyone who has them.

In oppressed cultures the question of beauty becomes complicated because both men and women are discriminated against for the way they look. Everyone of both sexes is ugly. In this both are equally oppressed. Under the weight of this ugliness the men, not surprisingly, look on their women as butts for all their feelings of unworthiness, self-hatred, and self-doubt. To go back to Morrison's example, within each group women become the ugliest of the ugly – Pecolas all. But for men there is always the ambivalence, the tension, of the visceral attraction, on the one hand, of their own women, and on the other hand, the admiration, and, even, adoration from a distance of the white women who represent the power that they are denied.

I don't know [a man of Mexican descent told us], I went down to Mexico and I saw the same thing there. All these really beautiful Mexican ladies . . . and I mean really beautiful . . . but if these blond women passed all the men's heads would turn. It didn't matter how ugly they might be. They'd rather go after an unattractive blond than a pretty Mexican woman. It's a real status to be seen with a blond. It used to be that way here. 'Gringas' are still 'in' in some parts. But not just any 'gringa.'

It is the same in other cultures. The attraction of black men to tall Germanic blondes is by now legendary. During the 1960s when blacks proclaimed that 'black is beautiful,' many black men could be found chasing white women, admiring their beauty, and making many black women feel uglier than ever. A black woman recalls,

During the period when the Civil Rights movement had taken hold, it certainly did strike me, as it did many other black women, that many of the men that we considered to be 'conscious' chose blond women to go out with. It certainly affected us. It affected our social life. It affected the way in which we thought about ourselves. . . . It set up again that fear. . . . black women . . . were not as valued as white women. . . . The men really did feel that white women were better looking.

Black men's disparagement of black women and their idealization of white women shows clearly how beauty becomes politicized. Eldridge Cleaver's autobiography *Soul on Ice* provides a raw account of the pain for black men in moving between two cultures, one intimate and familiar, and another oppressive and foreign, between black women and white women. Cleaver begins his work by telling of his obsession with the beauty of white women, an obsession that puts him in jail. 'I became a rapist,' he confesses. 'I started out practicing on black girls . . . when I considered myself smooth enough, I crossed the tracks and sought out white prey.' He sees his actions as deliberate and revengeful, revolutionary even. 'I was defying and trampling upon white man's law, upon his system of values. . . . I was defiling women,' he writes, 'I was resentful over . . . how the white man had used black women.'[4] But one wonders as one reads Cleaver how much of his act is conscious revenge and how much of it irrational hatred, not just of white women but of black women as well, on whom he 'practices'; whom he, like the white man, uses; whom he clearly believes are 'ugly.' He sees himself as a victim of his own self-hatred, of his powerlessness. (He calls himself a Black Eunuch.) We begin to understand this fully when he describes his chaste cell-bound love affair with paper playmates. He tells us of his calm, quarrel-free 'marriage' to a voluptuous white centerfold bride upon whom he freely bestows his affections until she is ripped from the wall on which she is displayed by a prison guard showing off his 'masculine' strength and power, who warns Cleaver that he must use a 'colored girl for a pinup.' (p. 8)

The anecdote offers a painful and dramatic example of the politics of beauty. The episode leads Cleaver to ask himself: 'did I really prefer white girls over black? The conclusion was clear and inescapable: I did.' (p. 8) He is bound to white man's values. He reveres them. But he is tortured by the realization. He talks to his friends to see if he alone among them is driven by an obsession with white women, but he finds that they too prefer white women, any other women for that matter, to black women. After one of the inmates, Butterfly, observes that 'we've had the white woman dangled before our eyes like a carrot on a stick before a donkey: look but don't touch,' Cleaver concludes that he was 'indoctrinated to see the white woman as more beautiful and desirable than ... [the] black woman.' (p. 10) There is no doubt that, in Cleaver's words, 'loving oneself less,' can lead to seeing oneself and one's people as ugly, as less than human, as divested of manhood or womanhood. The end of his autobiography ('To All Black Women, From All Black Men') reads like the reverse of the beginning. It is an encomium to the black woman, whom he now sees as 'Queen,' a 'Black Beauty.' He apologizes. He begs for atonement. He reveals his guilt for having substituted a paper bride, an image, a fantasy, for the 'Black Bride of My Passion.' Somehow, despite or rather because of the inflated rhetoric, it is hard to take the recantation as fully sincere. Cleaver's testimonial bursts with anger and one wonders if the man who later strutted in 'Cleaver pants' with their accentuated codpiece and who then embraced the values of the culture he once despised, doesn't still look at himself as ugly, as a black eunuch. One feels the cruelty of it all.

I spent 3 years hatin' white women so much it nearly made me crazy [a young black woman confesses]. It came from discovering how the whole world had this white idea of beauty. See, the western world concept of beauty is your kind of beauty, not mine ... the ads and all that – they still think in terms of narrow noses and light skin and straight hair. . . . And I mean, I just hated that so much that for 3 years I wouldn't speak to a white woman. And then I realized what I was doing to myself. I was losing my self-respect and even losing my looks. I finally had to work myself out of it. I had to find a new sense of my own dignity, what I really had to do was start *seeing* all over again, in a new way ... to see differently. That's hard!⁵

These stories are common. Men's troubled attitude toward white women and women of their ethnic group is matched only by the confusion of many women who are caught in the double-bind of hating not only other women but themselves as well.

Non-white men, like women, engage in the time-consuming and painful experience of worrying about how they look, about whether or not they are 'beautiful.' They, too, process their hair, bleach their skin, get permanents, and dress up to be noticed. (And, as women from some ethnic groups tell us, they *do* notice . . . the sway of their hips, the broadness of their shoulders, their walk, their clothes.) Many are caught in the belief that, if nothing else can, clothes make the man. They use clothes not just as a badge of group membership (although it is that too), but also (challenging the majority culture's view of them as indistinguishable from one another) as a way of calling attention to their individuality. Men of the majority culture would not be caught dead in such outlandish display – of course, since they have no need to.

The flashy display is one way of denying the feelings of impotence based on non-white skin color. Another way is through denial: claiming that it is not a problem. Richard Rodriguez, in his book *Hunger of Memory*, not only praises the public benefits of assimilation, but also concludes, 'My skin, in itself, means nothing. I stress the point because I know there are people who would label me "disadvantaged" because of my color.'[6] The statement is bold, especially since a significant portion of the book is spent detailing the psychological trauma that he endured growing up dark in America. He remembers his mother calling him 'negrito,' chiding him for not covering his skin.

You know how important looks are in this country. With 'los gringos' looks are all that they judge you on. But you! Look at you! You're so careless. . . . You won't be satisfied till you end up looking like 'los pobres' who work in the fields, 'los braceros.' (p. 113)

He remembers women in his family speaking with 'pleasure at having light children . . . of fear of having a dark-skinned son or daughter.' He remembers an aunt who 'prescribed to her sisters the elixir of large doses of castor oil during the last weeks of pregnancy (the remedy risked an abortion),' and children who were born dark having 'their faces treated regularly with a mixture of egg white and lemon juice' – in his case, he tells us, 'the solution would never take.' (p. 116) And he remembers how:

One night when I was eleven or twelve years old, I locked myself in the bathroom and carefully regarded my reflection in the mirror over the sink. Without any pleasure I studied my skin. . . . (In my mind I heard the swirling voices of my aunts, and even my mother's voice, whispering incessantly about lemon juice solutions and dark *feo* children).... I began soaping my arms. I took my father's straight razor.... Slowly, with steady deliberateness, I put the blade against my flesh, pressed it as close as I could without cutting, and moved it up and down across my skin to see if I could get out, somehow lessen, the dark.... the dark would not come out. It remained. Trapped. Deep in the cells of my skin. (pp. 124–5)

The episode is poignant: a child literally trying to scrape the color off his skin. But the story of his darkness does not end there. Even though he claims that at an early age language became his key to success in the 'public' world, it could not wipe out the envy he felt, in his adolescent years, at seeing his light-skinned brother sporting 'girl friends who seemed ... glamorous (because they were) blondes.' (pp. 114–15) Nor could it wipe out the feelings of 'shame and sexual inferiority' that he would feel years later because of his 'dark complexion.' (p. 124)

I judged myself ugly [he confesses], since the women in my family had been the ones who discussed it in such worried tones. I felt my dark skin made me unattractive to women.... I grew divorced from my body.... I denied myself a sensational life ... riding shirtless on a bicycle in the warm wind ... the sensations that first had excited a sense of maleness, I denied. I was too ashamed of my body. (pp. 125–6)

So, he tells us, he stayed out of the sun, shunned sports, and took instead to study, sometimes suspecting that 'education was making me effeminate.' (p. 127) And this is not all. His obsession with his looks, with his darkness, with his 'ugliness,' spills over to the rest of the book. He talks of his family in terms of their color. His mother, his brother, his father, his sister, are light of skin or they do not look Mexican, not, at least, in the sense of looking Indian. His father is white, recalling the faces of French men; his mother could easily pass for Portuguese or Italian, he tells us; his older brother is handsome, reminding him of Mario Lanza; his younger sister is 'exotically pale.' 'But,' he says, 'I never forgot that only my older sister's complexion was as dark as mine.... I guessed that she found her dark skin a burden. I knew that she suffered from being a "nigger".' (p. 115) He feels all this despite the fact that as he points out, in Mexican culture it is a mark of manliness to be 'feo, fuerte, y formal' (literally: ugly, strong, and responsible). Significantly, Rodriguez claims that 'During these years when middle-class Black Americans began to assert with pride, "Black is Beautiful," I was able to regard my complexion without shame.' (p. 136) It is during these years, he tells us, that he reclaimed his manhood.

'Dark-skinned.' To be seen at a Belgravia dinner party. Or in New York. Exotic in a tuxedo. My face is drawn to severe Indian features which would pass notice on the page of *National Geographic*, but in a cocktail party in Bel Air somebody wonders: 'Have you ever thought of doing any high fashion modeling?' (p. 3)

It is with this self-portrait that Rodriguez opens his autobiography. Proud, now, of his skin color, walking (one assumes) amidst the powerful and the wealthy, he stands out exotic among the rest. But, he says, towards the end of his work, it is all 'an attitude of *mind*, my imagination of myself.' (p. 138) So it may be, but this attitude is directed by the conviction that he, indeed, does look good, however different from the mainstream that look might be, and that conviction did not grow out of a void, but out of the collective efforts of people claiming their color.

It is not hard to see that in claiming their color, blacks were reclaiming their culture, something that had been denied to them because they were too 'ugly,' too 'beastly' to have one.

'Black is Beautiful' [one woman told us] means that not only looks but manner, talk and everything else are being reaffirmed. Historically it was absolutely necessary to go to the extreme and affirm blackness, whatever it was and whatever way it expressed itself, in order to begin to exorcise ourselves. The negative perceptions of blacks have been so deeply ingrained in black America that we needed some sort of extreme notion that 'Black is Beautiful'. . . . We had to redefine and recapture a term that was negative for us. . . . That was an enormous undertaking because how do you get at all the subtle ways in which you are told that you are ugly – and ugly meaning that you are bad and wrong and everything else. . . . we all know that stand-ards of beauty are ways of defining talent, work possibilities. . . . being black and having negroid features is something that is being perceived as an obstacle. . . . what more terrible way to reject someone than to attack their being. . . . It's terribly insidious.

Another woman summed it up simply: 'It means that someone is valued. . . . We're not as a race uglier than any other race.' Language may help break down barriers of communication. It may ease participation in this culture. But beauty ('ugliness') is really the last taboo.

We have been saying all along that divergence from the mainstream means 'ugly,' that the blue-eyed blond with free-floating hair has been this culture's ideal of beauty. But in the 1960s other possibilities asserted themselves. Blacks and other groups who said that not only were they different but, indeed, that they were proud of those differences, *forced* both themselves and mainstream society to take another look, to acknowledge, at least, the reality of different faces rather than to pretend that they did not exist, since their 'ugliness' made them invisible. They made themselves beautiful by saying that they were beautiful: Why hadn't the mainstream noticed? Some did notice finally. Fashionable parties for artists and intellectuals always included token representatives from non-white ethnic groups, the leaders usually, the more educated, the more visible, the more beautiful among them (and these often were the same because of the beauty-color caste system that tended to reward lightness economically and education-ally as well). By the end of the decade, blacks were beginning to make fashion news. The Afro was 'in,' not only among blacks, but also among whites who started to let their previously kinky hair go natural or who got Afro permanents. Mannequins in trendy stores in Europe and the United States started picking up the Afro look and their pigmentation got darker. But their features remained white. This was called 'exotic,' the new term used for 'beauties' who were not white but whose features were close enough to white not to shock the sensibilities of mainstream Americans. In fact, fashion magazines like *Vogue* and *Harper's Bazaar* started picking up the Afro, and using black models and other 'exotics.' From there, it was only a short leap to the advertising pages. Advert-isers realized that there was a whole new market to titillate. Designers such as Bill Blass quickly capitalized on the trend with slogans like 'Blass is Beautiful.' And in 1974 *Vogue* paid its tribute to blackness by putting a black face on its cover for the first time, acknowledging thereby that not only was black beautiful, but, better yet, profitable. People took notice, and attitudes began to change.

You know [a woman in her late thirties confessed to us], when I was in high school, I could never have conceived that blacks were beautiful, not because they aren't but because it never would have crossed my mind. No one had told me. So I didn't notice. Now they really do look different to me. . . . some are really beautiful.

The media can motivate social change. But the media are conservative, and would rather follow than innovate. The social changes of the 1960s led the way. Now it is not unusual to see a few exotics – blacks, Asians or Latins – smiling out from the pages of *Vogue* alongside the blonds who are still the bread and butter of the business. But there are only a few, and still fewer who appear on covers.

The participation of black models [says Beverly Johnson, one of the first black fashion models] is unjust in proportion to the amount of money that is put into the industry by Third World people. . . . We spend millions and millions of dollars, but we don't get a chance to participate in the actual advertising and marketing. . . . There are a few crumbs now, which is also economics. That's how we got into it, dollars and cents. When they took the first chance of putting me on the *Vogue* cover, which was the first to have a black woman, they didn't know it was going to double in circulation. Then they said in *Time* magazine that *Vogue* doubled in circulation based on the pictures of Deborah Turbeville. But it was because they had Chinese women buying it and Puerto Rican women buying it and Mexican women buying it. They can't deny it, but they don't publicize it.

The reason, she adds, that there are not more Third World women in the media is because 'They don't have to put us in them and we don't protest.'[7] The times of protest are over. The slogans are gone. The Afro is no longer 'in,' the ethnic look, so dominant in the 1960s, has been replaced by a quiet conservative elegance, on the one extreme, and, on the other, by 'punk chic.' Hair straightening is back, eye-rounding operations have never left, some women still think of lip reduction. But, somehow, things are different. Exoticism is still in, in Belgravia.

Well, we say as long as the features aren't too negroid, or the face isn't too round, or the eyes too narrow. . . . sure they're beautiful. Yes, they can be beautiful . . . Lena Horne, Bianca Jagger, O. J. Simpson, Rodriguez in a tuxedo. Mainstream Americans can now see that beauty comes in different shades. But there is yet to be a Black Miss America[8] or a Black Miss

Universe. The 'most beautiful girl in the world' is still white. While the young white women we interviewed felt that beauty was not limited to one ethnic group, the majority still preferred to look like Tiegs, 'healthy and fit,' and, we assume, blond and blue-eyed.

Nevertheless, whereas a couple of decades ago black or brown women, with very few exceptions, were treated as if they were invisible, now *Vogue* prints small news items such as one in its October 1982 issue entitled, 'Black, More Than Beautiful' announcing a 'Salute to the Black Model.' It is hard to determine what 'more than beautiful' can mean. The token inclusion of non-white women in national magazines has affected how these women see themselves. Although still not without conflict, especially among children, the gap between private and public image begins to narrow because of continued reinforcement within the individual ethnic groups.

I think there has been a tremendous change in attitude since the '60s [reflects Dr Greta Clarke, a dermatologist]. Now black women accept themselves and their inherited characteristics much better than years before when the Anglo-Saxon look was the standard of beauty and people did use a lot more bleaching cream and did try to straighten and bleach their hair. . . . In my practice women now come in because they have definite spots, melasma, on the skin, not because they don't like the color of their skin . . . I think that awareness and that concern that emerged in the '60s has caused people to look at themselves and accept themselves much better. Being black and being black and beautiful . . . accepting that the hair is curly or kinky, that the skin may be dark, the nose may be broad, or the lips full . . . that there is wide range of appearances that are attractive.

The image of a child trying desperately to scrub the color out of his or her skin is haunting; the idea that children might be able to feel that they are not Pecolas is encouraging. Dr Clarke, like other women we talked to, attributes this emerging acceptance of oneself and one's ethnic characteristics to the post-1960s proliferation of magazines and beauty pageants which cater to specific ethnic groups and which do not necessarily award first prize to the woman who comes closest to looking white. Unlike traditional beauty contests which encourage a homogenous Caucasian look among all, even non-white, contestants, these contests often emphasize ethnic features.

You have more of a sense of individualism [Margaret Wilkerson told us], even though it does have to work within certain perimeters of beauty – you don't see fat women for example. . . . You get more of an ethnic look because they mirror the range of options and styles within a certain culture.

Many women supported the ethnic beauty pageants and images of black fashion models in *Ebony* and *Essence* for this very reason.

The younger generation has an easier go of it than we had [one woman told us]. Younger children have more options, more choices, much more reinforcement in terms of beauty. You have *Essence* magazine, for example. You *have* to go out and buy *Essence* and put it on the coffee table to counteract all the negative images they see on television.

These magazines illustrate, in pictures worth a thousand words of racial-equality messages, that everyone – black, Asian, Indian, Mexican, Filipino – can be beautiful. Slogans have been replaced by visual proof. Cultural diversity is being celebrated. The fairest of them all no longer is necessarily the whitest. There are more choices, more options, but still the negative images proliferate: the bombardment of blonds, the force of history, culture, and money is still stronger than that of the Miss American Indian, or the Miss Filipina, or the Miss Latin American or the Miss Chinatown, and the Miss Black American pageants that so few hear about, and fewer still care about. Their pictures will certainly not be flashed on the 6 o'clock news. They will not get the thousands in prize money, or lucrative contracts that the winners of the major pageants receive. They will not be given worldwide publicity as 'the most beautiful girl in the world.' Habit is hard to break, but still it is slowly being broken. The young black, Asian, and Latin women we interviewed often described looks that approximated either their own ethnic group or another as their ideal, but they still had difficulty identifying themselves as beautiful. How did they see themselves? Some Latin women ventured to say 'attractive'; a number of Asian women called themselves 'cute'; the majority of black women put themselves in neither of these categories – in fact, they could not classify their looks. Whatever the case, young women are no longer subjected to the single authoritative message that those not born white are 'ugly.' In fact, many of the magazines directed towards non-white ethnic groups reflect a variety of looks, ranging from the ideal in white beauty on the one hand to, on the other, a more private, culturally-relative ideal. For example, in *Essence* magazine an ad which opens with the catch phrase 'Too Skinny?' announces how the 'Amazing NEW Ectopian GUARANTEES NEW CURVES IN 30 DAYS.' 'Your product gave me shapely legs, butt and rear . . . really helped me shape up in only 4 weeks,' a reader writes, endorsing the product. (Ads like that are almost unthinkable these days in magazines directed toward a predominantly white audience.) But curiously, only a few pages later the mainstream culture reasserts itself in an ad for 'London University "Crash-Burn" Wonder Diet' which promises 'the fastest weight loss method known to medical science! (Except for total starvation.)' And in *Blacktress* magazine, the cultural contradictions verge on self-parody, for example, an ad for Gain Products, with a drawing which details 'face and neck gain,' 'arms heavier,' 'fuller chest,' 'more inches on hips,' 'thigh heavier,' 'legs fuller,' followed on the other side of the page by the 'London University "Crash-Loss" Diet.' In the same way there are almost no ads for skin lightener, very common a decade ago, but virtually every other ad in *Ebony* or *Essence* or *Blacktress* is for hair relaxers. Still, models have the option of 'relaxed' hair or a modified Afro. Some models, especially for widely distributed products like Virginia Slims cigarettes, have white features (there is one ad where the model is a black Farrah Fawcett look-alike!) but other models, especially those for hair products, have identifiably black features. So there is variety in what young non-white women are being told today, about what being black (or brown) and beautiful, really means. 'I feel like Dr Jekyll and Mr Hyde,' a young woman of Mexican descent told us. 'The Mexican me and the American. Sometimes I wonder who I am.'

Quiet protests still.

I will not straighten my hair [one black woman tells us]. I am absolutely opposed to it. Not because intrinsically there is something wrong . . . but because it represents a particular legacy of mine and I think of most black people. . . . You try to change your hair to look white and as you're doing it, you're affecting your insides, you're saying there is something wrong about you and you communicate that to your kids. . . . I remember my great dream was to wake up . . . I wanted long, long hair that would come down to my hips . . . and my daughter has the same dream now and she should not. She is continually concerned with her hair, wanting it to be long and fly-away like on the TV ads. . . . I think she has a contradiction. On the one hand she wants to look like the models, on the other hand . . . she wants to believe that there is something right about her. There is that tension. . . . she looks at her friends' hair. She looks at their skin. I remember she once told me, 'I am the only person with choco-late skin.' It was like she was both upset about it and proud. . . . There's a lot of suffering involved in trying to make yourself into someone else.

Another woman talks of her daughter feeling a similar confu-sion, but she sees that there is change, that there is no longer a monopoly of one look.

At times [she says of her daughter], she sees a white figure somewhere and says she wished she looked like that white figure . . . she wished that her hair was long and straight or whatever. . . . But she is beginning to challenge her own perceptions. She is more aware of differences than I was. . . . I think that it makes her feel she has a right to her own standards and her own particular differences.

Challenging one's own perceptions is, finally, the most important thing, becoming able to acknowledge differences without assigning a negative value to those differences, without saying that one look is beautiful and another not, only because one look is what we have been accustomed to seeing, what we have been sold as an ideal.

The whole notion of difference [reflects Margaret Wilkerson] is some-thing that we have not come to grips with in our society. We are always saying, in subtle ways, that we assume that difference means inferiority. . . . that we are different from the majority, that's what is implicit in the word 'difference'. . . . We need to deal somehow in our society with the idea that we are a collection of very different kinds of people not only in looks but in terms of our cultural back-ground, and in terms of our goals and objectives. . . . It's frightening to people. It's saying that maybe we are all so different that we can never get back together again, that we can never have any common basis for working together as a country or as different people. We desperately need to understand how to deal with the notion of differ-ence, because, on the one hand, we have been talking about majority norms and how they have affected non-white concepts of beauty, but, on the other hand, even within our own cultural and racial groups we don't always deal with the notion of difference well.

We are at an exciting turning point in our perception of beauty, exciting because the ideal is being challenged. We, the dominant culture, must begin to challenge our own perceptions and accept that with the confluence of different cultures, our cultural diversity is beginning to create a whole new way of looking. A century ago the flood of immigration taught us to see our country as a 'melting pot.' Once again, in a deeper way, we have become a melting pot, a spicy mélange of all sorts of new possibilities, perceived in new and vibrant ways.

The neglect and the trauma that non-white women have undergone cannot be minimized. It has been painful. But the struggle has forced us all to face the question of what beauty is, what it means and why it's important. We have come to understand as a result, often against our will, that people see only what they want to see and what they have been told to see. The mirror has been telling whites for hundreds of years that they, with their fair hair and fair skin, are the fairest of them all. But as in the fairy tale, the mirror on the wall may be on the verge of challenging all those perceptions even to the point of saying that the name of the fairest is Pecola.

We were talking about the subject of this book to a roomful of women. During the question-and-answer period a young, blond woman raised her hand and protested that she has been feeling nondescript, rather ugly because so much is being made of the exotic look. You have to be exotic these days, she says, otherwise you're made to feel terrible, as if you don't rate. Too much emphasis is put on exotic looks. You know, all the emphasis on fashion models. We listen. She is dissatisfied with herself, however blond and blue-eyed, but she will never feel what Pecola felt.

# Chapter 10

# Some Final Thoughts

We have talked a lot about beauty in the foregoing chapters: its varying forms, its importance to us, its elusive definition, the lengths to which people will go to achieve it; our attitudes, our myths, and our language about it; men's feelings about beauty, and the predicament of those who cannot achieve beauty as we define it. But we have only sketchily explored what is suggested by the sub-title of this book: the political nature of beauty. We talked a little about it at the very beginning: beauty as the last taboo, separating woman from woman, women from men, and race from race as well; the power to define or at least determine beauty as power over other people. But we have not really located the source of the power of beauty, nor explained our thesis at any length: that beauty *is* an instrument of political control, that passive as it is, it has great power. We have insisted that beauty is passive, that it is dependent on its beholder for anything it can achieve; and yet at the same time we have said that people will sacrifice themselves for beauty – their own or someone else's.

We have observed the problem of having one's self-esteem depend on a commodity (if we can so think of beauty) that is not in one's power to create, or determine, or choose, and which will certainly disappear, through ageing or changes in the standards of the community, as time goes by. But beyond these truths, we must confront several popular allegations by commentators on the social effects of appearance, as well as by a large and ancient body of misogynistic literature, that women capitalize unfairly on their looks, using them manipulatively to acquire influence and material goods. From this assumption comes the conclusion that women – as possessors of beauty – have unreasonable power: unreasonable precisely because it is passive, not acquired by any real effort on their parts, not representing any active mastery over the universe

277

– like male virtues such as wisdom, political influence or physical strength.

Still another argument fuels the fires of misogyny. The distribution of this particular advantage seems so unfair: the chance to barter looks for influence, practically speaking, is restricted to one sex, and is based neither on actual work expended nor risks taken. Further, beauty is utilized to influence in an underhanded way: it works on the passions and the emotions, not allowing for intellectual judgment. In short, women, in gaining advantage through beauty, are perceived as acting unfairly in at least three ways; and since this is the only way 'real' women may ever achieve influence, it follows that women are either totally useless, or come by their effectiveness in illegitimate ways, and use it illegitimately – or are not 'real' women.

What this position fails to comprehend is that the disadvantage is not confined to men, by any means. First and most obviously, the woman who is not beautiful, or has ceased to be beautiful, has no recourse and no resources at all, while a man in that position has several avenues of accomplishment open to him and can select among them as his talents dictate. But more important is the very passivity of the power of beauty, the fact that it is not in the control of its possessor, in any but the most superficial ways: ways which can never be openly acknowledged or given credit. Because a woman cannot feel she has done it by herself, she cannot feel a sense of achievement, or true pride in accomplishment. There is only the empty vainglory of narcissism, rightly condemned but usually deplored in anger rather than pity, which is more appropriate. Narcissistic pride is gnawing, empty, and ungratifying, especially as the narcissist knows he or she has no control over the source of the 'pride,' and is not even sure that source really exists. The preening, the hours in the beauty salon, are more desperate attempts at reassurance – which can never come – than the self-congratulation which critics take them to be.

And worse: women are praised for beauty, and blamed for beauty – that is, given responsibility for it although they do not have control over it. They are expected to act so as to reap the rewards of their beauty, and are envied and censured for that. Yet we seem never to realize that women do not have power through beauty: *beauty* has power. Therein lies the paradox. Men – whose judgments are what give beauty what power it has – envy and resent women for their supposed 'power' through beauty over men's hearts and minds (and pocketbooks). Women fear and depend upon men, since only men can unlock the 'power' of beauty and make it function to women's advantage. Men are angry at women for possessing a power which, in fact, women do not possess; if anything, it possesses them. Women do not in general truly feel powerful through the possession of beauty, and therefore cannot use that power in simple direct ways. Men resent women for possessing a power which, in fact, is totally in the control of men. It is as if one person envied another for her possession of a diamond necklace: the necklace in fact reposes in the jewelry-box of the first woman, but the key is in the possession of the second, the envier. She, however, is not permitted to wear the necklace herself. Is it any wonder if the two feel continually yet irrationally angry at and resentful of one another, hardly knowing what the fight is about, but continually at odds none the less?

But beauty is a political problem in other ways than its tendency to divide women from men, to make it harder for the sexes to truly cherish each other and appreciate their complementarity. More obviously, it separates woman from woman. Contrary to any reality, beauty is considered a scarce commodity. We feel that there is a limited finite quantity to go around. Therefore, it is not possible, from this perspective, for everyone to be equally beautiful; one woman's beauty diminishes that of the next, subtracts from the latter's resources. To be beautiful is not in itself sufficient: one must be more beautiful than anyone else within range, or one's beauty is non-existent. Snow White's evil stepmother, chanting to her mirror on the wall, is but one example of this perception, hardly unique in her viewpoint and her anxiety.

Hence it becomes important for women to devalue one another's beauty – in the absence of the one being discussed, as well as in her presence (if she thinks she is not beautiful, the feeling goes, perhaps, indeed, very probably, she will not be so). Women's fabled 'cattiness,' their gossipy maliciousness, to the extent that it is real, is an offshoot of our view that beauty is a scarce resource, to be hoarded and counted up, only worth something if you have cornered the market. How do you know if you've cornered the market? Men make it clear. Beauty is measured by the number of men enslaved – preferably snatched from someone else. Given that women have in fact behaved in these ungenerous ways – and there is ample testimony that some always have and some still do – it can be seen as a necessary concomitant of the thesis that beauty is a scarce commodity whose possession can only be gauged by the unhappiness and jealousy of potential rivals. We need hardly point out that men benefit in several ways from this assumption: it forces women to depend all the more on men for self-esteem, it keeps women from forming bonds with other women and thus achieving real political power, it enables men to rule women's destinies. So it seems all the more ungenerous for men to revile women for their cattiness toward one another: it serves them well.

Beauty not only divides men from women and women from one another, but group from group – again to the enhancement of the dominant group. The latter typically possess a monopoly on beauty, and the ability to determine what constitutes beauty – defined according to their image. Since beauty is viewed as a scarce commodity, the dominant group – and particularly its women – must be vigilant in restricting the possession of beauty to members of their own group, and men in the dominant group, to protect their own right to judge beauty, must support them in this. Hence it is important to stereotype non-dominant appearance as ugly, not merely different, to perceive non-dominant groups stereotypically as being as different as possible from the dominant in looks. Hence, too, racist propaganda always seeks to accentuate the differences between dominant and non-dominant races, with the latter viewed insidiously, just as pornography, which is sexist propaganda, represents the sexes in as polarized forms as possible.

We might argue that everyone has the right to define beauty as he or she sees fit – indeed, that it is impossible that it should be otherwise, that we cannot legislate aesthetics, and that the very attempt would be abhorrent. Yet we can argue at least as persuasively that using 'beauty' to set group against group, to inculcate in one group an unwarranted – and therefore uneasy – self-pride, and in another an equally unwarranted, but relatively unbudgeable self-loathing, is a debasement of a noble concept, and that what could serve to enrich and uplift the human race should not be used for the reverse. 'Should not,' certainly; but as with so many 'shalts' we feel the need to impose on ourselves, the commandment is more easily stated than enforced. Those solutions that can be proposed seem facile; we learn to mouth pronouncements of equality of appearance, but in our hearts we feel the same leaps and bounds our ancestors did, confronted with 'same' and 'different.' Even where we most seem to transcend the old invidious ethnic stereotypes – as in intermarriage – deeper investigation often shows that the couple is enchanted by the very fact that it is going against stereotype, its own and that of society. It is perhaps a step up to love someone *because* they look so different and exotic, rather than to hate someone on the same grounds. But, in fact, not all that much progress is made. Looks, and the symbolic effect of differences in superficial appearance, have again carried the day.

And if the competition for the scarce goods tears society apart, what must it do to the individuals? We have seen how hope and fear divide woman from woman, but they also divide woman from herself. On the one hand, beauty is the one sure path to appreciation, power, and happiness. On the other, beauty is a sign of uselessness. On the one hand, it is a gracious gesture to others, as well as insurance for yourself, to spend time on your appearance, to alter, create, conceal. On the other, spending time on appearance is vanity, in both the word's senses, 'false pride,' and 'emptiness,' since such effort does not give one depth or substance, and has no permanency. So a woman feels apologetic and unworthy whichever route she chooses: to be obsessed with appearance or to ignore it. And the middle path is difficult to find, let alone keep to. If a woman uses her beauty to gain power, she is relinquishing all possibilities of autonomy, since beauty is in the eye of the beholder. But even when a woman goes after more autonomous forms of accomplishment, her looks remain paramount in the judgment of others,as is never the case for a man. If she is attractive, the verdict will be that she got where she is through her looks. If she is not, it will be assumed that she sought success elsewhere as a drab consolation prize, all she could hope to get. A man's looks embellish his worldly successes; a woman's define them. A woman therefore cannot be blamed if she feels unresolvable conflict draining time and strength. Who is she? What does she want? And how should she get it?

And how hard should she work for it? What sacrifice is worth making? Or, as some of us would put it, what sacrifice is not? Time and expense, most women readily grant. But health – and life itself? We have seen that the destruction of these, knowingly or not, for the sake of beauty is far from uncommon. And we sense that the connection is not fortuitous. The more a woman risks, the more beautiful she is seen to be – not because the risk enhances the actual beauty itself, so much as because the fact that the woman was prepared to chance so much for the sake of someone else's pleasure or approbation counts for a lot. It is not, we might argue, that cosmetics *ipso facto* enhance; rather, the fact that the wearer went to a lot of trouble – buying, trying, applying – is a signal to the viewer; 'I care enough about what you think of me to put a great deal into how I look to you.' Cosmetics are not merely a statement – 'I am an attractive woman' – but an offer: 'I want to be attractive to you, and I am willing to go to trouble to prove it.' Who could resist an enticement like that?

At the same time, it is wrong to be altogether negative about beauty. For one thing, what enterprise could be more futile and unpopular than attempting to give beauty a bad name? For another, what could be more inhumanitarian, more opposed to all the values that matter to us and that make civilization – indeed, the human race – worth belonging to and saving? What is more worthy of worshiping than beauty? And many would argue that, while of course we should not overrate beauty, none the less, beauty cannot be overrated. We value beauty highly because it gives us pleasure, often of a kind that unites intellect and heart in one. The thrill at the encounter with any kind of beauty, personal or not, has mystery and grandeur; the knowledge that we share this moment potentially with all who are human is a powerful force uniting the species, a force that, paradoxically (given what we have said about beauty's divisiveness), brings us all together, though it be just for an instant. Yes, beauty can be a cause of anger, envy, despondency; it can perhaps drive people to desperate acts. But that danger is more than outweighed by the blessings beauty brings in its train: the exaltation and pleasure, the sense of unity, the warmth kindled in the heart by the sight of someone or something beautiful, which makes the observer, for a moment's time, more human and more aware of the privileges and responsibilities entailed in being human, encouraging good deeds, kind acts. Without beauty, or without the ability to love it, we would be isolated and sad in a bleak and unforgiving world. Thus the power of beauty is underscored for us again, and we gain more understanding of why beauty is sometimes feared and even hated: it is a good part of what stands between us and savagery, and that is an awesome power. Is it not understandable that we feel fear and anger at a force we cannot control, but which makes such a difference to us?

We have to find a way to have the proverbial cake and eat it: to preserve our enjoyment of beauty, and allow us to appreciate and be appreciated without resentment and without obsession. It is not so much that we have to develop a 'new style' of beauty (one comes along on its own every so often anyway): whether beauty is perceived as weakness, plumpness, fitness, or whatever makes no real difference in our attitudes toward it and our use of it. We have to transcend, in the first place, dependence on 'style': for as long as we worry about the current fashion in beauty, not only must we worry about ourselves as individuals and how well we fare, individual to individual; but we also become dependent upon the whims of tastemakers beyond our acquaintance, forces we cannot see or touch, and that helps to create our confusion, as well as our sense that beauty makes its possessor passive and dependent. We must see beauty as an active force, and being or becoming beautiful as doing something, like running for office or playing football. Somehow we must cut the link between beauty and 'effeminacy,' all that seems to us deceptive, weak, and frivolous – and, therefore, stereotypically female.

It is easy to propose solutions and harder to talk about

implementing them, as well as thinking about the results should the changes take effect. A world in which beauty was perceived as doing would be most different from the present one. It would not be a simple trade-off: 'You-look-beautiful-throwing-that-discus,' in exchange for 'You-look-beautiful-wearing-that-diamond.' Women must reclaim beauty, somehow, as something that is their choice and their judgment – not in the eye of the beholder, but in the mind of the beauty (which would then no longer seem a peculiar juxtaposition).

At the same time – whether paradoxically or necessarily – beauty must be de-emphasized in the pantheon of feminine virtues. Not, we hasten to reassure the reader, that beauty itself, as an ideal and a reality, is to be devalued or compromised; but women must feel that their self-esteem stands on accomplishment, on achievements and skills that increase with age, that are a sign of autonomy and a means toward it. Beauty would be for women as it is for men – an extra, a source of pleasure to oneself and others, but not the be-all and end-all. That is, as we have seen, much too dangerous. It is dangerous for women themselves, as well as for men and women in their dealings with each other: the overvaluation of feminine beauty, coupled necessarily with the undervaluation of anything a woman achieves by her own visible efforts, makes real love and companionship between the sexes, too often, a romantic fantasy and no more.

Additionally, we must learn to separate our judgments about beauty from our learned expectations, that is, our social stereotypes. We must close the gap between what we really find beautiful, and what we think we find beautiful because we have been told to think that way. If we really like ourselves better through believing that beauty is the radiance of the good soul, or the keen mind, then we had better stop worrying about ugliness being the pimple on the chin, the two pounds on the behind. The doctrines are incompatible, and the incompatibility causes us distress. We must learn, somehow, to accept a wider range of physical attributes as potentially 'beautiful.' Where – outside the pages of a hundred diet books and fashion magazines, of course – is it written that beauty is indistinguishable from a size-three frame? A blond, flowing mane? Mascara and 6-inch stiletto heels? Male good looks cover a much wider range of possibilities, and female beauty could as well. We have to see as beautiful the perfection of a type – any type, rather than the perfections of one particular fantasy. This means, at its most obvious, that we must put aside our sense, overt or suppressed, of ethnic superiority, as it is realized in the feeling that our own kinds of features *are* the beautiful features, that the more different from ourselves someone else is, the uglier they are. To be able to do this with full sincerity, of course, requires true self-confidence – and this, in turn, requires among other things that we do not already feel ill-at-ease because of the way we look. Until we overcome the whole range of terrors we are subject to on the grounds of looks, it is not likely that a great deal of progress will be made in this direction.

But mainly, and most crucially, we must learn to think very differently about the quality of beauty. All of our competitive-ness, our fears, our anger stem ultimately from our innermost perception of beauty: we see it as a non-renewable as well as a scarce resource, a property of which there is a very finite amount to go around. We can, and do, use up our own beauty; we must husband it jealously, but sooner or later it will all be gone, like money. Like food in a famine, it is non-renewable: if I allocate some to you, I will have less, and I will never get it back. The more someone else has, the less (necessarily) I have. Beauty *is* currency for us, in all kinds of ways. It buys goods and services just like money. It opens doors, and makes its possessor welcome, just like money. And, like money, when one no longer possesses it, the door is apt to be slammed in one's face. Like money, it grants power to its owner. It is symbolic of value – of a radiance within – as money is symbolic of mineral wealth secreted elsewhere, out of our sight. While it is of value for itself, it is perhaps even more for what it represents, which we perceive only dimly with our conscious minds, but with crystalline clarity with other parts of our psyches.

Psychoanalysts refer to money as a 'deindividualized posses-sion,' thereby likening it to feces: for both, each individual has his or her own, but each individual's hoard looks just like anyone else's. One person's dollar bills look just like another's. In that sense, money is a possession that belongs separately to each of us, but at the same time, our own money isn't really unique to us, isn't really our own. We couldn't identify it as we could, say, our clothing. And, the psychoanalyst Otto Fenichel (1945) points out, 'deindividualized means necessarily losable,' (p. 281) because we could not identify the lost object as our own. The fear of loss of money is a symptom or a causal factor in many depressions. It is as if the deindividualization, the very non-uniqueness, of the possession rendered it the more precious.

At first glance nothing could be less similar than beauty to money, psychically speaking. Beauty is *par excellence*, we would say, an individualized, unique possession. Beauty defines and sets apart. One person's beauty is altogether different from another's, and indeed what defines a beauty is something special and individual about her looks. And yet, much of what has been said about beauty sounds remarkably like what has just been said about money, in terms of symbolic power. We might argue, besides, that, while one's natural looks are indeed unique, what we do to render ourselves truly 'beautiful' to the world – clothing, coiffure, cosmetics – serves in large part to obliterate that uniqueness. Fashion is paramount in all of these, and fashion is a leveling influence. In a literal sense, one woman's hairdo, or mascara, or dress, is altogether unlike another's; and indeed it is a staple of misogynistic stereotyping that nothing will infuriate a woman more than seeing another wearing an item of clothing identical to hers. Yet we must ask: why *is* this simple act so infuriating? Men wear clothing very similar to that of other men, and it is never an issue. Perhaps the act of dressing truly and literally 'identically' instead of only symbolically so acts, unconsciously, as a goad, an ironic statement. Certainly it is another stock in trade of misogyny to insist that all women are really interchangeably alike – that uniqueness of 'beauty' is recognized, in folklore of this kind, as only a sham. And in fact, while fashion claims to render each woman unique, each dress (ideally) the wearer's very own, this is really far from true. What fashion does, as we have seen, is to minimize the possibilities for difference, to fit everyone into the same mold. Fashion decrees a hemline, 'in' colors, the shape of a sleeve, the length of the hair, and so on. To step out of fashion – to be truly unique – is to invite the wrath of society, its contempt, its studied avoidance. Interesting: to be too much like someone else, and too much unlike everyone else provoke markedly similar responses, as if they both came, symbolically, to the same thing – as indeed they do. Beauty, that is, the beauty that comes of adornment and artifice, is for us on a symbolic level a deindividualized possession not unlike money. Unlike money, looks start out unique, but we labor to standardize them, and in that standardization lies the beauty we most readily appreciate.

Now, if we perceived beauty this way consciously, we would respond to it in a far less complicated and potentially dangerous way. We are perplexed about beauty – we are aware that our feelings and needs and responses don't make sense, but are powerless to alter them because we don't really know what they are, much less where they come from. Another reason why we find our responses to beauty so difficult to unravel is that they are, again to borrow psychoanalytic terminology in order to speak of matters psychoanalytic, overdetermined. Not only does beauty, as a partly deindividualized possession, recall unsolved excretory conflicts; but beauty can also be construed – and there is a good deal of evidence that we do so interpret it – as a phallic equivalent.

As we write these words, we hear the reader's incredulous voice in the background. This comes close – you have every right to say – to the worst sort of reductionism, the kind of airy theorizing that makes psychoanalysis the despair of science. By allowing any phenomenon in human experience to symbolize, or be symbolized by, virtually anything else, we render any comparison empty: something that is anything is nothing. How can beauty be feces *and* a phallus at once? Overdetermination with a vengeance! Illustrating, need anyone point out, the ridiculous extremes to which a theory based upon metaphor can be put. We are compelled to agree, and yet we cannot avoid the comparison. We don't want to suggest, in any case, that beauty *is* feces, nor that beauty and the phallic beast are one and the same. Consider, though, the ways in which we equate them – symbolically and pretty much unconsciously.

Beauty is for women, as we have remarked, as the penis is

said to be for men: the most important inalienable possession, the supreme desideratum. At the same time, we have to bear in mind another equation that fits in a rather complex way. The penis is often equated (for example by neo-Freudian writers like Karen Horney) with power. They suggest that it is not the physical penis *per se* that the little boy (and the big boy) so zealously treasures and the little (and big) girl so envies. Rather, the penis, especially for the child (who thinks concretely), symbolizes the differences between girls and boys, and being the sole visible difference, becomes for the child the 'explanation' of why boys seem to get the better deal: more freedom, more love, more power. The penis, then, is symbolically equated with power, and what the boy treasures and the girl envies is not the organ in its physical actuality, but the promise of power it signifies.

We have suggested elsewhere that beauty for a woman is equivalent to power for a man, as well as being a woman's sole permissible route to power for most of history. But how is that equation arrived at? Beauty is not, as we saw, powerful in itself: it cannot, and its possessor cannot, get things done by beauty. Beauty in this sense symbolizes power, which in turn symbolizes the phallus, which itself in turn symbolizes power again. Of course, the phallus: power equation, which is interesting because bidirectional, is a more typical metaphor because it relates abstract to concrete, where the beauty:power relation matches two abstractions. Or, we might say, the first substitutes a symbol for an organ, the second a symbol for a symbol.

Absurd as the equation may thus seem at first glance, let us put skepticism aside long enough to look at some of the relationships that exist between our psychic perceptions of beauty, and the phallus. Apologizing for a quasi-mathematicization (which does serve to clarify our points), we can represent these complex relationships schematically below:

| X | A | B |
|---|---|---|
| Beauty | Woman | Man |
| Penis | Man | Woman |

Then we say, for both X's: A has X; B doesn't and can't. And further, it is an insult to B to suggest B does wish for it for him/herself. The more A has of X, the more desirable A will be considered by B. X is in both cases a physical appendage to A, a part of A and inalienable, but not under A's control. It comes and goes (or works and fails) despite A, rather than because of A. And A uses it, when it is working, to attract B. It is an adornment or decoration (cf. the Yiddish *Schmuck*), but a vital one. A is in continual fear of losing X, and with it any influence over B. In both cases, the resource is felt to be scarce, and therefore all As are in competition over it: who has it, who doesn't; who has more, whose is better. Finally, B is jealous of A for having this resource, which is entirely off-limits to B, and displays anger and envy in various manifestations to A.

We see that virtually everything that has been said about the penis and males can be said about beauty and females. It is sometimes argued, again within neo-Freudian discourse, that the womb is the appropriate analogue to the phallus as what women possess and men envy. But it is also objected that the womb, being invisible, is meaningless to small children, of no real use to them until adulthood. On the other hand, while little girls can see their male sibling's organs, and perhaps, if Freud is right, equate them with the special marks of favor our society reserves for males, in the same way little boys can see that their sisters use their looks to garner those privileges that are reserved for the female. Little girls soon learn – very soon indeed – to rely on their prettiness to get away with behavior impermissible in their brothers, who are urged to act like 'a man,' and use their incipient strength, rather than flirtation based on passivity, to gain their ends. Similarly, although the womb and the penis are certainly more closely analogous to each other, both being organs of reproduction, than either is to the abstraction of beauty, our responses to beauty seem more like those to the phallus. The womb is not considered 'out of control,' something that has its owner, rather than vice versa; there is little real competition among women in terms of wombs, nor do women typically lead their lives in ways that demonstrate fear of the womb's passing. There is a sort of relationship, in that beauty in women is so closely related to women's years of fertility. But in our time, visible proof of fertility or fecundity is not a requisite for attractiveness. (In fact, maternity clothes are designed to de-emphasize their wearer's 'delicate condition' – if fecundity were truly admired, the reverse would be the case.) While there is certainly evidence of men envying women their repro-ductive capacity, there seems to be no body of folklore suggest-ing that women get special privileges by means of fecundity – as it is acknowledged they do by beauty, and men by the penis.

Of course, there is no real possibility of proof for these conjec-tures, in any scientific sense. All we can offer by way of support is, in fact, the basis for these suggestions in the first place – the mysteriousness and pervasiveness of the power beauty has over us, our unwillingness or inability to loosen its hold despite our knowing that our attitudes and behavior don't make sense. All these are typical of behavior that emanates from the deepest psychic wellsprings – we are under its power, and at the same time, we are unaware of the depths from which that power arises, and think we are being perfectly 'reasonable' in our attitudes toward beauty, when in fact those attitudes are but the thinnest of rationalizations. We can only gain back our capacity to deal with beauty intelligently by acknowl-edging how much we are under the sway of something else – and understanding what that something else consists of. If psychoanalytic metaphors – feces, the phallus – seem far-fetched or absurd, the reader is invited to construct others, as long as they capture the persuasive power of the fantasy. The obsession coupled with the unawareness – this is what requires explanation.

For half a century now advertisers have known how to use Freud's discoveries about the unconscious to create in our minds an irresistible urge to consume; the cult of unrealizable beauty is just one more example of their manipulative strat-egies. But if we are aware of what is within, we are no longer so subject to its manipulation – nor are we ourselves so desperate to continue as objects to be manipulated.

There are two thoughts here, jostling pessimistically at these suggestions. First, it's impossible. How can we become so self-aware? How can we resist the blandishments of a science of persuasion that has our number? And second, suppose we do . . . what then? Granting that we are too easily led by the nose where beauty is concerned, precisely because beauty plugs into such potent unconscious needs and hopes, suppose we somehow divest ourselves of those depths? what will be left of us? For we have already acknowledged the tremendous force for good, for love, and for creativity, that beauty engenders in human beings. If we could cast off the dark aspects, would the brighter ones survive meaningfully? Or, by discarding the web of fantasies, would we become stodgy, slow, and unimaginative – no more, in some ways, than animals? Can we retain beauty as a force for good, and diminish some of its power to do harm?

These are difficult questions, and not easily answered because we have no experience to fall back on. It has never been the case that large numbers of people have become aware enough of the origins in their minds of the force of beauty to do something to change the direction of that force. We appeal to religion, to poetry, sometimes even to science, to explain its power over us or to mitigate its fearful aspects – but we do not look within ourselves and harness our own innate strength. What will happen if we do? But it seems generally true that, in the long run, self-knowledge is always of value and its benefits necessarily far outweigh the pain it can cause at first. So since religion, poetry, and science have not saved us, we owe it to ourselves to try this one thing more, if we feel that we are too much at the mercy of beauty and those who have learned to use it to use us.

To say that beauty has great power over us because of its symbolic force is not to say that we approach it tied hand and foot, unable to do anything to dispel, mitigate, or alter that power. And as much as we attribute the pervasive influence of some of the worst aspects of our preoccupation to unconscious motivation – which we can only change individually, and only with considerable pain or at least discomfort – we still have to acknowledge that there are other forces at work, perhaps more malleable, certainly more accessible to our conscious selves. We see that, at a low level, fashions in beauty certainly can and do change: from the truly and frivolously insignificant (hemlines, lipstick colors) which in fact only exemplify the old proverb *plus ça change, plus c'est la même chose*, to somewhat more complex and significant changes: in the shift from the nineteenth-century beauty-as-illness to our current beauty-as-muscular-strength, we certainly see a difference in perspective. True, even this is only a change of a superficial nature, commercially encouraged because change in fashion is commercially necessary; and any standard imposed from outside ourselves is still the same old superimposition of standards which is more of the same old thing. But it proves that we can, as consumers, change our perception of what is beautiful in radical ways ... at least when we are told to do so. The crucial question: can we change from within – change our standards because we, as independent beings, have seen fit, on intellectual and true aesthetic grounds, to define beauty in an altogether new way – say, as each individual's unique striving toward his/her own expression of self (leaving aside false versions of this idea, the perfumes that are different for each woman, the 'being the best you can be' via hair rinses, and so on)? Can we decrease, or totally break, our dependency? Can we continue to enjoy the healthful fruits of beauty – the uncomplicated and rewarding fulfilment in seeing someone who has achieved that apotheosis – in enjoying our own successes in looking as good as we feel, and knowing we ourselves, as well as nature, have contributed through our efforts to making a bright spot in the day of many an onlooker? Vanity, narcissism – they have had a bad press, but without them, wouldn't everyone's world be a bit gloomier? We come to the same crossroads: the distinction between performing all those acts of self-perfection for one's own sake, directed by oneself, and doing the same because we are told to, because we are afraid of the results if we don't. The media's continual blandishments – 'this I do for me,' currently a popular commercial refrain, being a case in point – looked at from this point of view, show themselves to be a snare and a delusion indeed: 'This' you do not 'do for you' as long as someone is intoning that injunction over the airwaves to a few hundred million of you. This you do for someone else – whether for 'society,' for the 'media' – or whoever.

Society ... the media .... That sounds pretty good as a place to lay the blame for our predicament. We are accustomed to abusing these as agents of our corruption. It is 'society' that causes our obsession with beauty, or 'the culture' that provides our dubious values. It is 'the media' that tirelessly propagandize and proselytize, until it is only their voices we can hear, shutting out common sense. It is 'men' that coerce or trick women into becoming narcissistically intertwined with themselves and their looks, to the abandonment of other ambitions. In any event, it isn't *us*. We are the pawns, the sacrificial lambs, slaughtered on the altar of commerce, of conformity, of keeping things the way they've always been. Therefore (the argument inexorably continues) there's nothing for *us* to do but keep up an unrelenting pressure of complaint against these agents. When we yell loud enough, they'll hear us, and when they've heard us long enough, they'll change. Then we will be free to develop new concepts of beauty and new ways of achieving it and responding to it. Then we will truly be free.

But comforting as the litany is, it overlooks some rather critical details. Who, in the first place, are these faceless hordes? Who is 'society' but you and me? And the 'media' are not active, it is well known, but reactive; what they discern that their viewers/hearers/readers want, they provide. If we, the viewing public, are not stimulated to buy by the blandishments dangled before us, the media will be instantly responsive – there will be a whole new set of blandishments dangled faster than the eye can blink. So if the same tired messages, the same recycled pictures, pass across our weary retinas year after year, we cannot in all honesty blame the media for it.

'Men.' Feminists sometimes demonstrate the disquieting and discomfiting tendency to lash out at men as the people responsible for all our woes – women's and 'society's' as well, as victimizers and calculating planners of and benefiters from oppression. Certainly there is some justice in the complaint: if anyone has benefited from women's restriction to secondary roles, it is men; but it is far from clear that, in the long run, there is any benefit to be derived by anyone from the strict stereotyping of behaviors of the two sexes. In the short run, men benefit. But in the short run, women benefit as well from the double standard implicit in our views about beauty, male and female, and our unequal attribution of importance to looks in men's and women's lives. And in the long run both lose; in the short run, women probably lose more than men, but no one wins when freedom is denied to anyone.

This point suggests another issue that has to be dealt with: how responsible are women for their own enslavement to beauty? Can we call it 'enslavement,' indeed, if women are and have always been complicit in the determination of appropriate behavior for the two sexes? The more we look at history, at the record as it is available to us, the more the difficult facts glare in our eyes: we are complicit in our oppression. Women have helped – at least – to create the stereotype of woman as narcissistically dependent upon looks, and continue, with every evidence of pleasure, to reinforce that stereotype. Much as men reward women who obviously take pains on looks, and punish those who don't by avoidance and contempt, still more are women guilty of this behavior toward one another. Women are the arbiters of fashion; women are the super-critics who determine one another's standing; it is pointed out over and over again that women are much harsher on one another than men are on women. The pressure to be ever thinner, blonder, softer emanates from women more than from men. We learn from our mothers and our female peers in adolescence what is expected of us by way of looks, and how to achieve it. We learn from these hard taskmasters as well the penalties for not trying, or trying too hard, or trying the wrong way, or trying and failing.

But, the counterargument goes, how can women be complicit in their oppression – supposing we are willing to define this behavior as oppressive – if we have been trained to it by the promise that it will secure us men's approval, and we feel we must do all we can to win that approval? If the final arbiters are men, even if the intermediaries are women? Do women, in determining and enforcing the standards of beauty, act on their own, of their own free will? Only then can we talk of 'complicity' or responsibility. Otherwise, it is the same old story – men have the fun, reap the benefits, and put women in a position where they can be blamed: 'the woman me beguiled and I did eat.' If society is the serpent, what are the roles of Adam, and of Eve, in this particular fall?

Mary Daly (1978), for example, discusses the problem of complicity of women in their own oppression at length. She talks about problems very close to the ones we are concerned with – indeed, matters we have broached elsewhere, for example, Chinese foot-binding and Near Eastern clitoridectomy. In both these cases of pathological 'beautification,' women are the enforcers. Women traditionally do the disfigurement to other women; women declare that they would consider themselves and their daughters ugly if it were not done; women further assert that they would not welcome a daughter-in-law who had not submitted to the procedure. While foot-binding is a thing of the past, clitoridectomy is very much alive. And interestingly, when Western feminists have protested its continuance and sought to make the United Nations legislate against the practice, women from the cultures in which it is customary have expressed violent opposition, claiming that these women were interfering, in imperialistic ways all too typical of citizens of developed countries, in the indigenous affairs of other cultures, which they cannot hope to understand. Western feminists, it is claimed, do not understand the role such rites play in cultures which embrace them; and the result of Western influence, however well-meant, can only be the further weakening and ultimate destruction of fragile cultures, already undermined by the spread of Western ways. To Western eyes – which see the results of clitoridectomy as anything but beautiful – the complicity of these women in their own disfigurement is horrific. To the women involved, however, there is no disfigurement, but merely the creation of an illusion, not unlike certain Western practices that cause Western women not a raised eyebrow. And since we are complicit in those in the same way, what gives us the right to object to someone else's ritual?

But Daly argues that women, oppressed themselves, and totally dependent upon men's goodwill, cannot be complicit in the oppression of other women. Only a free agent can be responsible, and only someone who is responsible can be complicit. If we appear to take pleasure in our psychically (and occasionally physically) damaging beauty rituals, that is but surface show, the results of indoctrination. The brainwashed cannot be held to blame for their acts or thoughts. But who is to say that women have been brainwashed? And if so, by whom? For early education is largely in the hands of women, and has almost always been so. To absolve ourselves of complicity in the oppressions of beauty is necessarily to see ourselves as mentally weak and totally under the thumbs of others – the only others, in this case, being men. This is an even grimmer view of women's reality than the concept of women as complicit in their own narcissistic self-indulgence. And it seems likely that there is no way to tell, from the evidence available to us at present, what 'complicity' in this context really means. It does seem reasonable, on all grounds, to ask that women take the responsibility for their attitudes and behavior at present. We cannot speak for our ancestors, can never know truly to what extent, and under what levels of duress, women originally and over the millennia contributed to the difficulties we now are faced with. But we can decide that here – now – we can take a stand and regardless of how it was in the past, and how it still is for most of us at this moment, make some changes.

'Complicity' theory is attractive to many women precisely because it exonerates them from blame in the present state of things, and puts the burden for change on the shoulders of others – 'men,' or the faceless 'society,' or the amorphous 'media.' But to take that position is to assure that nothing will be done, either because the people who are expected to change are not the ones who stand to gain the most by such change, or because the forces we importune do not, in fact, exist outside of ourselves. We are the ones obsessed by beauty, whether our fathers, our mothers, or the media made us this way. Perhaps until recently women had so little else to make their lives comfortable, psychically as well as physically, that they needed the promise of beauty, and the thrill of competition with other women in this arena, to make living worthwhile. It is no longer so. We have changed enough of the conditions under which we live so that we do, in fact, have options if we choose to use them. It is true that the devisers of commercials are ever devious: a favorite current pitch is to confound the two: You're an executive – but still a lovely, desirable woman! (or you'd better be!) The message behind that message is very plain: we are being encouraged, once again, to entangle competence in the work sphere with feminine passivity, even though the time for that is, in fact, long past. Advertisers realize that we could make the break, could come to see beauty, competence, worthiness in general with newly-opened eyes, which would of course spell disaster for many commercial interests. It is necessary for them to reforge the broken link on the chain, and advertising is working away to that end. But if we see beyond the psychic tugs and twists that advertisers know how to do so well, we can still become ourselves, and our own people, with respect to beauty.

We have to recognize, ultimately, that anything that is packaged and sold for all women, however alluringly individual the pitch is, is *not* a true offer of beauty, but only of acceptability and blandness. Beauty must be understood as something achieved through individual experience, which shows in the face as a badge of a thoughtful, interested, and competent human being. The criteria for good looks in women must no longer be so dissimilar to the criteria we use for men. We can recognize for women – as we do for men – a certain childlike, dewy-eyed 'prettiness' that is ours only in youth, but we must not – as we do not do with men – confuse that with feminine beauty. Beauty is what shows in the crinkles around the eyes, the set of the chin, the stance of one who knows where she has been, where she is going, and how to get there. Whether the body is plump or muscular is not really the issue. The issue is autonomy, being one's own person. In that resides the first criterion of the beautiful person, male or female.

We would be naive to think that this new perspective would quickly be adopted. Too much that is comfortable stands to be lost. It is a general rule that, even where we clearly see gains for us in the future in changing, we resist change. What is old, however unsatisfying, is at least a *known* evil, and familiarity invests it all too often with a nostalgic glow. To cast off what we are accustomed to, the responses of others that we can calculate in advance and gauge, and know the reasons for – that is harsh and painful. To adopt a whole new set of values, to be unsure how to go about achieving them and not really to know what will create a positive response, or even perhaps what a positive response is; to know that for some time to come, the better you work at it, the more negative most people's responses will be; to work against the pressure of 'society,' 'the media,' and those we care about – all this is frightening and painful, and we could not blame anyone, contemplating these possibilities, for turning her back on the brave new world set forth. But some people have always been pioneers who faced the unknown, making the transition easier for later generations, and there will be pioneers here too. Human beings have flourished because of their adaptability, and we can certainly make this adaptation if we are convinced of its necessity.

And it is necessary if we believe in a world in which everyone has a chance for achievement, everyone can hope for autonomy, and everyone has the right to make choices. No other world will be fit to live in. We must take the problem of beauty in hand, and reshape that magical ideal which has always enhanced our lives into something that enriches our humanity even more deeply.

# Notes

## Chapter 2  The Problem of Beauty: Myth and Reality

[1]Quoted in Gilman (1975).
[2]In Chapter 5 we will discuss this topic at length.
[3]For example in Gorney (1968).
[4]Shakespeare, Sonnet LXV.

## Chapter 3  The Representation of Venus: An Ideal in Search of a Definition

[1]Cited in Rader (1935), p. 26.
[2]Freud (1964 [1930]), pp. 82f.
[3]Shakespeare, Sonnets, XVIII and CXXX.
[4]Byron 'She Walks in Beauty,' Hebrew Melodies.
[5]A rough translation of this poem into Modern English is as follows:

I Captivity.
Your two eyes will slay me suddenly; I may not endure their beauty, so much does it wound me keenly throughout my heart.
And your word alone will quickly heal the wound in my heart, as long as it is fresh. Your two eyes, etc.

## Chapter 4  Beauty in Our Time

[1]Strong, R. in Gibson and England (1969), p. 4.
[2]Devlin (1929), p. 116. Future references to this book will be noted in the text as *VB*.
[3]Stein (1982), p. 243.
[4]Farber (1981), p. 66. Future references to this book will be noted in the text as *F*.
[5]*San Francisco Chronicle*, September 22 1982, p. 33.
[6]*Time*, 9 February 1981, pp. 82–8.
[7]Juffe and Heden-Guest, 'Pretty Babies,' *San Francisco Chronicle. This World*, 5 October 1980, pp. 18–19, 22–3.
[8]*San Francisco Chronicle*, 2 September 1980, p. 21.
[9]*Time*, 30 August 1982, pp. 72–7.
[10]*Time*, 9 February 1981, p. 85.
[11]Ibid, p. 86.

## Chapter 5  Attitudes Toward Beauty

[1]Reprinted in the *San Francisco Chronicle*, 16 September 1982.
[2]E.g., in the *San Francisco Chronicle*, 16 September 1982.
[3]*San Francisco Chronicle*, September 1981 and 1982.

## Chapter 6  The Pathology of Beauty

[1]This discussion of silicone implantation is based on Larned (1977.)

## Chapter 7  Talking About Beauty

[1]A word here about the historical linguist's working assumptions. Proto-Indo-European (or PIE) is an abstract construct rather than a real, attested ancient language (like Hittite, or Sanskrit). It is a formula utilized by historical linguists, essentially the lowest common denominator or shortest distance between two or more linguistic points – the forms found in actual languages. The forms we reconstruct as PIE 'words' (preceded by asterisks which symbolize their hypothetical nature) are underlying forms from which, by the rules of sound-change, each of the attested forms can be derived using the fewest rules. But we do not assume that the forms we so represent were actually spoken by anyone, although we are happier with our reconstructions if they structure themselves as a plausible synchronic linguistic system – that is, we like it if PIE looks like real languages we know, in terms of the kinds of rules and the forms of words it is represented as containing.

Just as nearly all the languages spoken in Europe, and by the historical descendants of European peoples, are ultimately derived from PIE, so there is commonality at various other points. The Romance languages (e.g., French, Spanish, Italian, Rumanian) are all derived from a form of Latin and thus have much in common with one another. English, German, and Dutch, on the other hand, trace their descent to an early form of 'Germanic,' only distantly related to Latin. Other languages also pattern in families – for example, Balto-Slavic, including Russian, Polish, Czech, and many others.

Some of these families remain relatively pure, without a great deal of influence from outside sources: French, for instance, incorporates very little in its vocabulary from elsewhere, and that reluctantly. Others, of which English is far and away the best example, are readier to borrow, for historical reasons (i.e., invasion by a non-Germanic group) as well as, probably, because of its linguistic structure, which accepts borrowings of words and systems rather freely. Thus, the vocabulary of English is unusually large and unusually varied: words come from Old English directly; from Latin and Greek directly by learned borrowing; from other Germanic languages (especially Danish) as a result of early invasions; from Old French as a result of the Norman conquest (and since French is derived from

Latin, Latin words thus have two paths along which to enter English); and, less commonly, from all kinds of other sources reflecting the history of the speakers of English in Europe or elsewhere. Hence, when we speak, we often can select among almost an embarrassment of riches – near-synonyms, not precisely equivalent in meaning to one another, but all sharing a semantic base.

[2]Ernout and Meillet (1951)

[3]Ibid, p. 73.

[4]καλός sometimes means 'good, useful,' as well as 'beautiful.'

[5]*Roget's International Thesaurus* (1962).

[6]*Oxford English Dictionary* (*OED*), vol. V, pp. 67 f.

[7]*OED*, vol. VIII, pp. 1332 f.

## Chapter 8  Men and Beauty

[1]Lawrence (1928 [1956]), p. 196.

[2]Farber (1981), p. 77.

## Chapter 9  Beauty and Ethnicity

[1]Blake, 'The Little Black Boy.'

[2]Morrison (1970), p. 34. Hereafter page numbers for this work will be cited in the text.

[3]Fonda (1981), pp. 19–20.

[4]Cleaver (1968), p. 14. Hereafter page numbers for this work will be cited in the text.

[5]Carson (1970), pp. 243 f.

[6]Rodriguez (1982), p. 137. Hereafter page numbers for this work will be cited in the text.

[7]Farber (1981), p. 93.

[8]Actually, a black Miss America – light-skinned and with Caucasian features – was crowned in 1983.

# Bibliography

Adams, G. R. (1977), 'Physical attractiveness research,' *Human Development*, 20:217–39.

Alexander. S. (1933), *Beauty and Other Forms of Value*, London: Macmillan.

Ames, Van Meter (1931), *Introduction to Beauty*, New York and London: Harper & Bros.

Balfour, Arthur James (1910), *Criticism and Beauty*, Oxford: Clarendon Press.

Bartlett, E. M. (1937), *Types of Aesthetic Judgment*, London: Allen & Unwin.

Bascom, J. (1886), *Aesthetics; or The Science of Beauty*, New York: G. P. Putnam's Sons.

Baudouin, C. (1924), *Psychoanalysis and Aesthetics*, tr. Eden and Cedar Paul, London: Allen & Unwin.

Berne, E. (1959), 'The mythologic of dark and fair: the psychiatric uses of folklore,' *Journal of American Folklore*, pp. 1–13.

Blackie, J. S. (1858), *On Beauty*, Edinburgh: Sutherland & Knox.

Brain, R. (1979), *The Decorated Body*, New York: Harper & Row.

Broby-Johansen, R. (1968), *Body and Clothes: An Illustrated History of Costume*, New York: Reinhold.

Bruch, H. (1973), *Eating Disorders*, New York: Basic Books.

Burke, E. (1757), *A Philosophical Enquiry into the Original of our Ideas of the Sublime and Beautiful*, London: R. & R. Dodsley.

Carritt, E. F. (ed.) (1931), *Philosophies of Beauty from Socrates to Robert Bridges*, Oxford: Clarendon.

Carritt, E. F. (1932), *What is Beauty?*, Oxford: Clarendon.

Carson, J. (1970). 'Silent voices: the Southern Negro woman today,' in Watkins and David (eds), *To be a Black Woman*, Berkeley: Far West Laboratories.

Chandler, A. R. (1934), *Beauty and Human Nature*, New York and London: D. Appleton-Century Co.

Clark, K. (1956), *The Nude: A Study in Ideal Form*, Bollingen Series xxv.2, New York: Pantheon.

Cleaver, E. (1968), *Soul on Ice*, New York: Dell Publishing Co.

302

Coltera, J. T. (1965), 'On the creation of beauty and thought: the unique as vicissitude: a books review,' *Journal of the American Psychoanalytic Association* 13:634–703.

Corliss, R. (1982), 'The new ideal of beauty,' *Time*, 30 August 1982. 'Cosmetics vs. the consumer,' *Consumer Reports*, February 1963, pp. 90–1.

Daly, M. (1978), *Gyn/Ecology: The Meta-ethics of Radical Feminism*, Boston: Beacon.

Dermer, M. and Thiel, D. L. (1975), 'When beauty may fail,' *Journal of Personality and Social Psychology*, 31.6:1168–76.

Devlin, P. (1929), *Vogue: Book of Fashion Photography*, New York: Simon & Schuster.

Dion, K. & Al. (1972), 'What is beautiful is good,' *Journal of Personality and Social Psychology*, 24.3:285–90.

Erikson, E. H. (1962), 'Reality and actuality,' *Journal of the American Psychoanalytic Association*, 10:451–74.

Ernout, A. and Meillet, A. (1951), *Dictionnaire étymologique de la langue latine*, Paris: Klincksieck, pp. 543 f.

Erskine, J. (1925), *The Private Life of Helen of Troy*, Indianapolis: Bobbs-Merrill.

Farber, R. (1981), *The Fashion Photographer*, New York: Amphoto, American Photographic Publishing.

'Fashion: A shoe-in,' *Time*, 10 November 1961:57.

Fenichel, O. (1945), *The Psychoanalytic Theory of Neurosis*, New York: Norton.

Fonda, J. (1981), *Jane Fonda's Work Out Book*, New York: Simon & Schuster.

Frank, S. (1961), 'Brunette Today, Blonde Tomorrow,' *Saturday Evening Post*, 9 September 1961.

Freedman, David B. (1962), 'On the Phrase, "beautiful but dumb",' *Psychoanalysis and Psychoanalytic Review*, 49:100–2.

Freud, S. (1964 [1930]). *Civilization and its Discontents*. In J. Strachey and A. Freud (eds), *The Standard Edition of the Complete Psychological Works of Sigmund Freud*, volume XXI, pp. 59–145. London: Hogarth Press and the Institute of Psycho-Analysis.

Gibson, R. and S. England (1969), *The Masque of Beauty*, London: Southwark.

Gilman, R. (1975), *Decadence: The Strange Life of an Epithet*, New York: Farrar, Straus & Giroux.

Gorney, R. (1968), *The Human Agenda*, New York: Simon & Schuster.

Grinstein, A. (1963), 'Profile of a "doll" – a female character type,' *Psychoanalytic Review*, 50:161–74.

Guiles, F. L. (1969), *Norma Jean: The Life of Marilyn Monroe*, New York: McGraw-Hill.

Higgins, R. (1963), 'The perception of the body surface,' *British Journal of Medical Psychology*, 36:261–70.

Hogarth, W. (1753), *The Analysis of Beauty*, London: S. Bagster.

Hollander, A. (1975), *Seeing Through Clothes*, New York: Viking.

Hollander, A. (1982), 'Esprit de corps: How military uniforms have kept up with the march of time,' *Gentleman's Quarterly*, August 1982:94–5.

Hornik, E. (1932), 'Pleasure in disguise – the need for decoration and the sense of beauty,' *Psychoanalytic Quarterly*, 1:216.

Huxley, Aldous (1923), 'Beauty in 1920,' in *On The Margin: Notes and Essays*, pp. 115–21, London: Chatto & Windus.

Jacobson, E. (1959), 'The "exceptions": an elaboration of Freud's character study,' *The Psychoanalytic Study of the Child*, 14:135–54.

Juffe, M. and Heden-Guest, A. (1980), 'Pretty babies,' *San Francisco Chronicle. This World*, 5 October 1982, pp. 18–19, 22–3.

Lamb, R. de F. (1936), *The American Chamber of Horrors*, New York: Grosset & Dunlap.

Larned, D. (1977), 'A shot – or two or three – in the breast,' *Ms.*, September 1977, pp. 55, 86–8.

Lawrence, D. H. (1928 [1956]), *Lady Chatterley's Lover*, New York: New American Library.

Macgregor, F. C. and Ford, B. (1971), 'The other face of plastic surgery: the disappointed patient,' *Science Digest*, April 1971, pp. 16–20.

Miller, Marcia (1981), *Such a Pretty Face*, New York: Berkeley.

Moore, K. H. and Thompson, S. (1979), 'Plastic surgery: prostheses need more regulation,' *Science Digest*, August 1979, pp. 78–81.

Morrison, T. (1970), *The Bluest Eye*, New York: Washington Square Press.

Mussell, Kay J. (1975), 'Beautiful and damned: the sexual woman in Gothic fiction,' *Journal of Popular Culture*, 9:84–9.

Nashner, M. and White, M. (1977), 'Beauty and the breast: a 60% complication rate for an operation you don't need,' *Ms.*, Sept. 1977, pp. 53–5, 84–5.

Rader, M. (1935), *A Modern Book of Aesthetics*. New York: Holt, Rinehart & Winston.

Rodriguez, R. (1982), *Hunger of Memory*, Boston: Godine.

*Roget's International Thesaurus* (1962, 3rd edn), New York: Crowell, p. 584.

Rosenthal, R. (1966), *Experimenter Effects in Behavioral Research*, New York: Appleton.

Rudofsky, Bernard (1974), *The Unfashionable Human Body*, Garden City, NY: Anchor/Doubleday.

Sachs, H. (1940), 'Beauty, life and death,' *American Imago* 1:81–4.

See, L. (1982), 'A change of face,' *San Francisco Chronicle*, 2 June 1982: FF 1.

Skowe, J. (1981), 'Modeling the '80s look,' *Time*, 9 February 1981.

Stein, J. (G. Plimpton, ed.) (1982), *Edie: An American Biography*, New York: Knopf.

'A warning about "rainbow" diet pills,' *Consumer Reports*, 1983: 567.

Weiss, J. (1947), 'A psychological theory of formal beauty,' *Psychoanalytic Quarterly*, 16:391–400.

'What sort of man reads *Playboy*?', *Playboy*, January 1981, 28.1.

# Index

(Numbers in parentheses refer to illustrations)

307